THE OFFICIAL GUIDE TO
BODY MASSAGE

HAIRDRESSING AND BEAUTY INDUSTRY AUTHORITY SERIES

HAIRDRESSING

Begin Hairdressing: The Official Guide to Level 1 *Martin Green and Leo Palladino*
Hairdressing: The Foundations - The Official Guide to Level 2 *Leo Palladino*
Professional Hairdressing: The Official Guide to Level 3 *Leo Palladino*
The Colour Book: The Official Guide to Colour for NVQ Levels 2 & 3 *Tracey Lloyd with Christine McMillan-Bodell*
Men's Hairdressing: Traditional and Modern Barbering *Maurice Lister*
African-Caribbean Hairdressing *Sandra Gittens*
eXtensions: The Official Guide to Hair Extensions *Theresa Bullock*
Salon Management *Martin Green*
Mahogany: Steps to Cutting, Colouring and Finishing Hair *Martin Gannon and Richard Thompson*
Mahogany Hairdressing: Advanced Looks *Martin Gannon and Richard Thompson*
Patrick Cameron: Dressing Long Hair *Patrick Cameron and Jacki Wadeson*
Patrick Cameron: Dressing Long Hair Book 2 *Patrick Cameron and Jacki Wadeson*
Bridal Hair *Pat Dixon and Jacki Wadeson*
Trevor Sorbie: Visions in Hair *Trevor Sorbie, Kris Sorbie and Jacki Wadeson*
Trevor Sorbie: The Bridal Hair Book *Trevor Sorbie and Jacki Wadeson*
The Total Look: The Style Guide for Hair and Make-Up Professionals *Ian Mistlin*
The Art of Hair Colouring *David Adams and Jacki Wadeson*
The World of Hair Colour *John Gray*
The Art of Dressing Long Hair *Guy Kremer and Jacki Wadeson*
Essensuals, Next Generation Toni and Guy: Step by Step *Sacha Mascolo, Christian Mascolo and Stuart Wesson*
Professional Men's Hairdressing: The art of cutting and styling *Guy Kremer and Jacki Wadeson*

BEAUTY THERAPY

Beauty Basics: The Official Guide to Level 1 *Lorraine Nordmann*
Beauty Therapy - The Foundations: The Official Guide to Level 2 *Lorraine Nordmann*
Professional Beauty Therapy - The Official Guide to Level 3 *Lorraine Nordmann*
Aromatherapy for the Beauty Therapist *Valerie Worwood*
Indian Head Massage *Muriel Burnham-Airey and Adele O'Keefe*
The Complete Nail Technician *Marian Newman*
The Complete Guide to Make-Up *Suzanne Le Quesne*
The Complete Make-Up Artist *Penny Delamar*
The Encyclopedia of Nails *Jacqui Jefford and Anne Swain*
The Essential Guide to Holistic and Complementary Therapy *Helen Beckmann and Suzanne Le Quesne*
Hands on Sports Therapy *Keith Ward*
An Holistic Guide to Anatomy and Physiology *Tina Parsons*
An Holistic Guide to Massage *Tina Parsons*
An Holistic Guide to Reflexology *Tina Parsons*
Nail Artistry *Jacqui Jefford*
Nutrition: A Practical Approach *Suzanne Le Quesne*
The Spa Book *Jane Crebbin-Bailey, Dr John Harcup, and John Harrington*
The Art of Nails: A Comprehensive Style Guide to Nail Treatments and Nail Art *Jacqui Jefford*
The Official Guide to Body Massage *Adele O'Keefe*

THE OFFICIAL GUIDE TO
BODY MASSAGE

SECOND EDITION

ADELE O'KEEFE

standards information solutions

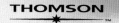

Australia • Canada • Mexico • Singapore • Spain • United Kingdom • United States

THOMSON

The Official Guide to Body Massage, Second Edition
Adele O'Keefe

Publishing Director	**Commissioning Editor**	**Development Editor**
John Yates	Melody Woollard	Jenny Clapham
Production Editor	**Manufacturing Manager**	**Editorial Assistant**
Emily Gibson	Helen Mason	Tom Rennie
Typesetter	**Production Controller**	**Senior Marketing Executive**
Tek-Art, Croydon, Surrey	Maeve Healy	Natasha Giraudel
Cover Design	**Text Design**	**Printer**
Harris Cook Turner	Design Deluxe, Bath, UK	Zrinski dd, Croatia

**Copyright © 2006
Thomson Learning**

The Thomson logo is a registered trademark used herein under licence.

For more information, contact
Thomson Learning
High Holborn House
50-51 Bedford Row
London WC1R 4LR

*or visit us on the
World Wide Web at*
http://www.thomsonlearning.co.uk

ISBN-13: 978-1-84480-330-9
ISBN-10: 1-84480-330-9

First edition published 2003 by
Thomson Learning.

Products and services that are referred to in this book may be either trademarks and/or registered trademarks of their respective owners. The publisher and author/s make no claim to these trademarks.

British Library Cataloguing-in-Publication Data
A catalogue record for this book is available from the British Library

Contents

Body massage case studies 307

THE OFFICIAL GUIDE TO
BODY MASSAGE
SECOND EDITION

ADELE O'KEEFE

standards information solutions

Australia • Canada • Mexico • Singapore • Spain • United Kingdom • United States

THOMSON
™

The Official Guide to Body Massage, Second Edition
Adele O'Keefe

Publishing Director	**Commissioning Editor**	**Development Editor**
John Yates	Melody Woollard	Jenny Clapham
Production Editor	**Manufacturing Manager**	**Editorial Assistant**
Emily Gibson	Helen Mason	Tom Rennie
Typesetter	**Production Controller**	**Senior Marketing Executive**
Tek-Art, Croydon, Surrey	Maeve Healy	Natasha Giraudel
Cover Design	**Text Design**	**Printer**
Harris Cook Turner	Design Deluxe, Bath, UK	Zrinski dd, Croatia

Copyright © 2006
Thomson Learning

The Thomson logo is a registered
trademark used herein under licence.

For more information, contact
Thomson Learning
High Holborn House
50-51 Bedford Row
London WC1R 4LR

or visit us on the
World Wide Web at
http://www.thomsonlearning.co.uk

ISBN-13: 978-1-84480-330-9
ISBN-10: 1-84480-330-9

First edition published 2003 by
Thomson Learning.

Products and services that are referred
to in this book may be either
trademarks and/or registered
trademarks of their respective owners.
The publisher and author/s make no
claim to these trademarks.

British Library Cataloguing-
in-Publication Data
A catalogue record for this book is
available from the British Library

Mapping grid

	G1, Ensure your own actions reduce risks to health and safety	G6, Promote additional products or services to clients	G11, Contribute to the financial effectiveness of the business	BT17, Provide head and body massage treatments	BT20, Provide Indian head massage treatment	BT21, Provide massage using pre-blended aromatherapy oils	BT29, Provide specialist spa treatments
1 The massage therapist at work	X						
2 Promoting products and services		X					
3 The therapist in business			X				
4 Anatomy, physiology and the effects of massage				X	X	X	
5 Client consultation and contraindications to treatment				X	X	X	
6 Preparation for massage				X	X	X	
7 Preheat treatments				X			
8 Massage techniques and procedures				X	X	X	
9 Modifications to massage treatments				X	X	X	
10 Indian head massage					X		
11 Aromatherapy massage						X	
12 Case studies				X	X	X	

Walk-through tour

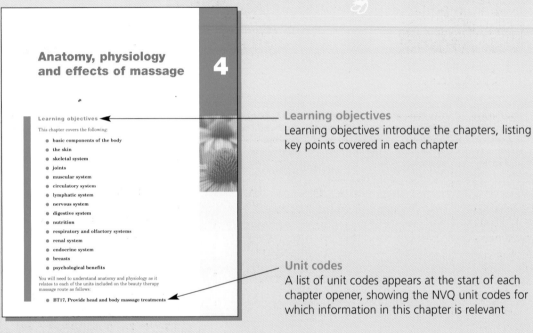

Learning objectives
Learning objectives introduce the chapters, listing key points covered in each chapter

Unit codes
A list of unit codes appears at the start of each chapter opener, showing the NVQ unit codes for which information in this chapter is relevant

Did you know boxes
Did you know boxes highlight extra points of interest to extend the core knowledge requirements for each chapter

Activity boxes
Activity boxes bring the text to life by providing practical exercises to reinforce the knowledge in each chapter

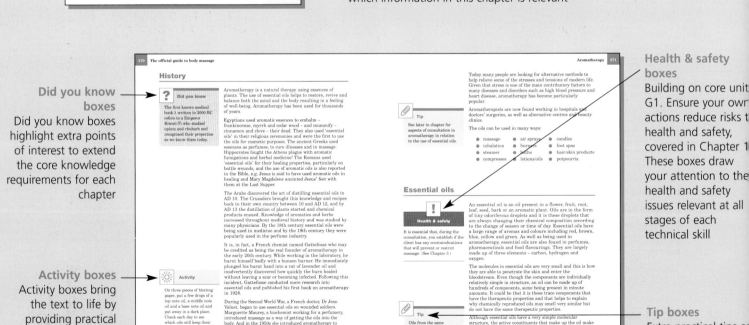

Health & safety boxes
Building on core unit G1. Ensure your own actions reduce risks to health and safety, covered in Chapter 1. These boxes draw your attention to the health and safety issues relevant at all stages of each technical skill

Tip boxes
Extra practical tips and suggestions to extend your knowledge of a topic in the chapter

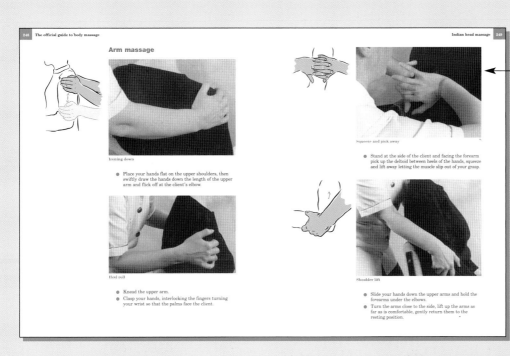

Indian head massage 249

Arm massage

Ironing down

● Place your hands flat on the upper shoulders, then swiftly draw the hands down the length of the upper arm and flick off at the client's elbow.

Heel roll

● Knead the upper arm.
● Clasp your hands, interlocking the fingers turning your wrist so that the palms face the client.

Squeeze and pick away

● Stand at the side of the client and facing the forearm pick up the deltoid between heels of the hands, squeeze and lift away letting the muscle slip out of your grasp.

Shoulder lift

● Slide your hands down the upper arms and hold the forearms under the elbows.
● Turn the arms close to the side, lift up the arms as far as is comfortable, gently return them to the resting position.

Step-by-step photos
Practical techniques are illustrated with detailed photographic sequences

Knowledge review
An extensive list of review questions is provided at the end of each chapter to assess your knowledge and understanding. These questions relate to the knowledge and understanding requirements for the unit or units relevant to that chapter.

Equipment lists
To assist in preparing for practical treatments an essential equipment list is provided illustrated with images of the tools, materials and products required

Find out more
A list of websites is provided at the end of the book with addresses of key massage-related associations and suppliers

Aromatherapy 291

✔ Checklist

Equipment check
● Treatment couch
● Towels
● Pillows
● Trolley
● Client's footstool – to assist the client to step onto the treatment couch
● Stool
● Bowls
● Tissues
● Record card/pen
● Gown
● Cleansing lotion – to remove client's makeup prior to the treatment
● Damp cotton wool – to gently wipe away the client's makeup
● Toner – to freshen the client's skin after cleansing
● A range of essential oils and carrier oils
● Glass measuring jug – to ensure that the quantity of carrier oil is accurate
● Blending bottles – ensure that the carrier oil and carrier oils are thoroughly blended. These can also store the remaining oil after treatment and can be given to the client to take home
● Bin

palms of the hands and rubbing backwards and forwards. A friction rub helps to warm the skin and brush off dry, superficial skin cells, therefore aiding efficient absorption of the oils.

Procedure

Back

1 Apply oil.
2 In the stride standing position, perform friction rub.

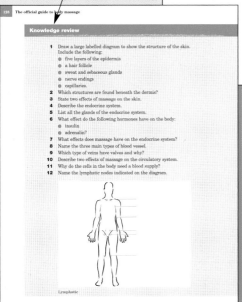

128 The official guide to body massage

Knowledge review

1 Draw a large labelled diagram to show the structure of the skin. Include the following:
   ● five layers of the epidermis
   ● a hair follicle
   ● sweat and sebaceous glands
   ● nerve endings
   ● capillaries.
2 Which structures are found beneath the dermis?
3 State two effects of massage on the skin.
4 Describe the endocrine system.
5 List all the glands of the endocrine system.
6 What effect do the following hormones have on the body:
   ● insulin
   ● adrenalin?
7 What effects does massage have on the endocrine system?
8 Name the three main types of blood vessel.
9 Which type of veins have valves and why?
10 Describe two effects of massage on the circulatory system.
11 Why do the cells in the body need a blood supply?
12 Name the lymphatic nodes indicated on the diagram.

Lymphatic

Find out more

Associations

British Massage Therapy Council
7 Rymers Lane
Oxon OX4 3JU
Tel 01865 774 123
www.bmtc.co.uk

Federation of Holistic Therapies
18 Shakespeare Business Centre
Hathaway Close
Eastleigh
Hants SO50 4SR
Tel 023 8062 4399
www.fht.org.uk

Hair and Beauty Industry Authority (HABIA)
Fraser House
Nether Hall Road
Doncaster
South York DN1 2PH
Tel 01302 380 000
www.habia.org.uk

Institute Federation of Aromatherapists
182 Chiswick High Road
London W4 1PP
Tel 020 8742 2605
www.ifparoma.org

Introduction

Massage has existed in one form or another since early civilisation. This introduction chapter traces the key stages in the development of massage.

Massage is the manipulation of the soft tissues and muscles of the body for therapeutic purposes. Rubbing parts of the body is a natural and instinctive way to relieve pain and discomfort and it was probably this instinct that led to most primitive forms of massage. The sense of touch is one of the first to be developed and is essential to our growth as human beings.

In its various forms, massage can be used to stimulate or relax. It has been used throughout history for both its physical and psychological benefits and is used to treat conditions ranging from headaches, both stress and posture related, to abdominal, pelvic, muscle and back pain, either general or as a result of specific injuries like falls, sports and car accidents and even for stress. From a treatment initially used for its physical or 'medical' benefits, the 'feel good' factor of the therapeutic touch has led to its use as a truly holistic treatment, one that treats body and mind as a whole.

Did you know

The word massage is generally believed to derive from the Arabic 'mass' or 'mass h', which means to press softly. Practised in many cultures for thousands of years as one of the earliest forms of healing, massage is an art that can be said to be as old as mankind itself. It was usually practised by doctors and priests.

Did you know

The Cong Fou of Tao-Tse describes a form of massage that involves the use of pressure points and is known as *amma*. It is still used in China today.

A brief history of massage

3000BC   Records documenting the use of massage in China have been found dating back as far as 3000BC. Some of these records, including the ancient book *Cong Fou of Tao-Tse*, which describes the use of plants, exercises and massage to maintain good health, can be found at the British Museum in London

Did you know

Early writings of Chinese Taoist priests state:

> Early morning effleurage with the palm of the hand after a night's sleep, when blood is rested and tempers more relaxed, protects against colds, keeps the organs supple and prevents any minor ailments.

Did you know

The origin of ayurvedic massage, like that of the Japanese for shiatsu, is believed to have originated in China. Evidence has been found that the ancients used massage for both cosmetic and therapeutic purposes, combining massage with oils.

Did you know

In ancient Greece, women used massage combined with aromatic oils as a beauty treatment, just as women do today.

Did you know

Massage played an important part in the daily life and system of medicine of ancient Greece.

1800BC	Writings documenting massage have been found by Hindu priests dating back to 1800BC, for example ayurveda
1600BC	Aesculapas, a priest and physician in ancient Greece, is said to have combined massage and exercise to produce a form of 'gymnastics' to treat disease and promote health. The ancient Greeks believed that massage had potent healing properties and they used it to treat injuries, enhance the performance of athletes and induce relaxation and sleep
700BC	Homer referred to the use of massage in treating war injuries in *The Odyssey* and it is also known that massage was used by the Greeks in the 776BC Olympic Games
400BC	Herodotus, in the 5th century BC, documented the benefits of massage
300BC	Hippocrates, later credited with being the father of medicine, wrote in his *Corpus Hippocratus* in 380BC:

> The physician must be experienced in many things but also assuredly in rubbing, for things that have the same names have not always had the same effect, for rubbing can bind a joint that is too loose and loosen a joint that is too tight, can make flesh or cause parts to waste, hard rubbing binds, soft rubbing loosens, much rubbing causes part to waste, moderate rubbing makes them grow.

100BC	The Romans learned the therapeutic benefits of massage from the Greeks. Galen, a physician to

? **Did you know**

Pliny, a Roman naturalist, was regularly rubbed to relieve his asthmatic condition and Julius Caesar was pinched all over every day to relieve neuralgia and headaches. Later, massage became an art that was carried out by their slaves. It is thought it was applied as a substitute for exercise and partly to try to reduce the effects of too much food and drink.

? **Did you know**

All the massage strokes in Ling's Swedish massage system relate to the body's circulatory and lymphatic systems. The massage helps to relieve tension, alleviate fatigue and enable deep relaxation. It encourages the body's organs and systems to function more efficiently and helps speed the healing process for any damaged tissue. Ling believed in combining massage with a lot of exercise and physical activity. Today, Swedish massage is far more refined and more relaxing for both client and masseur or masseuse. Although the techniques have changed, the original movements of effleurage, petrissage, fraction and tapotement have remained the same.

several emperors in the 1st century AD, was an advocate of massage in the treatment of certain diseases and injuries

Around this time we see massage being used for pleasure rather than simply as a medicinal treatment

AD400	During the Middle Ages there is not much reference to or development in massage. By and large, the scientific use of massage disappeared and little progress was made within the context of medicine. The religious conservatism of the west meant that 'touching' became taboo
AD1400	The Renaissance brought a renewed interest in the writings of the ancient Greek and Roman physicians and there was a revival in massage with a basis in anatomical and physiological science
AD1700	In the late 18th century, Pehr Henrik Ling, a Swedish physiologist, reintroduced massage into the mainstream of European life. It is said that he cured himself of rheumatism using techniques he learnt while travelling around China. On his return to Sweden, he formalised a system of massage and exercise based on these techniques, together with Greek, Egyptian and Roman techniques as well as some of his own. He is often credited with being the father of modern massage as the creator of today's well-known and internationally used Swedish massage
	At around the same time John Grosvenor was using massage to ease stiff joints. It was probably the Dutch physician, Dr Johann Metzger, who established massage as part of medical practice, as he used it successfully for rehabilitation and made his techniques consistent with the anatomical and physiological knowledge of the time
AD1813	A college in Stockholm offered massage as part of the curriculum for the first time. It later became popular in other institutes and spas all over the country
AD1838	A Swedish institute was opened in London
AD1899	Sir William Bennett opened a massage department in St George's Hospital, London, establishing massage as an accepted form of treatment in the medical profession
AD2000	Within complementary therapies, massage has become increasingly common and universally accepted

The massage therapist at work

1

- **Consumer Protection Act 1987**

- **Manual Handling Operations Regulations 1992**

- **Health and Safety (Display Screen Equipment) Regulations 1992**

This chapter relates to the following core mandatory unit:

- **G1, Ensure your own actions reduce risks to health and safety**

This chapter explores the various issues that will be vital to good practice in your everyday working life practising body massage. It assumes that you will be working in an established salon; however, most of the chapter is also applicable if you are a mobile therapist or if you are setting up your own business. It covers the rights and responsibilities of everyone at work, whatever their status, unpaid, paid, full time or part time and covers 'all persons' whether employees, employers or self-employed.

Working relationships

Colleagues

It is essential that you have a good working relationship with all the other members of staff at your place of work both for your own benefit and the benefit of your clients. Everyone should have a job description specific to their job role, duties and responsibilities. This helps to ensure that everyone knows exactly what they are doing.

You should be polite and courteous at all times and never talk down to colleagues. Avoid losing your temper and never ridicule colleagues in front of clients. If you have disagreements or personality differences with colleagues, do not show these in front of the client. Settle any differences as soon as possible so it does not affect your work. Should you ever experience any problems that you cannot resolve yourself, you should report the problem or incident to your supervisor who will take the appropriate action. Most companies will have a written procedure for grievances.

Tip

Remember, good practice concerns not only the way you carry out massage but also the way you relate to clients and colleagues.

Clients

It is important that clients enjoy their visit to the salon or clinic and that they feel totally relaxed and comfortable. You should always remember that every client is an individual with different needs. You need to know how to approach them in order to make them feel important and relaxed, and this process often begins before you even speak. Non-verbal communication is very important in service professions such as beauty therapy. Even when we are not speaking we are transmitting our feelings by the way we look and act, for example the way we smile at the client or make or avoid eye contact.

The manner in which you speak is also very important.

Do:
- speak clearly
- use a courteous tone and manner
- listen to what your client has to say, as this will help you to identify their needs
- guide the conversation to find out the client's needs but avoid interrogating them.

Don't:
- shout
- use slang
- interrupt the client when they are speaking
- use jargon or technical terminology
- talk about controversial subjects like sex, religion and politics.

Ellisons

Client record cards

Tip

It is helpful to make notes on the client's record card of topics that are of particular interest to them. You can bring up these topics on their next visit. This will make them feel special.

Remember that you need to gain their confidence and build up a good professional relationship. Often when the client gets to know you they will start to share confidences with you. **Never** pass judgement and always maintain their confidence by not discussing what you have been told.

Health and safety

Tip

You can find out about your health and safety responsibilities as an employer and as an employee at www.businesslink.gov.uk

It is important to be aware of the different areas of legislation. There are a number of health and safety laws that must be followed whether you are working in a salon, leisure centre, clinic or you are offering home visits. Health and safety legislation is part of criminal law and employees, employers and customers/clients all have certain duties imposed and owed to them under these laws. You are legally obliged to provide a safe and hygienic environment and it is very important that you follow health and safety guidelines. The laws are designed to protect you and your clients and penalties for contravening these laws can be severe. It is therefore important that you are aware of the relevant publications that highlight your responsibilities and your rights.

Health and Safety at Work Act 1974

This covers all aspects of health, safety and welfare at work. It identifies the responsibilities of not only the employer but also the employees. Under this act, employers are responsible for the health and safety of anyone who enters their premises. They must provide a safe working environment in terms of equipment, systems of work, training, supervision, storage, welfare and personal protection. The act states employees must take reasonable precautions to ensure/protect the health and safety of themselves, clients and colleagues.

Workplace (Health, Safety and Welfare) Regulations 1992

These regulations incorporate the Health and Safety at Work Act 1974 and also other earlier legislation including the Offices, Shops and Railway Premises Act 1963, as this is being phased out (although there is a requirement to register your business with the local council).

The new regulations state the minimum standard of health, safety and welfare required in each area of the workplace.

Health and Safety at Work Act

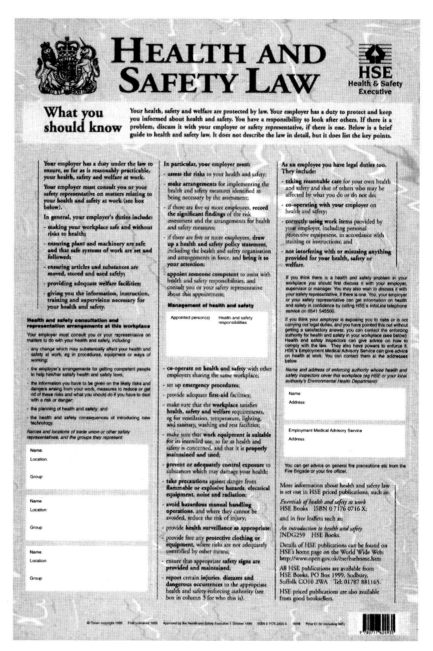

Personal protective equipment

If an employer has more than five employees they must have a health and safety policy for the establishment and this must be available to all staff members. Regular checks must be made in the workplace to check that safety is being maintained at all times. It is the employer's responsibility to implement the act and to ensure that the workplace is safe for the employees and clients. Under these regulations, employers must:

- ensure the safe use of equipment and the safe working of systems
- ensure safe storage and use of substances and equipment
- provide necessary training, information and instruction
- provide personal protective equipment that will ensure health and safety
- ensure the place of work is a safe place
- maintain and provide access to the place of work ensuring that escape routes are kept clear and emergency evacuation procedures are understood and adhered to.

Failure to comply with these duties may result in criminal liability and a claim for damages. Minor offences may result in fines up to £5000 and for more serious offences up to £20 000 and/or six months' imprisonment. Very serious offences may result in fines being unlimited as well as up to two years' imprisonment. If a hazard is identified it must be reported to the relevant authority and then it will have to be rectified by the employer.

The regulations cover issues such as maintenance of the workplace and equipment, ventilation, temperature and lighting, access to drinking water and eating facilities, etc.

Maintenance of the workplace

Cleanliness

All areas of the premises must be kept clean and tidy at all times.

A clean treatment room

Restrooms

There should be clean toilet facilities for both men and women. In small salons, men and women may share the same WC if the toilet is in a separate room and can be secured from the inside. There must be washing facilities near to the WC or urinal that supply hot and cold water, soap and a hand dryer or paper towels.

Food and drink

If staff eat and drink on the premises then a suitable area must be provided for them in which to eat, drink (a supply of wholesome drinking water must be available) and rest.

Clothing

An area must also be provided for the staff to hang up their outdoor clothes.

Salon temperature

The ambient temperature should be 16°C minimum (61°F) within one hour of the employees arriving for work. The working environment must be well ventilated and the lighting must be adequate to ensure that all treatments can be carried out safely with no risk of an accident occurring.

Ventilation

Ventilation must be good, as it provides a healthy environment for the clients and employees. Ventilation allows fresh air to replace stale air, so good ventilation may be achieved by opening doors and windows, but clients may be distracted by the additional noise and also feel a lack of privacy. Artificial ventilation may be more appropriate:

- Free-standing fans are usually portable, but only really provide air movement and are therefore not particularly effective.
- An exhaust system pushes air from inside the clinic to the outside.
- A supply system draws in fresh air from outside and filters it to remove any dust.
- Exhaust and supply systems can be combined with an air-conditioning system. Air-conditioning units can either warm the air if it is cold or cool the air if it is too hot. If the humidity is not right it can dry or moisten the air to create the correct humidity. Air conditioning also filters out dust particles.

Humidity

If humidity is not controlled properly and becomes too high, it can lead to problems such as headache, fatigue and irritability.

Lighting

Lighting must be suitable in all work areas. Light fittings, windows and skylights must be cleaned on a regular basis and any broken tubes or bulbs replaced. It is extremely important that there is sufficient lighting for the therapist to work efficiently, but at the same time the clients will not like to have the lights too bright when they are trying to relax. The best solution to this is spotlights that can be pointed in any direction and dimmed when required.

Glass

Windows, partitions and doors that are glazed must be made of safe materials (toughened or laminated glass should be used) and marked appropriately.

Privacy

Dedicated treatment rooms are ideal for privacy, but in many clinics there is not enough space to allow for them. In this case, treatment areas should be provided with curtains around them to provide privacy for the client.

Health and Safety (Information for Employees) Regulations 1989

The health and safety policy must be in written format and must be available to all staff members. It must include the following information:

- details of chemicals that are stored on the premises
- details of the stock cupboard or dispensary
- records of checks carried out by a qualified electrician on any specialist equipment
- escape routes and emergency evacuations
- names of key holders.

Accidents

Accidents often occur as a result of unsafe working conditions or negligent employees. As a matter of good practice, all

Health & safety

Always determine:

- whether the spillage is a potential hazard
- what action is necessary
- to whom it should be reported
- how the spillage should be removed
- how you should dispose of the material correctly.

Tip

Incident Contact Centre
Caerphilly Business Park
Caerphilly CF83 3GG
Tel 0845 300 9923
Fax 0845 300 9924
Email: riddor@natbrit.com
Internet: www.riddor.gov.uk

accidents that do occur in the workplace should be recorded, for example in an accident book, regardless of how minor the accident appears at first. Legislation exists with regard to the recording and reporting of more serious accidents.

Reporting of Injuries, Diseases and Dangerous Occurrences Regulation (RIDDOR) 1995

This places duties on employers, self-employed people and those in control of a workplace with regard to reporting injuries, diseases and dangerous occurrences. Unless you are self-employed and the incident relates to you, all deaths, major injuries and dangerous occurrences to employees, self-employed contractors and members of the public on your premises must be reported to the Incident Contact Centre or your local HSE office/authority without delay.

If an act of violence occurs in the workplace and there is an injury, it must be reported but only if it is connected to work. If any industrial disease such as asthma occurs, it must be reported once you receive a letter from the doctor saying the employee has an occupational disease. All dangerous occurrences such as gas leaks and fires must be reported.

This should then be followed up by submitting an F2508 report form within 10 days of the incident. This latter requirement also applies to the self-employed. Any injuries that result in the affected person being unable to perform their usual work duties for over three days should also be reported on the same form within 10 days. Any reportable work-related disease must be reported on form F2508A.

All reporting should be to the Incident Contact Centre (ICC) at Caerphilly and can be done by telephone (Mon–Fri, 08:30–17:00), fax, post or via the internet. You can also report by telephone and send a completed form to your local HSE office or local authority, which will forward the report to the ICC.

In addition to this reporting, an employer, self-employed person or person in charge of a workplace must ensure that the following points are documented and kept for three years after the injury, disease or dangerous occurrence:

- personal details of those involved
- date and method of reporting
- date, place and time of the event
- brief description of the nature of the event or the disease.

HMSO

Report of an injury or dangerous occurrence

ACCIDENT REPORT FORM

Date of accident: _____

Time of accident: _____

Location of accident: _____

Address: _____ Postcode: _____

Telephone number: _____

Name of injured person: _____

Address: _____ Postcode: _____

Telephone number: _____

Injuries

Part(s) of the body affected: _____

Nature of injuries: _____

How did the accident happen?

Provide as much information and detail as possible. _____

_____

First aid given, record details: _____

Name of first aider: _____

Witnesses

Name/s: _____

Address: _____ Postcode: _____

Telephone number: _____

Details recorded in accident record book? _____

Signature of injured person _____

Signature of first aider _____

Signature of witnesses _____

Signature of supervisor _____

An accident report form

This can be done by keeping a copy of the report form on file, maintaining a separate written log or recording the details on a computer.

If you have any query about RIDDOR or any other legislation enforced by the HSE, you can ring the HSE's InfoLine. More information about RIDDOR, a copy of F2508 and F2508A and a list of reportable major injuries, reportable dangerous occurrences and reportable diseases is available in the free booklet *RIDDOR Explained* or the priced publication *Guide to the Regulation*, both published by the HSE.

Accident prevention

It is essential that you learn to recognise and identify hazards and risks in your workplace and that you know the

Activity

Hazards include:

- spillages
- breakages
- obstructions to fire exits

Discuss other hazards that may occur in your workplace. What would you do to minimise risk from these hazards?

Activity

Discuss how you would remove and dispose of broken glass, so as to avoid injury to yourself and others.

difference between the two. The Health and Safety Executive (HSE) define the two concepts as follows:

Hazard: 'a hazard is something with potential to cause harm'

Risk: 'a risk is the likelihood of the hazard's potential being realized'.

It is important that the employer provides a safe and healthy environment and if a hazard is identified it is the responsibility of employers and employees alike to report it to the designated person in order for the problem to be rectified.

Spillages

If something is spilled in the salon, you must first establish if the spillage is a risk to health and the action that must be taken. You must know to whom it should be reported (the 'responsible person'), what equipment is required to remove the spillage and how it should be disposed of.

If any spillage occurs in the workplace it is essential that it be removed immediately to avoid someone slipping and falling.

Obstructions

An obstruction is anything that blocks the traffic route in the workplace. This would represent a hazard. If a fire exit were blocked, this would delay people from exiting the building or prevent the emergency services entering the premises, if the need arose.

The employer must be aware of any potential hazards and rectify them before health and safety is compromised. Some basic guidelines include:

- All entrances and exits must be kept clear.
- There must be adequate lighting in all areas of the premises.
- All staff should be trained in the use of any equipment.
- All electrical equipment should be well maintained and correctly wired.
- Power points should never be overloaded.
- Regular checks should be made for any cracked plugs, frayed wires, etc.
- All electrical equipment should be switched off before being cleaned and never touched with wet hands.
- All chemical containers should be clearly marked.

Accidents often involve spillages and breakages and these should be dealt with straightaway before further accidents are caused. Broken glass can cause cuts, so the hands should be protected with gloves and broken glass should be made safe before being deposited in the waste bin.

Regardless of the environment in which you are practising massage, whether it is a salon, leisure centre, clinic or if you offer home visits by a mobile service, you are working in a service industry and you are legally obliged to provide a hygienic and safe environment. It is therefore essential to follow the health and safety guidelines. If you put your clients at risk or cause them any harm, you will be held responsible and will be liable to fine and prosecution. You must, therefore, be aware of the relevant publications that highlight both your rights and responsibilities.

Working Time Regulations 1998

These regulations came into force in October 1998 and are concerned with the working hours, holidays and rest periods for full- and part-time workers. Employees may not work more than 48 hours a week averaged over 17 weeks, unless the employee agrees in writing, with an agreed notice period in which the employee can withdraw. If the employee also works elsewhere, their hours must be adjusted accordingly.

All adult employees are entitled to at least one day a week off (under 18 year olds are entitled to two days a week off).

Minimum rest periods

All employees are entitled to at least 20 minutes' rest, if they have worked more than six hours (a young person is entitled to 30 minutes if they have worked more than 4½ hours).

Holiday

After an employee has been employed for 13 calendar weeks they are entitled to at least four weeks' paid holiday (bank holidays and paid public holidays can be counted towards these).

Management of Health and Safety at Work Regulations 1999

This regulation requires employers to appoint a responsible person, trained and aware of the procedures involved, to assess risks to the health and safety of employees, clients, visitors or anyone entering the premises and to take the appropriate action to minimise or eliminate the risks.

If the employer has more than five employees, the named responsible person must document the findings of their assessment and it is advisable to document the findings in any case. If any risks have been identified, an action plan must be drawn up and all staff members made aware of the risks and the procedures that will be enforced in order to control the risks. Health and safety training for all staff must be ongoing.

Data Protection Act 1998

This is designed to protect the client's confidentiality and privacy. Whatever system you use to store records and client information, this act requires you to register with the Data Protection Registrar.

The Data Protection Act states that you must register with the Data Protection Register and that you must comply with the following:

- Only hold information that is relevant and only for the purpose stated in your register entry.
- Only ever obtain and process data lawfully.
- Never hold information for longer than is necessary.
- When required, always allow individuals access to the information that is personally relevant to them.
- Always take relevant security measures to prevent accidental or unauthorised access to, loss of, alteration, disclosure or destruction to the information.
- Ensure that the information is kept up to date and accurate.

Health and Safety (First Aid) Regulations 1981

Under these regulations, employers must ensure that the appropriate equipment and facilities are provided to deal with first aid and injury. It is the employer's responsibility to assess the first aid needs of a workplace that are deemed to depend on a number of factors, including the number of employees, the type of work being carried out and the proximity to emergency medical care.

The regulations state that the place of work must have at least one adequately stocked first aid box, preferably located close to handwashing facilities.

 Checklist

The kit should be identified by a white cross on a green background, and as a guide could contain at least the following items:

- basic first aid guidance leaflet
- 20 individually wrapped assorted sterile adhesive dressings
- 4 individually wrapped triangular bandages
- 2 sterile eye pads
- 6 safety pins
- 6 medium sized (approx. 12cm × 12cm) individually wrapped sterile wound dressings (non-medicated)
- 2 large (approx. 18cm × 18cm) individually wrapped wound dressings (non-medicated)
- individually wrapped moist cleaning wipes
- disposable gloves

 **Health & safety**

When an accident occurs the appointed person or first aider must:

- assess the situation
- try and identify the problem
- provide the appropriate treatment
- arrange transport to the hospital or doctors (if necessary).

The contents should be examined regularly and restocked as soon as possible after use. It should not contain any tablets or medication and should only contain items that the first aider has been trained to use.

The regulations detail the number of first aiders or appointed persons required, which is dependent on the risk of the occupation and the number of employees. There must be at least one member of staff to take charge in an emergency and record details of accidents. There should be a list of emergency phone numbers – ambulance, fire services and doctor – displayed in the first aid box. All staff should know the location of the first aid box and the identity of the first aider.

First aiders should record incidents to which they are called. The information should include the date, time and place of the incident; the name and job of the ill or injured person; details of the injury or illness and any first aid given; what

Activity

Even if you are not the appointed person or first aider in your place of work, it is in everyone's interest to have a basic knowledge of first aid so assistance can be given when required. Find out about attending a recognised first aid course in your area.

happened immediately after; name and signature of the first aider.

The following section simply highlights some of the conditions that you might come across when working as a massage therapist.

Unconsciousness

Unconsciousness is caused by an interruption to normal brain activity. When a person becomes unconscious, there is a danger that they will lose control of the muscles that normally keep the airways open and the cough reflex that keeps the throat clear of saliva and could choke on the contents of their stomach.

If a person becomes unconscious for no apparent reason, you should call for an ambulance straightaway. If they regain consciousness within three minutes, it is best to advise them to seek medical advice. If the casualty has had an accident or does not regain consciousness after three minutes, you should also call for an ambulance. You should stay with them until the ambulance arrives, checking and recording the pulse and breathing. If you have the qualifications, you should be prepared to resuscitate. If it is safe, move the person to put them in the recovery position.

Checklist

Recovery position

1 Loosen any tight clothing and spectacles.

2 Place the person on their back with legs straight.

3 Tuck the hand that is nearer to you under the thigh with arm straight and palm facing upwards.

4 With the other hand, grasp the thigh that is further away and pull up the knee, keeping the foot on the floor.

5 With one hand, keep the casualty's hand pressed against the cheek and pull them towards you using the other hand on the upper leg.

6 Make sure the airways are open by tilting the head back. The head needs to be well back, so adjust the cheek hand, so the head is well supported and turned to the side to prevent choking.

7 The top leg should be bent, at right angles to the body, while the other leg is only slightly bent. Check that they are not lying on their lower arm and the palm is facing upwards.

8 Check the breathing and pulse rate every 10 minutes.

Recovery position

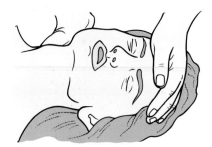

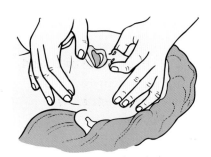

Artificial ventilation

If you are not aware of any medical conditions, you should check to see if they have anything that identifies a medical condition. For example, they might be carrying a medical card identifying them as diabetic, epileptic, on steroids or with an anti-coagulant condition. Bracelets, necklaces or key rings are sometimes worn or carried by people with specific medical conditions. If you can find any of these, it will help the ambulance personnel to administer the correct treatment more quickly. Any syringes, inhalers or medicines they are carrying will also provide the paramedic with vital clues as to their condition.

The recovery position is a safe and comfortable position in which to place an unconscious or injured person.

Artificial ventilation

If the casualty has stopped breathing and the first aider is competent, they should use artificial ventilation. Knowing how to administer resuscitation techniques could save a person's life and prevent brain damage. First aid courses run by organisations such as the British Red Cross or St John Ambulance teach these techniques. You should not try to learn these techniques from a book as you may do more harm than good, if you are called on to use them. The basic technique outlined here is for reference only:

1 Make sure the airways are free.
2 Tilt the head back to open the air passages.
3 Pinch the casualty's nose.
4 Take a deep breath, sealing your lips around the person's mouth and blow until you see the chest rise.
5 Take your mouth away and allow the chest to fall.
6 Continue at a rate of 10 breaths a minute and check the pulse every 10 breaths.
7 If the heart has stopped (there is no pulse), artificial ventilation needs to be combined with chest compressions.

Chest compressions

Remember, these must only be carried out by a qualified first aider. This book should only be used as a reminder of how this technique should be performed in an emergency:

1 Lay the casualty on the floor or a firm surface flat on their back.
2 Place the heel of one hand two finger widths above the point where the casualty's bottom ribs meet the

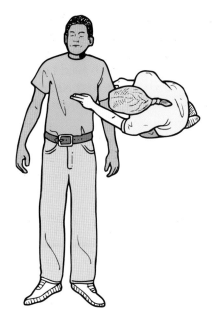

Chest compressions: top view

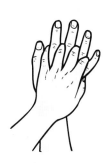

Hand position

Side view

breastbone. Place the heel of the other hand over it and interlock your fingers.

3 Press vertically down on the breastbone with arms straight to depress their chest by 4–5cm.

4 Release the pressure and repeat at a rate of approximately 80 compressions a minute.

Chest compressions need to be combined with artificial ventilation in order to oxygenate the blood. The two techniques used together are known as cardiopulmonary resuscitation or CPR. To administer CPR the ratio is two breaths every 15 compressions for one first aider or one breath every five compressions if there are two first aiders.

Measuring pulse rate: the neck

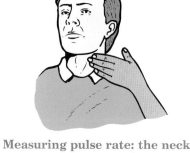

Measuring pulse rate: the wrist

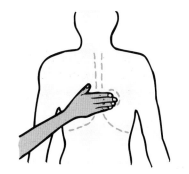

Measuring pulse rate: the chest

Pulse rate

In normal adults, the heart beat or pulse rate varies from 60 to 80 beats a minute at rest. This may be slower in very fit individuals. In a child, the resting pulse/heart rate is between 90 and 140 beats a minute. The pulse rate may increase with exertion, fear, blood loss, certain illnesses and fever. It may also decrease with certain heart disorders and when someone has fainted.

If you need to measure someone's pulse rate, you should count the number of beats in 30 seconds and then double it to find the beats a minute. The pulse can be taken in various places on the body, but the easiest sites are the neck and wrist. The neck is usually the easiest as the pulse is strongly felt. Using the first and second fingers feel the pulse in the carotid artery, which is just under the angle of the jaw in the hollow between the voice box and adjoining muscle, nearly level with and below the corner of the mouth. To find the pulse in the wrist, you should also use the first and second fingers. The pulse can be felt about 1.5cm in and down from the thumb side of the wrist. The thumb should never be used to take a pulse as it has a pulse itself.

The following are some of the injuries or conditions you may come across when working in massage therapy.

Cramp

Cramp is a painful involuntary muscle contraction, usually caused by poor circulation. It can be brought on by not warming up before an exercise session or through excessive perspiring resulting in loss of body salts. To treat cramp, you should stretch and massage the affected muscle as much as possible.

Allergies

Skin allergies occasionally occur during treatment. They can be identified by excessive redness, accompanied in some instances by swelling, itching, a severe burning sensation and vesicles in the area in which the offending product has been used. To treat an allergic reaction you must first of all remove the product that has caused the reaction. This can be done by using tap water. If necessary, you should apply a cold pack or a cold compress to the affected area. This will help to reduce swellings or inflammation. If the reaction does not subside, you should refer the client to their doctor. Remember to enter all the details onto the client's record card so that you and your colleagues know not to use the product on the client in future treatment.

Fainting

Fainting occurs when there is lack of blood flowing to the brain, which results in the person losing consciousness for a short period of time. This can be caused by emotional or physical shock or spending a long time in a room that is hot or poorly ventilated. Quite often the affected person will know they are going to faint as they tend to feel dizzy and unsteady. Sometimes they may lose colour or start to sweat excessively, especially from the hands, face and neck.

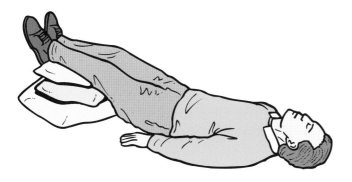

Dealing with a faint: lie down, sit down

If the client feels faint either lay them down and raise their feet by placing pillows under their lower legs to stimulate blood flow or sit them down and bend them forwards placing their head between the knees. Make sure that you loosen any tight clothing and instruct them to breathe deeply. Open windows or doors if possible to allow fresh air in. If they have any problems breathing or they faint and do not regain consciousness quickly, put them in the recovery position and call for an ambulance.

Nosebleeds

Nosebleeds may be spontaneous or caused by a blow to the face. To treat a nosebleed, you should sit the person down with their head bent well forwards, loosen any clothing around the neck, ask the casualty to breathe through their mouth and firmly pinch the soft part of their nose (bridge) for about 10 minutes. When the bleeding does stop, it is better if the casualty rests quietly for an hour or so and does not blow their nose for about four hours, so that the clot is not disturbed. If the bleeding does not stop after half an hour, the casualty must seek medical advice.

Stings

If the casualty has been stung by a bee, the sting with the poison sac will be in the skin. If you can see this, pull it out with tweezers, grasping the sting below the poison sac and as close to the skin as possible. You should take care to remove the sac with the sting and on no account attempt to squeeze the sting out as this will spread the poison. You should remove wasp stings in a similar way.

Once the sting has been removed, you should apply a cold compress to the area. You should advise the casualty to seek medical advice if the pain and swelling continue over several

Applying pressure to a cut

days. If the casualty is stung in the mouth, give them ice to suck on to minimise swelling. There is a danger that the swelling may interfere with their breathing, therefore it is advisable to send for an ambulance.

Some people are allergic to bee and wasp stings. Their bodies react in such an extreme way that within minutes they can stop breathing. If you have any doubts, call for an ambulance straightaway.

Cuts

If a person cuts themselves it is best to cleanse the area by rinsing under running water. If bleeding occurs, you should either place sterile gauze or a pad of clean cotton wool over the wound, applying pressure for a few minutes and keeping the area elevated. If the bleeding does not stop after a time, medical assistance must be sought. Any cut through the entire skin thickness must be covered with a sterile dressing and medical assistance sought.

Shock

Shock can be caused by many things such as an emotional upset, severe bleeding, a heart attack or some other kind of emergency situation. The face will often become pale and greyish in colour, the hands and face start to sweat but the skin will feel cold and clammy. The person may feel weak and dizzy and their breathing becomes shallow and rapid. There may be an increase in the pulse rate, followed by a weak pulse rate that appears to come and go.

It is best to reassure the casualty, try to make them comfortable, loosen any tight clothing, lay them down and raise their feet above their head. Try to keep them warm by covering them with a blanket. If they feel sick put them in the recovery position or just turn their head to one side. If you suspect that the shock is caused by electrocution or a heart attack, you should call an ambulance immediately.

Burns and scalds

There are several types of burn, classified by how it is caused. Burns can be caused by various agents.

Regardless of the cause, all scalds and burns can cause intense pain and are usually accompanied by redness and swelling. Minor scalds and burns can usually be alleviated by the immediate administration of the correct first aid procedures outlined later. Severe burns lead to blisters and

Table 1.1 *Types of burn and scald*

Type	Cause	Treatment
Electricity	Contact with lights, plugs or faulty electrical equipment	Area should be cooled with water for 10 minutes and a dry dressing applied. Medical attention should be sought as these burns are usually very much deeper than their size indicates
Dry heat	Touching a hot object, such as a flame or cigarette	Area should be cooled with water for 10 minutes and a dry dressing applied
Corrosive chemicals	Undiluted disinfectants and antiseptics	Can produce severe skin burns. It is best to flush the area with large quantities of cold water immediately to dilute the solution
Moist heat	Scalds can be caused by hot drinks, showers, boiling water	Area should be cooled with cold water. Remove anything tight from the area, such as a ring or watch, before swelling starts. If blisters occur these should not be broken as this could cause infection

Health & safety

Remember: if first aid is to be administered while waiting for an ambulance, it must only be carried out by a trained first aider.

the casualty is also in danger of shock, which is directly related to the extent of the injury. Anyone who has suffered severe burns or scalds must be taken to the hospital.

It is important to cool down the injured area by flushing with cold water for about 10 minutes. If this is impossible, for example because the area is too large, it is better to submerge the area, for example in a bath. If neither of these options is available, use a bowl of cold water. Keep submerging the area and constantly splashing it. This will stop the heat in the tissues spreading and will minimise the pain.

If the casualty is wearing any jewellery on the affected area, it is best to remove it before any swelling starts. If a scald occurs over clothing, the clothing should be removed or held away from the body while cold water is sought. However, if there is any clothing stuck to a burn, it should not be removed as any blisters that occur must not be broken, as this will leave the area open to infection. The injury should be dressed with a lightweight, clean, non-fluffy material. (If nothing else is available, cling film can be used.) This is to keep the wound from getting infected.

Asthma

Asthma can affect people of any age and seems to be on the increase. When a person suffers an asthma attack, the breathing tubes go into spasm and narrow so that normal breathing becomes impossible, as they are only able to use the upper lung lobes. Breathing becomes difficult, shallow and wheezy. An attack can be caused by nervous tension, overexertion, infection, extremes of emotion or an allergy. It is best to keep the casualty sitting up or leaning slightly forward in a comfortable position, and loosen tight clothing. You should reassure the casualty. If this is not their first attack, they will probably have personal medication that they can take. If the attack persists or is severe, you should call for an ambulance.

Making a person comfortable during an asthma attack

Epilepsy

Epilepsy exhibits itself either as convulsions or loss of consciousness due to abnormal activity in the brain. When a person is having a minor epileptic attack, their eyes become fixed and tend to stare for a few minutes. The person becomes pale and is not aware of what is going on around them. When they come round, they often will not know what has happened. A minor epileptic attack can take the form of a faint. With both types of attack, the person may be a little confused after the attack and unaware of what is going on.

A major attack can be quite frightening for both the victim and any other people present. The casualty may suddenly lose consciousness, remain rigid for a few seconds and then start to experience convulsions. The jaw often becomes clenched, with saliva appearing at the mouth. If the tongue has been bitten, the saliva may be bloodstained. During an attack, the casualty may become incontinent due to the loss of muscle control. All of a sudden the person will completely relax and regain consciousness, remembering nothing of the incident.

To treat epilepsy, the first aider must first try and prevent self-injury, by removing anything within the vicinity that the victim could injure themselves on in an attack. Ask onlookers to move away. Do not restrain the casualty but try to protect their head and loosen any clothing around the neck. Keep checking that their airway is clear and the person is breathing. As they start to relax, place them in the recovery position and stay with them until they have fully recovered, reassuring them if necessary. If they are not recovering, send for an ambulance.

Control of Substances Hazardous to Health (COSHH) Regulations 2002

Tip

These regulations do not apply to substances that are only hazardous to health because they are inflammable, although employers and employees must ensure that these are stored correctly.

Hazardous substance symbols

Many substances that seem quite harmless can prove to be hazardous if incorrectly used or stored. The employer has to carry out a risk assessment to assess those that could be a risk to health from exposure and to ensure these are recorded. This must be carried out on a regular basis.

Hazardous substances must be identified by symbols on their packaging and stored and handled correctly.

Try if possible to replace high-risk products with lower risk products.

An assessment should be carried out on all staff members who may be at risk.

Carry out training for all staff members and provide personal protective equipment if required, although this should only be as a last resort.

Substances that are hazardous may enter the body via:

nose – inhalation

mouth – ingestion

skin – contact/absorbed

body – injected or via cuts

eyes – contact.

Each supplier is legally required to make available the guidelines on how their materials should be stored and used.

Provision and Use of Work Equipment Regulations 1992 (amended 1998)

The 1998 regulations address the specific regulations surrounding the potential risks and dangers that could occur when using the equipment. They state the duties for employer and employee. This regulation affects both old and new equipment. It identifies:

- requirements in choosing suitable equipment and maintaining it
- that the manufacturers must provide instructions and training in safe use of the equipment.

Personal Protective Equipment at Work Regulations 1992

Usually the requirements from these regulations are met if you comply with the COSHH regulations. All employers must provide suitable personal protective equipment (PPE) to all employees who may be exposed to any risk while at work.

Environmental Protection Act 1990

This act states that all waste must be disposed of safely. It is important to exercise care when disposing of surplus/out-of-date stock and manufacturer's guidance should be sought. If in any doubt, ask the manufacturer to dispose of the stock for you.

Electricity at Work Regulations 1989

These state that every piece of electrical equipment in the workplace must be tested every 12 months by a qualified electrician. An electrical fault can result in an electrical burn, shock or fire, which could obviously have adverse effects on your business.

Local authority byelaws

These are laws that are made at local level by the local council. If, for example, you want to make major changes to the business or even just change the shop window, you need to apply for permission to the planning department and the public highways department. They will decide if the proposed changes will cause any inconvenience to the local residents, for instance, if parking facilities are adequate or the volume of traffic would increase.

Building regulations

These must be strictly adhered to and are administered by the building control officers working for the local council. This ensures good health and safety for the public.

Fire regulations

The local fire service will provide all the necessary advice on fire-fighting equipment and the correct procedures for evacuation. If any structural alterations are made, you must enquire about the fire regulations and carry them out.

Certification of registration

If the business provides treatments such as ear piercing, epilation, tattooing or any form of body piercing, the person who is carrying out these treatments must be registered with the local council.

Licensing

Some local councils require a licence if certain treatments such as body massage are being carried out. These are usually valid for one year and are granted with a set of standards and conditions for a fee. The standards must be met or the licence will be revoked.

Inspection and registration of premises

The local authority's environmental health department enforces the Health and Safety at Work Act. The environmental health officer visits and inspects the premises. Any area of danger is identified by the inspector and it is then the employer's responsibility to remove the danger within a stated period of time. If the employer fails to comply, this can lead to prosecution. The inspector has the authority to close the business until he or she is satisfied that all dangers to the public and employees have been removed.

Fire precautions and acts

Fire Precautions Act 1971

A fire certificate is required if there are more than 10 people employed on more than one floor or 20 people employed on one floor at any one time. All premises must be provided with fire-fighting equipment and an escape route in the event of fire. Fire drill notices should be displayed and fire exits clearly marked with appropriate signs.

Fire Precautions (Workplace) Regulations 1997 and Fire Precautions (Workplace) (Amendment) Regulations 1999

These state that all the staff must be aware of and trained in emergency evacuation and fire procedures for their workplace. A fire risk assessment should always be carried out and the following in place:

- A smoke alarm should be fitted.
- Fire doors should be fitted within the business to help keep the fire from spreading.
- All escape routes must be kept clear of obstruction and there should be emergency lighting.
- Fire-fighting equipment must be located in specified areas. This equipment includes fire extinguishers, blankets, buckets and water hoses and these should be checked on a regular basis.

Fire fighting and extinguishers

As there are different types of fire-fighting equipment, it is important that the cause of the fire is identified before using

Fire extinguisher symbols

anything. Using the wrong extinguisher could possibly make the fire worse.

There are four causes of fire:

1   **Class A** fires involve paper, wood, hair and other solid materials.
2   **Class B** fires involve flammable liquids such as petrol.
3   **Class C** fires involve vaporising gases such as butane and propane.
4   **Class D** fires involve electrics.

A fire caused by solid materials like paper or wood must be extinguished with a water extinguisher. This has a red label and can only be effectively used on Class A fires.

A fire caused by flammable liquids should be extinguished with a foam extinguisher. This is red with a cream/buff label. It should only be used for Class B fires and small Class A fires.

An electrical fire could be extinguished with a dry powder extinguisher. This is red with a blue label. It is also suitable for Class B and Class C fires.

A carbon dioxide extinguisher can be used on all fires but is particularly useful on Class B and electrical fires. It is red with a black label.

Fire blankets can be used on small localised fires and are used to smother the flames. Sand is used on liquids. This will again smother flames and soak up liquids. Water hoses are used on large fires usually caused by paper materials. Buckets of water are used to put out small fires. Always remember to turn off the electricity first.

Public liability insurance

This protects the employers and the employees against any injury or death to a third party while they are on the premises. It is not a legal requirement but should be taken out to cover any claims made by the public as a result of damage or injury to personal property by the employer or employee at work. Every employer must have employer's liability insurance; this provides financial compensation to an employee if they are injured while at work.

Employer's Liability (Compulsory Insurance) Regulations 1998

It is the duty of all employers to take out and maintain an insurance policy against liability for all employees within their employment that covers them for bodily injury or disease. The insurance certificate must be displayed in the place of work.

Consumer Protection Act 1987

This act safeguards the consumer against unsafe products. The act covers general safe handling requirements, product liability and prices that are misleading.

Manual Handling Operations Regulations 1992

Health & safety

Make sure you assess the weight of a load and only lift it if it is safe. With feet shoulder width apart, firmly grasp the object, lift from the knees, not the back. When carrying, balance the weight in both hands and carry the heaviest part of the load nearest to the body.

Many accidents are as a result of incorrect lifting, carrying, pushing, pulling and handling techniques whether by hand or bodily force. Certain sprains and strains are caused over a period of time, others are a result of a single incident. Employers are required to provide appropriate training for employees after carrying out an assessment of risks.

In some instances it may be just a case of reorganising shelves and storage areas or providing car insurance to enable them to pick up stock and equipment from the wholesaler. Wherever possible it is advisable to avoid manual handling. If this cannot be avoided, you need to consider the following factors:

- load, weight and size of things being moved
- area, whether it is wet or dry and how much space there is
- person's capability in relation to the task being carried out.

It is important to assess the weight of the load and only lift if it is safe. Feet should be shoulder width apart. Firmly grasp the object; lift from the knees, not the back. When carrying, balance weight in both hands and carry the heaviest part nearest to the body.

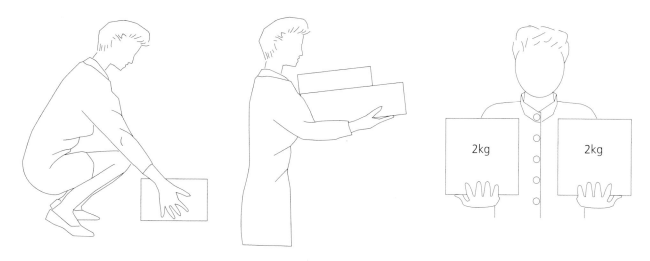

Lifting a box   **Carrying several boxes**   **Carrying equal weights in both hands**

Health and Safety (Display Screen Equipment) Regulations 1992

If you have an employee who is working with display screen equipment, such as a receptionist, you will need to pay for eye tests given by an optician or doctor and special spectacles if required.

It is also the employer's responsibility to provide information and training for display screen equipment users and ensure there are regular breaks or a change of activity.

Knowledge review

1 Why are positive working relations with your colleagues essential?

2 If you have a grievance, to whom would you report it?

3 Name two acts of parliament concerned with health and safety in the workplace.

4 Explain your main legal responsibilities under the Health and Safety at Work Act 1974.

5 Why must regular health and safety checks be carried out in the workplace?

6 If a serious accident occurs in the workplace who must be informed within 10 days of the accident taking place?

7 Explain the Reporting of Injuries, Diseases and Dangerous Occurrences Act.

8 What is the procedure for dealing with an accident in the workplace?

9 What hazards may exist in your place of work?

10 Why must you be aware of potential hazards?

11 While checking the audio sonic electrical leads for safety before treatment application, you notice that the wires in the lead are exposed. What action would you take?

12 Explain the Data Protection Act 1998.

13 Name six essential items in the workplace first aid box.

14 What does the abbreviation COSHH stand for?

15 Why is it important to enforce COSHH regulations in the workplace?

16 How often should electrical equipment be tested? Who carries out this procedure?

17 What is a fire drill?

18 What is the fire evacuation procedure in your place of work? How often should this be carried out?

19 In the event of a real fire, once you have safely evacuated the building, how would you contact the appropriate emergency service?

20 Which fire extinguisher(s) would put out a fire caused by paper or wood?

21 In your place of work, you discover a bin that has smoke coming out of it, caused by an unextinguished cigarette. How would you extinguish this fire?

22 What is employer's liability insurance?

Promoting products and services to clients

2

Learning objectives

This chapter covers the following:

- **gaining knowledge of the additional services or products available**

- **informing the client of the additional services and products**

- **gaining client commitment to using additional products and services**

- **importance of staff knowledge on the products and services available to the client**

- **importance of sales**

This chapter covers essential knowledge and understanding for the following unit:

- **G6, Promote additional products or services to clients**

Retail sales

Retail sales are a key way of greatly increasing the income of the business without too much extra time or effort. Treatments themselves are time consuming and labour intensive, so selling a product as well as providing a treatment will greatly increase profitability for the business.

In the same way that you would adapt treatments to suit individual clients, it is important to treat the client as an individual when promoting further products and services. Initially, you should find out the following:

- Is the client allergic to any particular substance?
- Does the client have any disorders or diseases that may be contraindicated?
- When and how often is the client planning on using the product?

Bearing the answers to these questions in mind, you can now guide the client into buying a product suitable to their needs using your product knowledge and expertise. It is important that you know your products thoroughly in order that you can discuss and advise the client, as well as answer any questions clearly and professionally.

Health & safety

If the client has not tried a product before and you are in doubt as to how their skin may react you must carry out a patch test.

Ensure that the skin is clean and apply a little of the product either behind the ear or on the inner elbow. Leave area for 24 hours, asking the client not to wash or touch the area over that time.

If there is no reaction, the client is not allergic to the product, but if the client reacts and experiences erythema, soreness, itching or swelling to the area where the product has been applied, the client must not use the product as they are allergic to it.

Staff training

All staff should be trained in the products and salon services that are being offered. Regular staff training in product and

Activity

Select a range of massage products from those available in your college or place of work and discuss their key features and benefits with your colleagues.

service knowledge will ensure that all employees have regular opportunities to update their knowledge and skills. Some companies offer free training on their products, which are good ways of keeping up to date with the latest ranges. Make sure that whenever certificates are received from attending training courses, you display these publicly in the salon. This will instil further confidence in your knowledge and expertise.

It is possible to send one representative from the business to these training sessions and then hold a meeting in which this representative can present the new information to the other members of the team. This is also a good forum for discussing new ideas, new product ranges or services or future promotions.

Product promotion

Activity

Start collecting leaflets and promotional material from department stores and salons. Analyse the material. Is it well designed? What particular features make it eye catching or attractive? If you think it's badly designed, identify features that prevent it working for you.

Ensure that promotional displays are set up in prominent communal spaces in the salon, for example the reception area. These displays should include information on benefits and costs for the client to read while they are waiting for their treatment. This can be in the form of window stickers, posters or information leaflets. Samples, or at least testers, should be made available for clients to try before they buy. A page on the business website could also be set up outlining the products and services available, along with their costs and details of the benefits of each.

Displays

Displays should always be eye catching and attractive. It is essential that they are changed on a regular basis to reflect any promotions, are always kept well stocked and are checked and cleaned on a regular basis. Testers should be checked to ensure they are still in good condition.

Activity

Write an imaginary treatment menu for a salon including the name of each treatment, its key features and benefits, along with the treatment time and price.

Range of products

Ensure that a wide variety of products and ranges are stocked. Sales should not be lost because of a lack of product variety.

Legal responsibilities

It is important to be aware of your responsibilities and the customer's legal rights when providing services and selling products.

If you feel after the consultation has been carried out that the client is not suitable for a particular product or treatment, you must tactfully explain to the client why and ask them to seek out permission from their GP before either the treatment is carried out or you sell them the product. Some clients' expectations can be unrealistic. If this is the case, explain the situation clearly, so that the client understands why treatment cannot be carried out. Aim to agree to a more realistic treatment programme.

It is your duty under the Health and Safety at Work Act 1974 to avoid harm both to yourself and the client. Never use equipment that you are not qualified to use, as you would not have the expertise to adapt the treatment to meet the client's needs and would not be able to provide treatment advice, in order to ensure the best possible effects.

Data Protection Act 1998

During a consultation you will need to ask your client many necessary but often personal questions before agreeing on a treatment plan. These client details are confidential and should be recorded onto a client card, which must be stored in a secure area. Always ensure that the client understands the reason for asking these questions. Information that is confidential about staff or clients should only be made available to those people to whom consent has been given.

Prices Act 1974

Product prices must be displayed clearly to prevent misunderstandings on the part of the buyer.

Resale Prices Act 1964 and 1976

A manufacturer can supply a recommended price, but the seller is not obliged to sell it at the price that was recommended.

Sales and Supply of Goods Act 1994

This has replaced the Supply of Goods Act 1982 in order to include service standards requirements. Goods must be fit for their intended purpose, as described, and of merchantable quality. This act also covers the terms and conditions under which a customer may return goods.

Consumer Protection Act 1987

This implements a European Union directive to ensure that the consumer is protected against unsafe products and services. Clients who are unsatisfied may contact several organisations that deal with legal advice on consumer protection. If a business is found to be at fault, it will face legal action.

Consumer Safety Act 1978

This act reduces the consumer's risk from products that are potentially dangerous.

Consumer Protection (Distance Selling) Regulations 2000

These are derived from a European Union directive. They cover the supply of goods or services made between suppliers acting in a commercial capacity and consumers. They are concerned with purchases made by digital television, telephone, fax, mail order and the internet.

The consumer must receive clear information on services and goods, including the payment, delivery arrangements, supplier's details and the consumer's cancellation rights, which should be in writing. The consumer has the right to cancel their purchase during a seven-day cool-off period.

Equal opportunities

The United Kingdom has equality legislation specific to protecting employees and covers the goods and services provision.

Race Relations Act 1976

This act makes it unlawful to discriminate on the grounds of colour, race, nationality, ethnic or national origin.

Disability Discrimination Act (DDA) 1995

This act makes it unlawful to discriminate on the grounds of disability.

Under the DDA, as a provider of services, goods and facilities your workplace has a duty to ensure that no clients are discriminated against on the grounds of disability.

It is unlawful, due to a disability, to:

- provide a service to a lesser standard or on worse terms
- fail to make reasonable adjustments to the way the services are provided
- fail to make reasonable adjustments to the service premises physical features, in order to overcome physical barriers to access.

Services can only be denied to a person who is disabled if it is justified and other clients would be treated in the same way.

It is the employer's responsibility to ensure that adequate training is provided to employees to prevent discriminatory practices taking place and that reasonable adjustments are made to the workplace to facilitate access for people who are disabled.

Equal opportunity policy

The Equal Opportunity Commission (EOC) states that it is best practice for all workplaces to have a written equal opportunities policy. This will include an equal opportunity commitment by the employer and details of a structure on how the policy will be implemented. All employees should know and understand this policy and it should be monitored regularly to review its effectiveness.

Informing the client about products and services

Think about the best times to inform the client about additional services and promotions. They may be informed before their treatment, when the consultation is being carried out. During a treatment is usually not the right time, as the client generally wants to close their eyes and relax. After the treatment, when giving advice and discussing aftercare, is an ideal time to open the discussion. This will give the opportunity to reinforce the importance of further services or products that may enhance the benefits of the treatment or treatments you have just provided.

Communication

When discussing products and services, be aware that communication with the client can be both verbal and non-verbal. Listen to what your client is saying – this will identify their treatment requirements. Always observe their body language – if the client is interested in what is being said, they will agree and their body language will be attentive but at the same time relaxed. However, if the client is uninterested they will not agree and will appear inattentive. If this happens, suggest alternatives and try to regain their interest without pressurising them.

Remember, if a sale is made, smile and be positive – this will ensure that the client feels that they have made the right decision.

Promotions

Promotions are a great technique to increase awareness of the services and products you offer to both new and existing clients.

Internal promotions can be run for existing clients, whereas external promotions will attract new clients. Whatever the aim of the promotion, it is essential that thorough planning is required to ensure its success.

Checklist

Why promote?

- Motivates employees
- Helps to improve business profits at quiet times of the year
- Helps the success of the launch of a new treatment or product
- Increases the client base
- Gives clients an incentive, such as financial discounts on services booked following a promotion

It is important that the aim of the promotion is identified and understood by all employees. A team approach is vital when discussing and sharing ideas on the best way forward. This can take place at a formal team meeting (see Chapter 3). Tasks should be listed with deadline dates for completion and staff responsible for the completion of each task.

Preparing for a promotion:

- Always work within your budget.
- Ensure that the event is advertised properly.
- Use your existing client database to invite and inform clients of the event.
- Ensure the venue is suitable by inspecting the facilities. Will there be enough room for the attendees? Check that all the required resources are provided: for example, is the car parking adequate?
- Check on lighting and audio equipment.
- Refreshments – do you require external caterers or does the venue provide this service?
- Ensure that all employees can answer questions confidently when asked about the promotion.

Advertising and PR

Advertising your promotion will require high-quality, well-designed promotional material and flyers. It is a good idea to set up a business website that you can keep updated with all the latest treatments and product ranges, as well as forthcoming promotions. As well as this, consider advertisements in the media, for example radio, newspapers, journals, magazines and television.

Local press

The local press may have a regular feature that could help promote the business. It can be beneficial for public relations to offer a free treatment to a journalist for them to experience, evaluate and report on. Alternatively, you may work with them by offering a special prize for a competition feature, where the winner would receive a complimentary treatment and the business would be promoted.

Local radio and television

Radio advertising is an effective way to promote the business. Alert the local television to anything different or unique you may wish to feature. Once good links are established with the media, your expertise may often be sought out for future features.

All these techniques can be included in the term public relations (PR). Public relations can market your business very effectively and can be self-organised. Larger organisations usually employ a PR consultant.

Demonstrations

When organising a demonstration in front of an audience, careful planning must be carried out in order to achieve maximum benefits.

Ensure everything that is required is in place, including all products, electrical equipment and any literature to be given out to the audience.

Plan what type of demonstration will be required. Will it be demonstrating a treatment on a client, demonstrating as a group or selling a product or a range of products? The presentation should include an introduction to the event and an introduction to the demonstrator or product and a conclusion, remembering to thank the audience and models.

Written promotion material can be handed out as members of the audience arrive, placed on the seats or given out at an appropriate point during the demonstration. It is a good idea to hand around samples for the audience to try.

Ensure the demonstration is simple, clear and not too long and that everyone in the audience can see what is being done and hear the commentary. Give the clients the opportunity to buy the products immediately. If this is not possible ensure that clients leave with a voucher to exchange for the products. This should act as an incentive, such as a discount encouraging potential clients to come into the salon and buy.

Never sell the benefits and features to potential clients *without* giving them a chance to buy.

Clients who want to purchase products or a service must be questioned accurately. This will ensure that you are selling the right product to the client. Remember, you are the expert with the knowledge, so show your knowledge.

Listen carefully to the answers your client gives, do not interrupt or talk over the answer. Once the client has finished, you should give a considered, informed reply. Ask further questions if you are still unsure what the best product may be for their needs.

Use of client questionnaires is a good exercise in which to evaluate your promotion. These can be used at random and the results analysed and the appropriate action implemented to improve areas of weakness, building on the strengths as well as investigating areas that are potential for development and growth.

Targets

The setting of targets for the employees and the business is important to analyse overall performance. The employer must have an overall idea on productivity against targets set. Targets tend to vary from employee to employee according to their workload, experience and length of service.

Productivity

Treatments are costed on products used (remember those hidden costs, such as laundering of towels), overheads and the therapist's time.

Sales can be increased through:

- promotions
- incentives
- personal targets.

In some instances, poor levels of productivity and performance may indicate a development need for training. It could also be that there is a skills gap, where there are not enough staff qualified to offer a popular treatment. Through regular and thorough staff training, increased productivity and profits can be achieved.

Reward for high-achieving employees, known as commission, is a good method of rewarding individuals for meeting or exceeding their personal targets.

Client feedback

Feedback from clients is very important when measuring service levels, as this will allow you to evaluate the services offered and the business image.

Informal methods

Ask the client if they enjoyed their treatment.

Formal methods

Client questionnaires can be used to evaluate performance at the end of the treatment (see Chapter 3).

Client focus groups

This is another effective way of gathering views and opinions, and incentives for the client's time can be offered in the form of a thank-you voucher.

Knowledge review

1 Explain why it is essential to have a good knowledge of the services and products available in your workplace.

2 Why are retail sales important to the workplace?

3 Briefly explain when would be an ideal opportunity to promote a service or a product.

4 Why is it important to keep up to date on the products and services you offer in your workplace?

5 Explain what is meant by body language.

6 Why is it important to observe the client's body language when promoting a product or service?

7 If a client wanted more information on a product or service that you were not qualified to advise on, what action would you take?

8 Briefly explain the different ways you could promote products and services available in the workplace.

9 Explain how a retail display should be maintained and why.

10 Explain what is meant by 'consumer rights'.

11 Why is it important to give accurate information on a product or a service?

12 Why is it important to ascertain a client's requirements before selling them products or services?

13 Explain briefly why it is important for the client to use additional products at home as advised by the therapist.

14 Briefly explain the benefits of setting sales targets for the individual employees in the workplace.

15 Explain the benefits of staff training.

16 Why is it important, when selling a product or service to a client, to speak with authority and confidence?

The therapist in business

3

Learning objectives

This chapter covers the following:

- **The effective use and monitoring of resources:**
  - **human resources**
  - **stock**
  - **tools and equipment**
  - **time**
- **meeting productivity and development targets**

This chapter covers essential knowledge and understanding for the following unit:

- **G11, Contribute to the financial effectiveness of the business**

Contributing to effective use and monitoring of resources

There are four factors that contribute to the financial effectiveness of a business. These are:

- human resources
- stock
- tools and equipment
- time.

Human resources (HR)

This refers to the people employed in a business. They are the most important asset of a business.

When running a business it is essential to understand and abide by certain legislation:

- employment legislation
- Working Time Directive.

This aims to ensure that all employees:

- are working within health and safety guidelines
- do not work more than 48 hours a week
- have a daily rest period of 11 hours
- have a rest break when working longer than six hours in a day
- have a minimum rest period of one day a week
- do not exceed more than an average of eight hours when working at night.

Tip

Human resources (HR)
This is the term used to refer to the abilities, qualifications and talents of the people employed in the business.

Tip

See Chapter 1 for full details of the relevant health and safety legislation.

Tip

Any discrimination on the grounds of disability, race, sex, marital status or union membership is breaking the law.

Tip

Race Relations Act 1976
This act exists to prevent discrimination on the grounds of race, colour, ethnic or national origins.

Tip

Sex Discrimination Acts 1975 and 1985 and the Equal Pay Act 1970
This was implemented to prevent less favourable treatment of a man or women on the basis of gender and to promote equal opportunities as well as covering pay and conditions.

Tip

Disability Discrimination Act 1995
This has been introduced to prevent people who are disabled being discriminated against during selection, recruitment and employment. Employers have a duty to adjust working conditions to prevent discrimination of a person with a disability.

Tip

Trade Union and Labour Relations Act 1992
This act is to prevent trade union members being treated less favourably than non-members and vice versa. Employees who have been penalised can complain to an employment tribunal.

Activity

Discuss what other external legal documents may be required.

Information systems

Information systems can be either manual or computerised. Manual systems, for examples file and record cards, need to be indexed into an organised filing system, while computer systems allow you to input client information (for example, personal details and treatment history) into a digital filing system. Computer systems can also store data on staff (including targets they have met, salon performance and so on) and stock details including retail sales and daily takings.

Information systems ensure that the business runs smoothly and provide all the legal information required for external agents and the supervisor, including information required by the Inland Revenue at the end of each financial year.

Job descriptions

It is essential that each member of staff has a written job description that details their job role, duties and responsibilities. As well as this, each new staff member should receive a staff induction to thoroughly familiarise them with their job and work environment. Staff should also agree development targets and personal productivity targets with their manager against which their performance will be reviewed at regular interviews. This procedure ensures that all staff know exactly what is expected of them and what their limitations are.

Grievance and disciplinary procedures should be in place to ensure that staff discipline is adhered to. This is vital in the event of misconduct, complaints or poor performance issues.

Contract of employment

A written contract of employment must be given to an employee within two months of their commencing work, detailing when employment started and when the period of continuous employment began. The contract should also lay out the terms and conditions of employment including:

- rate of pay
- payment interval, e.g. monthly
- hours of work
- holiday entitlement including bank holidays
- place of work
- job title
- responsibilities
- eligibility for pension schemes, sick pay etc.

Working with others

It is important to keep working relationships with your colleagues and clients professional at all times. This will increase productivity with regard to individual and business targets. It is important to:

- be polite
- resolve any personal issues between yourself and a colleague as soon as possible
- always keep your temper
- treat everyone as you would expect to be treated yourself.

Grievances

If you feel you are being treated unfairly, report the incident to your supervisor. All staff should have an awareness of the appeals and grievance procedures.

Staff training

Tip

Remember that when you're speaking on the phone your face cannot be seen – your entire manner is conveyed through your tone of voice.

Staff training is essential. The more effective the staff training, the better the quality of services, financial performance and business productivity.

Technical training, product knowledge and retail knowledge are important to increase sales and boost the client's confidence (see Chapter 2). Staff must work as a team, even though each person may play a different role to ensure the effectiveness of the business overall.

It is important that communication systems are in place. The two types of communication are oral and written.

Oral communication is used when speaking on the phone or when talking in person with a client, another member of staff or with external bodies. Pay attention to your tone of voice and your body language and ensure that the information you are giving is clear and concise. The more experience you have of communicating, the more you will improve your skills in this area.

Internal communication can be improved through regular staff meetings. These are an invaluable way for the employer or supervisor to update the whole team on new initiatives, discuss any issues and to share ideas.

Meetings can be formal or informal. Formal meetings are planned in advance and include an agenda (circulated to all the participants before the meeting) listing the topics to be discussed. The meeting venue should be appropriate for the job, ensuring that there is room for everyone to be seated and involved in the proceedings. One person (the chairperson) should be elected to lead the meeting and one person should be allocated to take the minutes of the meeting, which will be distributed later either by email or as paper copies to the staff members who were in attendance and to the ones who could not attend. Unplanned, informal meetings may occur from time to time when necessity arises.

Stock

Stock describes the total quantity of consumables, services and retail products within the workplace. It is important that procedures are in place to keep accurate, up-to-date

Tip

Legislation surrounding the sale of retail goods includes:

- Prices Act 1974
- Trades Description Acts 1968 and 1972
- Resale Prices Acts 1964 and 1976
- Sales of Goods Act 1994
- Consumer Protection Act 1978
- Consumer Safety Act 1987
- Consumer Protection Regulations 2000.

See Chapter 2 for details.

Activity

Do a search on the internet for stockists in your area of equipment and products you may need in your business. Compare prices on a few similar items. Which stockists would you choose to use and why?

Health & safety

Before handling any damaged goods, it is important to check that they are not hazardous. Dispose of damaged stock promptly and safely.

stock records. Responsibilities should be allocated to various staff members for the maintenance of stock records, ordering stock, checking deliveries when they arrive, unpacking stock and putting it away in the correct area.

You need to be aware of the legal requirements relating to the sale and retail of goods. These are identified in Chapter 2, page 36.

How to order stock

Stock can be ordered from wholesalers, usually cash and carry outlets that sell products to business, or from company representatives. Sales representatives are useful as they can provide the business with all the latest promotions and any new ranges that may be on the market.

Some companies send out sales representatives on a regular basis to the workplace, where orders can then be placed. The order is then taken back to the company, processed and sent out to the business.

When ordering stock the supplier will open a credit account for you and explain how to order and pay for the goods. Cash and carry wholesalers do not usually have minimum orders. Mail-order companies usually charge postage on small orders under a certain amount.

Stock control

It is important to keep accurate records on how much stock the business is holding at any one time. This avoids either running out of stock or having too much of any one product and reduces the amount of money that is tied up on the shelves.

It is important to order stock on a regular basis before it runs out. Orders should be placed as stock becomes low, ensuring that as the existing product lines are sold new stock will be arriving.

When an order arrives it must be carefully checked off against the delivery note. This is a list that arrives with the order, listing the items sent and any that are out of stock and to follow shortly. Any inaccuracies must be reported to the supplier immediately, before signing to confirm the delivery is correct. Damaged products must be reported to the supplier and either sent back or replaced with the relevant paperwork.

Ensure that all the stock is put away immediately, avoiding any accidents that may occur. Stock should be taken to the appropriate storage area on arrival, that is, to the treatment room, storage shelves or cupboard or into a retail area.

Tip

When to return goods to the supplier:

- If they had not been ordered.
- If they have been incorrectly supplied.
- If they are damaged.

Tip

Manual Handling Regulations 1992
The employer is required to carry out a risk assessment of all activities that requires manual lifting. (See Chapter 1, page 28.)

Tip

Employers must have employer's public liability insurance to provide cover for disease or injury that an employee may get as a result of their work. Ensure that the employer's liability certificate is updated and displayed in the workplace.

Health & safety

It is important to carry the goods carefully; don't struggle with a heavy load but ask for assistance when needed. If an employee suffers a personal injury at work that results in a major injury, spending more than 24 hours in hospital or unable to work for three calendar days, the injury must be reported under the Reporting Injuries, Diseases and Dangerous Occurrences Regulations (RIDDOR) 1995. (See Chapter 1, page 9.)

Health & safety

Lifting techniques
The feet should be shoulder-width apart. Firmly grasp the object, bending from the knees and not from the back. When carrying, balance the weight in both hands and carry the heaviest part nearest to the body.

Both employers and employees have a duty under the Health and Safety at Work Act 1974 to work in a safe and healthy environment. Employers are responsible not only not to endanger themselves, but also to ensure that rules are laid down to ensure safe working practices. They must:

- provide safe systems for handling, carrying and storage of all materials
- train all staff in safe working practices.

Stock rotation

When new stock is purchased it must be put to the back of the shelf and the existing stock brought forward. A lot of stock has a shelf life because of the minimum amount of preservatives that they contain. Any products that exceed their shelf life must be disposed of immediately.

Stock systems

Efficient stock systems allow the person responsible to assess quickly the amount of stock that is available.

Regular stock checks show:

- how many stock items you started with and what is left
- a description of each product and its size
- how much of each product is in stock
- when stock needs to be reordered
- minimum and maximum stock levels.

This can be achieved by having a simple stock record card or by feeding the information into a computer. Both these methods need to be carried out regularly.

The computer will analyse the sale details, calculate stock levels and when to reorder. When a manual stock take is performed, it will provide a printout in order that stock can be checked off against the information.

At the point of sale, the person making the sale will either complete a sales bill, which includes stock information, or the computer will read the price ticket via barcodes printed on the package. This will then recognise the product and automatically update the stock records.

Theft

If you suspect a client of stealing and have evidence to support the allegation, you have the right to make a citizen's arrest under the Police and Criminal Evidence Act 1984. It is important to know your employer's policy on theft.

Security

Security is important for theft prevention. Open display areas should be stocked with 'dummy' products. The retail area should be designed in order that all staff have a clear view and, where possible, a security camera should be fitted. Resources should be kept in a secure area only accessible by authorised staff.

Health & safety

Tools and equipment must be sterilised in the appropriate way before and after each treatment. (See Chapter 6, page 171.)

Tools and equipment

All tools and equipment should be provided in sufficient quantity and be of a suitable standard to comply with the relevant health and safety legislation and requirements. This legislation is covered in detail in Chapter 1. All staff must be given the appropriate training in the safe use of equipment.

Health & safety

It is important that electrical equipment is checked and serviced every 12 months by a qualified electrician and a record kept for each piece of equipment.

When purchasing equipment for your business make sure you consider the following:

- Where the equipment is very expensive to purchase, could it, perhaps, be leased?
- Is there client demand?
- What backup service will be provided by the manufacturer in the event of it breaking?

Time

Time management is important; time is money. When booking clients in for treatments it is essential that enough time is allowed for that service to be carried out.

It is important to carry out the treatments in the allocated time, to avoid the next client having to wait for their treatment.

Tip

Service (excluding consultation and preparation)	Maximum service times
Indian head massage	45 minutes
Aromatherapy body massage	60 minutes
Aromatherapy face and body massage	75 minutes
Full body massage including head	75 minutes
Full body massage without head	60 minutes

It is important to remember that at times you will be very busy and perhaps feeling very tired. On these occasions, try to bear in mind that it is not the client's or your colleagues' fault – try to remain helpful and cheerful. Often you will have to cope with situations where your client arrives late for their appointment, you overrun on the allocated treatment time, two clients arrive for the same treatment time, unscheduled clients arrive or bookings change suddenly. Working as a team with your colleagues will usually help to overcome these situations.

If a client is dissatisfied, they will either voice their opinions or alternatively keep quiet but not return for further treatment. To prevent this, always ensure that:

- the client has a thorough consultation before their treatment to ensure they are suitable for the treatment

Tip

Utilities that include power and water must be used in an economical way to contribute to the profitability of the business.

- the client is satisfied and, if there are any concerns, address them straightaway
- the client is informed, particularly if there is any disruption to their service.

Inconvenience can usually be compensated for, however it is therefore important to resolve any problems promptly and keep the client satisfied.

Complaints

Sometimes the client cannot be appeased and therefore a complaint will be made.

A complaints procedure is a formal approach adopted by the business to handle any complaints. Employees must be trained in how to deal with a complaint.

To prevent complaints from occurring it is important that an experienced staff member is always available. Careful planning of holidays or of days off during the week must be considered when drawing up staff rotas. Christmas periods usually require more staff to maintain an efficient service and avoid the loss of clients that could, in turn, result in loss of revenue.

Meeting productivity and development targets

It is important to have personal targets in which achievement can be measured. Targets should be SMART, that is:

- **s**pecific
- **m**easurable
- **a**greed
- **r**ealistic
- **t**imed.

Productivity and development targets need to be set for each individual, for the team and for the business as a whole.

These will review:

- efficiency
- quality
- results.

Personal targets should include:

- what standards are to be expected
- review dates for any progress that was agreed, actioned and achieved
- what tasks need to be performed
- what productivity targets need to be achieved regarding retail and technical sales.

It is important that you always perform to the highest standard, presenting and promoting a positive and professional image not only of the business, but of the industry you represent.

Appraisal

These are progress reviews, in which supervisor or employer looks at how another member of staff is performing in their job role.

Appraisals give the opportunity to review an individual's performance and to plan future actions and personal goals. They also allow you to:

- look at additional accomplishments
- measure the results achieved against the targets set
- look at achievements to date
- identify training needs
- identify any barriers affecting progress
- identify what you feel should be accomplished and how this can be met
- identify and amend any changes to your job role
- identify any additional responsibilities you may want
- update your action plan.

At the following appraisal, the agreed action plan and targets set from the previous appraisal are reviewed.

Sometimes an appraisal is not a positive experience. It is therefore important to try and remain positive about any improvements and recommendations that are agreed at the appraisal, in order that you improve your performance and work towards achieving them. In some circumstances, failure to meet targets can result in a disciplinary procedure, which can later lead to a dismissal.

Tip

Remember your individual productivity targets lead to the long-term financial effectiveness of the business.

Knowledge review

1 Explain briefly what a job description should entail.

2 What are the benefits of an induction process?

3 How would you correctly dispose of broken glass if found when unpacking an order?

4 Why must accurate stock records be kept?

5 Briefly explain when you should return goods.

6 What could be the consequences if goods were not stored correctly?

7 Explain how flammable liquids should be stored correctly.

8 Explain the main points of good stock keeping.

9 Why should stock that is blocking access be removed immediately?

10 What does the abbreviation COSHH stand for?

11 What is the correct lifting procedure when lifting a large box from floor level to a work surface?

12 What security methods should be taken to prevent stock from being stolen?

13 Give two legal requirements regarding the sale of retail goods.

14 How often should a piece of electrical equipment be tested?

15 Who should carry out the electrical equipment testing?

16 Give two examples of how the relevant workplace health and safety regulations are implemented and monitored in the workplace.

17 Why is it important to work to commercial treatment times when carrying out a treatment service?

18 What is the purpose of an appraisal?

19 Why is it important to meet development and productivity targets?

20 Give two examples of how you could achieve your development and productivity targets.

21 Explain briefly what action you would take if you found you could not achieve your individual targets.

22 Give examples of what an effective team is.

23 Why is it important to communicate well with others?

24 Why is it important to have a positive relationship with your colleagues?

25 If you had a grievance, to whom would you report it?

Anatomy, physiology and effects of massage

4

Learning objectives

This chapter covers the following:

- **basic components of the body**
- **the skin**
- **skeletal system**
- **joints**
- **muscular system**
- **circulatory system**
- **lymphatic system**
- **nervous system**
- **digestive system**
- **nutrition**
- **respiratory and olfactory systems**
- **renal system**
- **endocrine system**
- **breasts**
- **psychological benefits**

You will need to understand anatomy and physiology as it relates to each of the units included on the beauty therapy massage route as follows:

- **BT17, Provide head and body massage treatments**

● **BT20, Provide Indian head massage treatment**

● **BT21, Provide massage using pre-blended aromatherapy oils**

The essential anatomy and physiology you need to know and understand for each unit is indicated with a tick in the following table:

Unit	BT17, Provide head and body massage treatments	BT20, Provide Indian head massage treatment	BT21, Provide massage using pre-blended aromatherapy oils
Structure and function of cells and tissues	✓	✓	✓
Skin structure and function	✓	✓	✓
Factors affecting skin condition (this is covered in Chapter 5, Client consultation and contraindications to treatment)	✓	✓	✓
Skeletal system and joints	✓	✓	✓
Muscular system	✓	✓	✓
Circulatory system	✓	✓	✓
Lymphatic system	✓	✓	✓
Nervous system	✓	✓	✓
Digestive system	✓	✓	
Respiratory and olfactory systems	✓		✓
Renal system	✓		✓
Endocrine system	✓		✓

Tip

When carrying out any massage treatment, remember that all the body systems work together – the functioning of one will affect all the others.

Massage can have both physical and psychological effects. In order to gain a proper understanding of the physical benefits of massage and perform it safely, it is essential to understand the anatomy and physiology of the human body. This chapter looks at each of the major body systems that can be affected by massage and then explains the effects of massage on each discrete system before moving on to explore the psychological effects of massage. However, you should remember that in the same way that the physical and psychological cannot truly be separated, each system of the body is interconnected and affected by the functioning of other systems.

Basic components of the body

Checklist

Remember the composition of the body as follows:

- The **organism** is made up of a number of **systems**.
- A **system** is made up of **organs**.
- An **organ** is made up of **tissues**.
- **Tissues** are made up of groups of **cells**.

The human body is made up of billions of cells. **Cells** are the smallest structures that show all the features of living things. In multi-cell organisms like the human body, cells combine in groups to do certain jobs effectively. Common groups of cells are known as **tissues**. Different tissues combine to form specialised **organs**, each of which has a particular function, for example the stomach. Organs are then organised into **systems**, for example the digestive system, that combine to form **organisms**.

Cells

Although cells can differ in size, shape, structure and function, there are seven characteristics that the cells of all living things have in common. These are:

1 growth
2 reproduction
3 sensitivity
4 excretion
5 movement
6 metabolism/nutrition
7 respiration.

All cells contain three key components:

- The **nucleus** controls chemical activity and contains the genetic information of the cell. One of the main functions of the nucleus is to control cell reproduction.

Structure of a cell

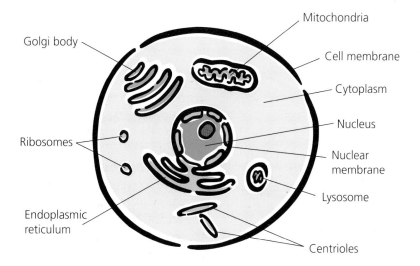

- **Cytoplasm** surrounds the nucleus and fills the cell. It is liquid consisting mostly of water but also contains various organelles as well as salts, dissolved gases and nutrients. The organelles can be involved in energy production, e.g. mitochondria, protein production, e.g. endoplastic reticulum; or have other specialities.

- The **cell membrane** forms the outer surface of the cell surrounding the cytoplasm and controls the passage of soluble substances into and out of the cell.

Tissue

There are four main types of tissue found in animals (including humans) and each carries out a different function. (See Table 4.1.)

Table 4.1 *Tissues and functions*

Tissue type	*Function*	*Example*
Nervous	To detect, monitor and respond to internal and external stimuli forming a communication system between different parts of the body	Neurones/ nerve cells
Connective	To support surround and connect different parts of the body	Bones, areolar, cartilage
Muscular	To contract and produce movement	Skeletal, voluntary, involuntary
Epithelial	To form surface linings for protection	Epidermis

Nervous tissue

Nervous tissue is made up of nerve fibres and nerve cells or **neurones**, which are very sensitive to stimulation. Neurones respond to stimuli and conduct and transmit nerve impulses throughout the body from their origin to their destination. Neurones connect all parts of the body to the central nervous system (CNS), which consists of the spinal cord and the brain.

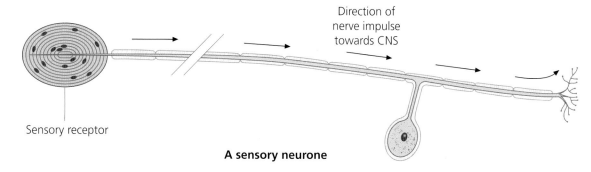

Sensory receptor

A sensory neurone

Direction of
nerve impulse
towards CNS

A sensory neurone

Neurones can be either sensory or motor. Sensory organs include the ears, nose, mouth and eyes, but sensory receptors can also be found in joints, tendons, muscles and the dermis of the skin. When stimulated, impulses pass from the receptor, along the neurone fibre to the central nervous system. This gives us sensations such as touch, taste, sight, smell and hearing. Motor effector neurones conduct impulses away from the central nervous system to the muscles and glands of the body to stimulate them to carry out their work, for example voluntary muscle contractions. Since a nerve is a collection of single neurones (surrounded by a protective sheath), nerves can contain only sensory neurones, only motor neurones or a combination of the two.

Connective tissue

Connective tissues support and connect various parts of the body. They consist of cells, collagen fibres and networks, elastin and a matrix that can be fluid, solid or gel. There are a number of types of connective tissue including:

- adipose tissue, which stores fat under the skin and around organs
- cartilage, much firmer than the other connective tissues, contains no nerves or blood vessels
- bone
- blood
- fibrous tissue, assists in maintaining the elasticity of skin.

Muscular tissue

There are three types of muscular tissue. (See Table 4.2.)

Table 4.2 *Muscle tissues*

Type	Function	Location
Skeletal	Produces body movement and maintains posture	Skeletal system
Cardiac	Under involuntary control and maintains heartbeat	Only found in the heart
Smooth	Peristalsis	Digestive and circulatory systems, e.g. walls of blood vessels and intestines

Epithelial tissue

The most common example of epithelial tissue can be found in the epidermis (the outer layer of the skin), but tissue of this type can also be found in the linings of the lymph, blood and heart vessels, respiratory and digestive organs. Epithelial tissue can be either **simple**, i.e. composed of a single cell layer or **compound**, i.e. composed of multiple cell layers.

There are four basic types of simple epithelial tissue:

- squamous
- cuboidal
- cilated
- columnar.

Squamous tissue	Like flat stones, fit closely together	Provide a smooth lining for lymph and blood vessels and the heart	
Cuboidal cells	Cube-like in shape	Found in some glands and in the tubules in the kidneys. Involved in secretion and absorption	
Cilated cells	Rectangular with hairs	Found in respiratory passages and uterine tubes. Contain hairs that force the contents of the tube to move in one direction	
Columnar cells	Retangular	Found in the lining of the gall bladder, organs in the alimentary tract and in the ducts of glands. Some of the cells absorb nutrients during digestion and others secrete mucus	

Compound or stratified epithelial tissue is less delicate than the simple type. It can also be:

- squamous, lining the mouth
- cuboidal in ducts of sweat glands
- columnar in the anus
- transitional (hollow – found in urinary bladder and prevents organ from rupturing) – lining the bladder.

Rather than lining organs as the simple type do, compound epithelial tissue tends to protect underlying structures. The top layers tend to be flat in shape, but in deeper layers the cells are columnar in shape. In compound tissues, the basal cells are constantly producing new cells by multiplying, which causes them to push the cells above outwards with a flattening effect. These cells are either keratinised, such as the hair, skin and nails, which provide protection and stop the cells underneath from drying out, or non-keratinised, such as the conjunctiva of the eyes, the mouth lining and the oesophagus.

Each system of the body is usually built up around one of the body's organs, for example the circulatory or cardiovascular system is built around the heart, the digestive system around the stomach and the integumentary system around the skin. Most of the body's systems can be affected by massage and we will look at each in turn, together with the effects massage can have.

Skin

Did you know

The skin is the largest organ in the human body. If you took off your skin and laid it flat, depending on your body size, it would cover an area of about 1.9m².

The skin forms part of the integumentary system along with the hair and nails and as far as massage is concerned, the skin is the most important aspect. It is the largest organ of the body and serves as an interface with the environment and as protection for the body.

Structure

The skin consists of three main layers:

- the epidermis
- the dermis
- subcutaneous layers.

Layers of the skin

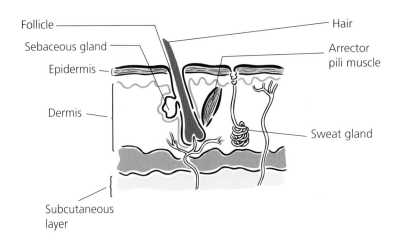

Follicle
Sebaceous gland
Epidermis
Dermis
Subcutaneous
layer

Hair
Arrector
pili muscle
Sweat gland

Epidermis

The epidermis, interlocked with the upper layer of the dermis by papillae, is made up of five layers:

- stratum corneum
- stratum lucidum
- stratum granulosum
- stratum spinosum
- stratum germinativum or basal layer.

Tip

The epidermis is self-sufficient in reproducing itself.

It is within the layers of the epidermis that the process of **keratinisation** takes place. This is the process by which living cells transform to dead horny flat cells with no nucleus. The epidermis contains cells at every stage of this process, from basal cells with well-defined nuclei to superficial flaky debris in which the nuclei and all evidence of cell structure has disappeared. As the cells become

Layers of the epidermis

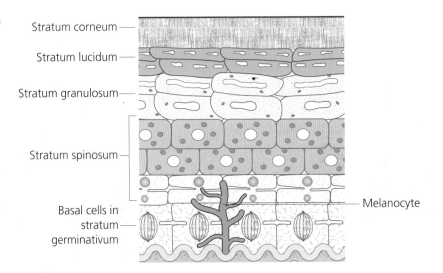

Stratum corneum
Stratum lucidum
Stratum granulosum
Stratum spinosum
Basal cells in stratum germinativum
Melanocyte

Skin layer	Functions
Stratum corneum	The cells contain an epidermal fatty material that keeps them waterproof and helps keep the skin from cracking and becoming open to infection
Stratum lucidum	This layer derives its name from its clear translucent almost transparent appearance. Only a few cells deep, the stratum lucidum lies between the outer horny layer and the inner granular layer. It is thought that this layer is the barrier that controls the transmission of water through the skin
Stratum granulosum	The thickness of this layer may vary from one to several cells in depth and is at its thickest on the palms of the hands and soles of the feet. The cells are flat and becoming keratinised. These cells reflect light and give the skin a white appearance. Loss of fluid is an essential process in the stages of keratinisation and the cells in this layer are believed to represent the first stage in the transformation of the epidermal cells into the horny keratin material
Stratum spinosum	This prickle cell layer (rounded cells with short projections) is often classed with the stratum germinativum to form the **malpighian layer**
Stratum germinativum or basal layer	This is the deepest section of the epidermis and is in contact with the dermis from which it derives its nutrient fluids via the capillary blood vessels
	It is in this layer that the process of **mitosis** – cell division – takes place as the development of new cells leads to a gradual displacement of the older cells towards the surface. The basal layer is at its most productive between midnight and 4am and this is one explanation for the term 'beauty sleep'
	Melanocytes (melanin-forming cells) are found in abundance in this layer with one in every 10 cells a pigment-forming melanocyte. Melanin protects the skin against ultraviolet radiation and is responsible for differences in skin colour. Exposure to sunlight increases the production of melanin, as the skin works harder to increase its protection levels. The visible evidence of this is a suntan

Health & safety

If you sunbathe you must always protect the skin with a suitable sunscreen and use a moisturising after-sun product to lessen the effects of premature aging and the risk of cancer.

keratinised, the epidermis provides a thick, tough outer barrier to protect the body

The thickness of the epidermis can be altered by external stimuli. It will become thicker if it is subject to friction or exposed to sunlight in order to protect the deeper tissues of the body. Radiation, including that from sunlight, damages the epidermis. It causes the upper layers to burn and peel and can affect the dividing basal layers, which increases the risk of cancerous growths. If the rays penetrate through the epidermis into the dermis, the connective tissues can be damaged, which leads to visible signs of aging such as wrinkling (due to connective tissue losing elasticity) and thicker, leathery skin.

Dermis

The dermis is thicker than the epidermis and lies underneath it. It is a dense fibrous structure, which itself consists of two layers: the papillary layer and the reticular layer. The **papillary layer** is the upper layer and connects the dermis to the epidermis above. It has an uneven surface that consists of fine strands of elastic tissue extending upwards into the epidermis in looped finger-like projections (or **dermal papillae**). These dermal papillae enable oxygen and nutrients to be transported into the basal layer of the epidermis. The **reticular layer** contains fat cells, blood vessels, lymph vessels, sweat glands, hair follicles and nerve endings.

There are three kinds of fibre that intermingle with the cells of the dermis:

- collagen fibres, which make up 78% of the dry weight of the skin
- recticulum fibres, which form fine branching patterns in the connective tissue helping to link the bundles of collagen fibres
- elastin, which is contained within the collagen fibres. Elastin has elastic qualities and helps to give the skin its resilience.

The dermis is thinnest on the eyelids. It is thickest on the palms of the hands and the soles of the feet and tends to be thicker in men than in women.

Other structures of the dermis are now discussed.

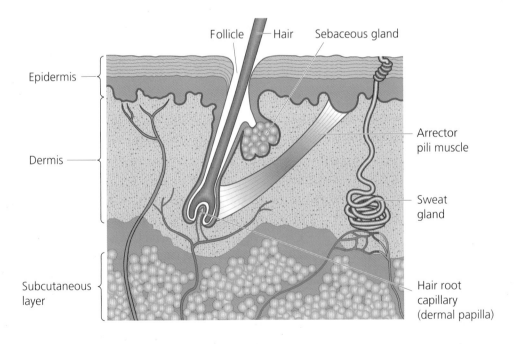

Follicle — Hair   Sebaceous gland

Epidermis

Dermis

Subcutaneous layer

Arrector pili muscle

Sweat gland

Hair root capillary (dermal papilla)

The dermis

Sensory nerve endings

Situated in the dermis, these register any pain, pressure, touch and changes in temperature. It is the sensory nerve endings that send messages to the central nervous system and the brain to let us know what is happening on the skin's surface.

The dermis contains structures that are called skin appendages. These are:

- sweat glands
- hair follicles
- sebaceous glands
- nails.

Sweat glands (subodiferous glands)

These glands extend from the epidermis to the dermis and are found all over the body. The function is to regulate the body temperature. There are two types of sweat gland:

1 Eccrine glands – these are coiled in the dermis but look straight in appearance to the epidermis. They are found all over the body and appear as tiny ducts that open directly onto the skin's surface, commonly referred to as pores. Their function is to maintain body temperature (36.8°C) by continually secreting small amounts of sweat.

2 Apocrine glands – these are attached to a hair follicle and are controlled by hormones. Their activity increases when we become nervous or excited. The fluid that is secreted contains small amounts of protein, urea, fats and sugars and is thicker in consistency than the secretion from the eccrine glands. If good personal hygiene is not adhered to, an unpleasant smell is produced when sweat is broken down by the skin's bacteria.

Hair follicles

These are found all over the body except on the lips, the soles and the palms. The hair follicle is connected to the base of the epidermis by the arrector pili, which is a small muscle. When the arrector pili contracts, it causes the hair to stand up in its hair follicle, which results in a goose pimple. The hair is composed of cells called germinal matrix formed in the hair bulb (lowest part of the hair). The follicle is supplied by nerves and blood vessels that nourish the cells in the area as they reproduce. The cells move up the follicle from the bulb and their structure changes to form the hair.

Sebaceous glands

These are found all over the body except for the palms and soles. The sebaceous glands produce the skin's natural oil, referred to as sebum. Sebum is made up of fatty acids and waxes that have fungicidal and bactericidal properties and also reduce the amount of moisture evaporating from the skin and prevent it from becoming dry.

Nails

Nails protect the nail bed which is the living part of the nail. Nails are composed of dead epidermis cells that are keratinised and therefore hard.

Subcutaneous layer

This layer contains **adipose tissue**. As well as in the skin, adipose tissue can also be found around the organs of the body. It stores fat that is used as a reserve when energy intake from food falls below energy output. It is composed of specialised cells known as **adipocyte cells**. Adipose tissue varies in thickness according to age, sex and general health and tends to be thicker in women than men. The fatty adipose tissue gives smoothness and shape to the body and serves as a protective cushion for the upper skin layers. Massage is thought to aid the reduction of adipose tissues.

Function

It is essential to life that the skin functions both efficiently and effectively. It has six main functions.

Health & safety

Although one main function of the skin is to protect the body from the outside environment, some substances can still be absorbed through the skin. Remember always to wear disposable gloves when dealing with harmful substances.

? Did you know

About 80% of household dust is made up of dead skin cells shed from the epidermis.

Function

Function	
Protection	The skin protects the body from bacterial infection and injury
Heat regulation	It compensates for changing temperatures outside the body. Sweat glands make the necessary adjustment to their functions in order to maintain the normal temperature of a healthy body (36.8°)
Secretion and excretion	The skin acts as both an excretory and secretary organ. Subodiferous glands excrete perspiration, which is a waste product. Sebaceous glands secrete sebum, which coats the skin's surface and helps to waterproof it at the same time as slowing down the evaporation

▶

of moisture. The skin also creates a barrier that inhibits the growth of harmful bacteria

Absorption	The skin only has limited powers of absorption. Some chemicals, cosmetics and drugs can be absorbed in small amounts through its pores
Respiration	The skin breathes through its pores in the same way as we breathe through our lungs. Oxygen is taken in and carbon dioxide is discharged
Sensation	Heat, cold, pain, pressure and touch receptors are found in the papillary layer of the dermis. Nerves supplying the skin register these basic sensations

Tip

Never massage over an area if there is any sign of skin infection or if it is severely bruised.

Tip

When massage is applied on the skin, it produces the following effects:

- Improvement in skin condition caused by an increase in circulation, which will improve the functions of the sebaceous and sweat glands by opening them if they are blocked.
- Sebaceous glands are nourished by fresh blood supply, leading to an increase in sebum production, which softens the skin and makes it more supple.
- Subodiferous glands are stimulated, which results in the production of more sweat and the excretion of waste products.
- Desquamation – removal of the top layer of dead cells – takes place, which leads to improved skin condition and a healthier appearance.
- It is claimed that massage can soften the hard fat in the adipose tissue in the dermis and speed up its removal dispensing it into the circulatory system.

Skeletal system

Did you know

There are 206 bones in the human body.

and 600 muscles in the body,

The skeleton is made up primarily of bones, the hardest structure in the body. Bones come in many different shapes, depending on their function and are connected to each other at joints by less dense connective tissues, cartilage and ligament. Supported by skeletal muscles, the skeleton makes up the framework of the body.

Human skeleton

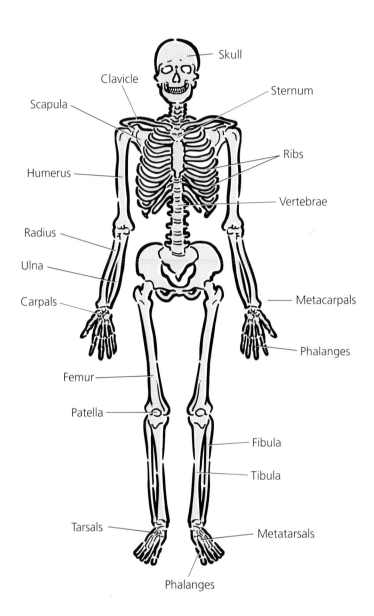

Structure

The human skeleton consists of 206 bones divided into two main groups: the axial skeleton, which is made up of the bones around the centre of the body, that is the skull and vertebral column together with the ribs and sternum, and the appendicular skeleton, which consists of the bones of the upper and lower limbs together with the pelvic and pectoral girdles.

Axial skeleton

The three main groups of bones that form this part of the skeleton are the bones of the head, the spine and the thorax.

Bones of the head

The skull consists of two parts, namely the **cranium** and the **face**. There are eight bones in the cranium and 14 in the face. The function of the skull is to protect the brain and, together with the muscles that cover the bones of the face, the skull determines the shape of the face and head.

The cranium

There are eight flat bones forming the cranium that surrounds the brain. These bones are slightly curved and thin. They are held together by connective tissue. As we grow from childhood, the joints, called **sutures**, become immovable:

- **The frontal bone** forms the front part of the roof of the skull, the forehead and the upper wall of the eye sockets.
- **Two parietal bones** form the sides and roof of the cranium, the crown.
- **Two temporal bones** form the sides of the head, the lower region and sides of the cranium around the ears. They provide two attachment points for muscles, the zygomaticus process and the mastoid process.
- **The occipital bone** forms the back and base of the cranium. It leaves a large hole, the foramen magnum, through which pass the spinal cord, blood vessels and nerves.
- **The sphenoid bone** forms the anterior part of the cranium base at the back of the eye sockets. It is bat shaped with wings on either side that form the temples. It joins all the bones of the cranium.
- **The ethmoid bone**, between the eye sockets, forms part of the nasal cavities.

Bones of the cranium

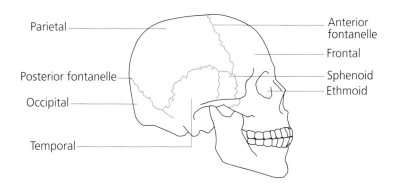

The bones of the face

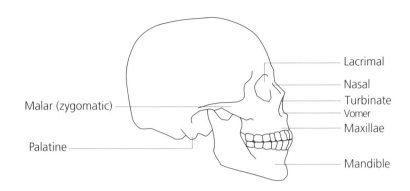

The face

The facial bones form the facial features and support structures such as the teeth and eyes. The 15 facial bones are as follows:

- **Two nasal bones** form the bridge of the nose.
- **Two maxillae** form the upper jaw, the side walls of the nose and part of the roof of the mouth.
- **Two malar bones** (zygomatic) form the cheekbones.
- **Two palatine bones** form the floors and side walls of the nose and the roof of the mouth.
- **Two lacrimal bones** form the inner walls of the eye socket.
- **Two turbinate bones** form the outside of the nose.
- The **vomer bone** forms part of the nasal septum, the dividing bony wall of the nose.
- The **mandible**, the only movable facial bone, forms the lower jaw. This is the strongest and largest facial bone.
- The **hyoid bone** supports the tongue (not shown in diagram). It is a u-shaped bone at the front of the neck.

Vertebral column

The spinal column extends from the skull down to the pelvis. It lies on the posterior side of the skeleton, providing the body with a central flexible axis. It protects the nerve pathway of the spinal cord and provides a surface for muscle attachments.

The spinal column is composed of 33 irregular bones called vertebrae. Some of the vertebrae are fused together and there are 26 movable bones. The spinal column consists of:

- **Seven cervical vertebrae** at the top of the spine. The **atlas** vertebra (first vertebra) supports the skull, the **axis** (second vertebra) allows the head to rotate.

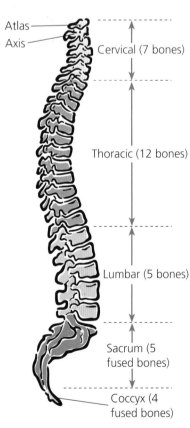

Vertebral column: lateral view

- **Twelve thoracic vertebrae** lie mid-spine in the thorax region where they articulate with the ribs.
- **Five lumbar vertebrae** are positioned in the lower region of the back and help support the weight of the body.
- **Five sacral vertebrae** lie in between the bones of the pelvis.
- **Four coccyx vertebrae** are collectively known as the tailbone.

The thorax

The thorax protects internal organs such as the lungs and heart and consists of the **ribs**, **sternum** and the **thoracic vertebrae**.

There are 12 pairs of ribs. The first 10 pairs are attached at the back to a thoracic vertebrae. The first seven pairs attach at the front to the sternum. The next three pairs attach to the ribs above them and are called false ribs. The final two pairs do not attach to anything at the front and are called floating ribs.

The pelvic girdle supports the vertebrae and the weight of the body and also protects some internal organs such as the uterus. It is composed of two hipbones joined at the back by the **sacrum** and at the front to the **symphysis pubis**.

The sternum is the breastbone, and it provides a surface for muscle attachment, allowing muscle movements and protecting the internal organs.

Appendicular skeleton

Two **clavicles** form the collarbone. These are long slender bones that meet at the base of the neck. The collarbone allows movement of the shoulders, forming a joint with the **scapulae** and the sternum.

Two **scapulae** are the shoulder blades in the upper back. They are triangular and provide attachment for muscles that move the arm. The shoulder girdle, composed of the scapulae and the clavicle, allows movement at the shoulder.

Upper limbs

The **humerus** is the bone in each of the upper arms. The humerus meets the scapulae in a ball and socket joint and allows movement in any direction.

The **ulna** and **radius** are the long bones of the forearm. They are tied together by a fibrous ring and allow a rotating

Bones of the arm and chest

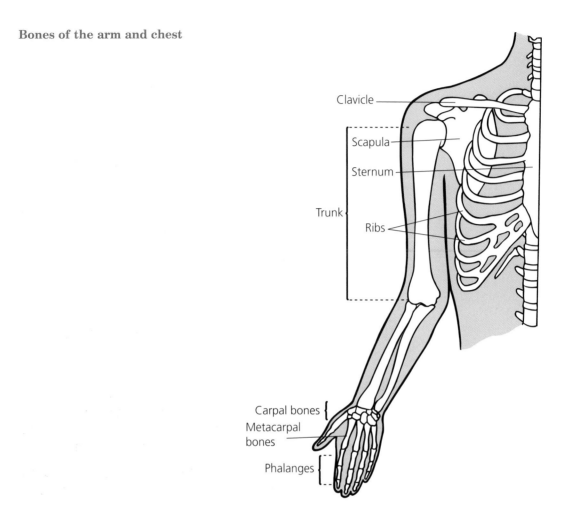

Bones of the hand

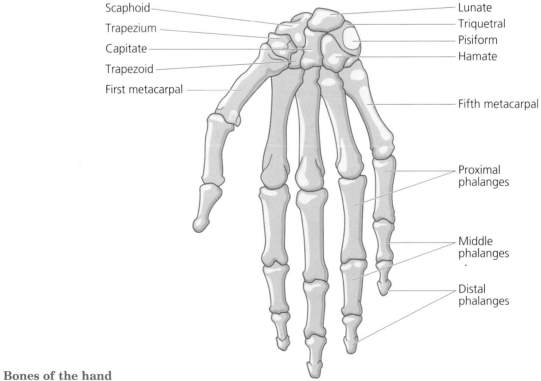

movement. The radius is shorter than the ulna bone and is positioned on the thumb side of the forearm. The ulna is positioned on the little finger side. The joint between the two bones produces a movement called pronation. This is when the radius moves obliquely across the ulna, resulting in the thumb side of the hand being closer to the body.

The wrist contains eight **carpals**. These are irregularly sized bones that are very close together and held in place by ligaments.

The hand is made up of five **metacarpals** making up the palm and 14 **phalanges** making up the fingers – two in each thumb and three in each finger.

Lower limbs

The **femur** is the longest bone in the body and can be found in the upper leg. The head of the femur fits into a socket in the **pelvis**, which forms the hip joint and the distal end articulates with the **patella** (kneecap).

The lower leg is composed of the **tibia,** which is the larger of the two bones carrying body weight and is positioned on the lateral side of the body, and the **fibula**. Both bones have joints at the knee and at the ankle.

The foot is composed of seven **tarsal** bones, five **metatarsal** bones and 14 **phalanges**. These fit together to form the arches that support the foot and absorb the impact when running, jumping and walking.

Bones of the lower leg

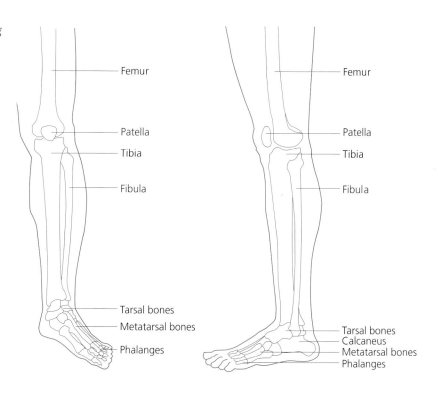

Femur

Patella

Tibia

Fibula

Tarsal bones
Metatarsal bones

Phalanges

Femur

Patella

Tibia

Fibula

Tarsal bones
Calcaneus
Metatarsal bones
Phalanges

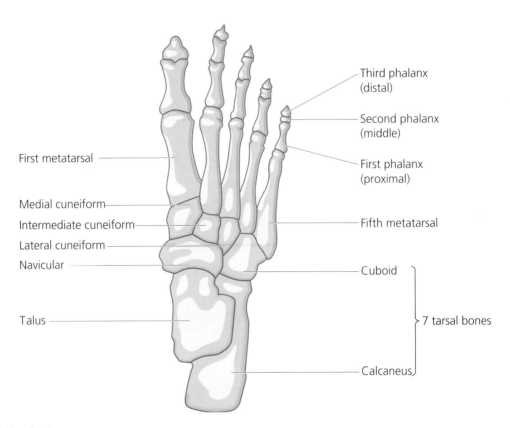

Third phalanx (distal)

Second phalanx (middle)

First phalanx (proximal)

First metatarsal

Medial cuneiform

Intermediate cuneiform

Lateral cuneiform

Navicular

Talus

Fifth metatarsal

Cuboid

7 tarsal bones

Calcaneus

Bones of the foot

Tip

Never massage over any painful bones if you do not know the reason for the pain. Make sure that any fractures or breaks have healed completely prior to treatment and seek medical advice if the client has any metal pins or discs.

Functions of the skeletal system

The skeletal system:

- protects the underlying structures such as the brain, lungs and the heart
- provides a structure from which many of the internal organs are suspended and kept securely in position
- provides an attachment point for the muscles to allow movement
- supports the softer tissues
- gives shape to the body.

Blood cells known as the bone marrow are made inside the bone.

Tip

When massage is applied to bones, it does not have any direct effect. What *does* happen is that because of increased blood circulation the bones are fed fresh oxygen and waste products are absorbed more quickly.

Joints

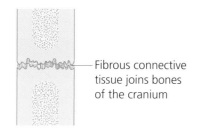

Fibrous connective tissue joins bones of the cranium

A fibrous joint

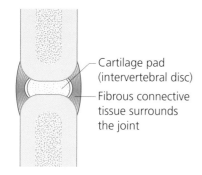

Cartilage pad (intervertebral disc)

Fibrous connective tissue surrounds the joint

A cartilaginous joint

A joint is where two or more bones meet. There are three main types of joint:

1. Fibrous joints or sutures that do not allow movement between bones. The bone edges are effectively fused together. The joints between the bones in an adult's skull are fibrous joints as is the joint between the maxilla and mandible of the jaw, between the teeth.

2. Cartilaginous joints that allow slight movement between bones by means of **fibrocartilage** pads between the bones, which act as shock absorbers by allowing slight movement. The joints between the vertebrae in the spine are cartilaginous joints.

3. Synovial joints that allow free movement between bones because the bones are held loosely together by **ligaments**, a form of connective tissue.

From the point of view of massage, it is synovial joints that are the most important because the synovial fluid is stimulated, which in turn lubricates and nourishes the joint by helping to increase movement. There are a number of different classifications of synovial joint, depending on the type of movement that they allow. These are hinge, gliding, pivot, condyloid, saddle and, finally, ball and socket. (The main synovial joints in the body are detailed in Table 4.3.) Their basic formation is a sleeve-like ligament (or **articulating capsule**) that holds the bones loosely together and surrounds the joint creating a cavity. The capsule is lined with a **synovial**

A synovial joint

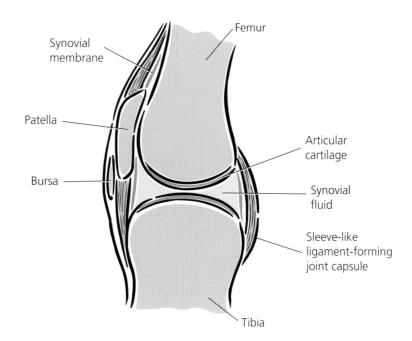

Synovial membrane

Femur

Patella

Bursa

Articular cartilage

Synovial fluid

Sleeve-like ligament-forming joint capsule

Tibia

membrane, which secretes **synovial fluid** that lubricates and nourishes the joint. **Articular cartilage** provides a smooth coating that covers the end of each bone, protecting them from wear and tear brought about by friction. Extra

Table 4.3 *Synovial joints and their functions*

Position	Type	Movement
Hand	Gliding	Flexion (angle between two bones at a joint decreases); extension (angle between two bones at a joint increases)
Foot	Gliding	Eversion (plantar foot surface turns outwards); inversion (plantar foot surface turns inwards)
Toe	Hinge	Extension, flexion, the joint at the base of the toe allows abduction (movement away from the centre of the body) and adduction (movement towards the centre of the body)
Finger	Hinge	Extension and flexion, the joint at the base of the finger allows abduction and adduction
Wrist	Condyloid: formed between bones of the lower arm which are the radius and the ulna and the wrist bones which are the carpals	Flexion, extension, abduction, adduction
Ankle	Hinge: formed between the bones of the lower leg tibia and fibula and also the talus of the foot	Dorsiflexion (produced by the foot pulled up towards the knee); plantar flexion (produced when the foot is being pointed)
Forearm	Pivot: formed between the ulna and head of the radius	Supination (when the palm of the hand turns up); pronation (when the hand is turned downwards)
Elbow	Hinge	Flexion and extension of the arm

Humerus
Radius
Ulna

Elbow joint

Table 4.3 *(continued)*

Position	Type	Movement	
Knee	Hinge: formed between the femur and tibia	Femur Joint stabilised by internal ligaments and pieces of cartilage Tibia Fibula **Knee joint**	Extension and flexion of the leg
Shoulder	Ball and socket: the head of the humerus is ball shaped and this fits into the socket on the scapula	Shallow socket (scapula) Ball (head of humerus) Tendon of biceps muscle runs through the joint capsule Humerus **Shoulder joint**	Abduction, adduction, extension, flexion and rotation. Also arm circling, which involves movement of this joint together with the shoulder
Hip	Ball and socket: the femur head is shaped like a ball and this fits into the pelvis socket	Intracapsular ligament Socket (pelvis) Ball (head of femur) **Hip joint**	Abduction, adduction, extension, flexion and rotation

strength is produced by the ligaments that run outside the articular capsule or inside the joint itself.

Discs of cartilage are contained in some joints to maintain stability and cushion movement, very much like that found in cartilaginous joints. Some synovial joints also contain a **bursa**, a sac-like extension of the synovial membrane, which provides additional cushioning where tendons rub against bones or other tendons to prevent excessive friction and damage.

Tip

Joints are nourished as the blood supply is increased to the area. Massage can also help to loosen any adhesions in a joint's surrounding structures.

Muscular system

Structure

There are two types of muscle: **voluntary** and **involuntary**. Voluntary muscles are used, for example, in walking, talking or writing; they are muscles that are under our conscious control via the nervous system. Involuntary muscles are muscles we cannot control; they keep the heart beating and allow food to be digested.

There are three types of muscle tissue:

- smooth
- cardiac
- skeletal.

Smooth muscle tissue

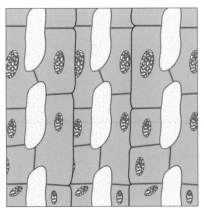

Cardiac muscle tissue

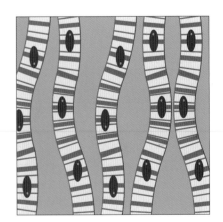

Skeletal muscle tissue

These muscle tissues operate as follows:

- Smooth or visceral is under involuntary control. This type of muscle tissue is involved in automatic functions in the body, for example peristaltic movement in digestion.
- Cardiac is only found in the heart and is under involuntary control.
- Skeletal is under voluntary control. This accounts for the majority of the muscular system. Skeletal muscle tissue covers the bones of the body and is attached to them by connective tissue that protects the muscle and gives it its shape. We use it for voluntary movements of the skeleton.

Muscle tissue is composed of 20% protein, 75% water and 5% mineral salts, fats and glycogen. On average, it makes up about half of a person's total body weight. Muscles are well supplied with blood in order to provide energy and nerves to deliver messages to and from the brain. Muscles can be either *superficial*, laying just below the skin, or *deep*.

A muscle consists of a number of elastic fibres bound together in bundles. The bundles are usually spindle shaped and held in a sheath. At the end of the sheath are tendons, strong fibrous bands that attach the muscles to bones.

Voluntary muscles

Structure and movement

Voluntary muscle is made up of cylindrical cells that, in turn, make up fibres. Each fibre contains several nuclei on its outer membrane or sheath. All the fibres run longitudinally and form bundles as described earlier. Voluntary muscle looks as if it were striped. This is because the fibres are made up of two different coloured protein filaments,

Voluntary muscle tissue

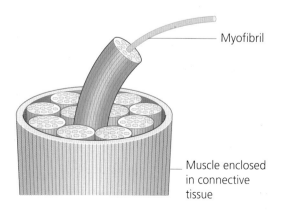

Myofibril

Muscle enclosed in connective tissue

myosin, the thicker filament, and **actin**. These play a significant part in the mechanism or muscle contraction.

Each muscle has an **origin** and an **insertion**. The origin is usually the attachment or most fixed point – **proximal** part. The insertion is usually the most movable point of attachment – **distil** part. When muscles contract, this is called an action.

The attachment of muscles can be by muscle fibrous bands, tendons and muscle fibres, to each other, skin, fascia, bones, ligaments or cartilage.

Muscles work in groups. There will be more than one muscle involved in generating any movement or action. Muscles usually work in pairs. One will be the **agonist** or **protagonist**, whose function is to contract, and the opposing muscle is the **antagonist**, whose function is to relax. Agonists are the prime movers in all muscle action and while the agonists contract, antagonists have the

Plantar flexion
(toe pointing)

Dorsi flexion
(foot raised)

Adduction – muscles
pull limb towards
body/fingers together
to their usual position

Pronation

Supination

Abduction – muscles
move limb, etc. from
usual position

Extension

Flexion

Diagrams showing the main muscle actions

controlling influence. **Synergists** help the protagonists to produce the best possible movement and prevent inefficiency. **Fixators** cut out any unnecessary movements that may hinder the prime movers. They are the stabilisers – they work to hold and fix.

When the muscle is stimulated to contract by the nervous system, a sliding movement occurs within the muscle's contractile fibres. The actin protein filaments move inwards towards the myosin and the two filaments merge. This causes the fibres of the muscle to shorten and thicken and pull on their attachments (bones and joints) to achieve the movements required. When relaxing, the muscle fibres elongate and return to their normal shape.

Properties

Muscle tissue has a number of properties that allow it to function. These properties are:

- the ability to contract and extend
- elasticity, i.e. ability to return to its original shape after contracting or extending
- responsiveness, i.e. contracts in response to nerve impulses.

Voluntary muscles work together with the nervous system and will only contract when stimulated. In order to contract, muscles require energy. This is produced by tissue respiration, which is when the glucose delivered by the blood and stored in the muscle in the form of glycogen, combines with oxygen, also supplied by the blood. Lactic acid is created as a result of energy production and must be removed from the muscle in order to prevent muscle fatigue. In order to work effectively, therefore, muscles require a good blood supply to deliver oxygen and nutrients and take away lactic acid. If the blood cannot supply enough oxygen, muscles can respire without oxygen for short periods of time. This is called **anaerobic respiration**.

When muscles respire anaerobically, glucose is broken down into lactic acid. As lactic acid builds up in the muscle tissue, it causes fatigue, which is not only painful but also causes the muscle to stop contracting. Muscle fatigue causes a delay in muscle response and can result in the muscle not working at all. Anaerobic respiration results in an oxygen debt in the muscle tissue that must be repaid. After strenuous exercise where anaerobic respiration occurs, it is essential that the muscles receive a good supply of blood, as oxygen is needed to break down the lactic acid into water and carbon dioxide so that it can be removed from the body. If any traces of

Health & safety

Warming down after exercise ensures adequate blood flow to the muscles so that enough oxygen is available to break down the build-up of lactic acid. This prevents cramps and stiffness.

lactic acid remain, stiffness will result. Cramps can also occur if the accumulated waste products are not removed quickly.

Muscles work more effectively when warm, which is one reason why warming-up exercises are advised before participating in any vigorous exercise. They help not only to prepare the muscles, but also to improve the blood supply through the muscles. Body massage also helps to improve the blood supply, by relaxing and warming the muscles.

Muscle tone

> **Tip**
>
> A certain amount of muscle tone can be maintained superficially by some massage movements.

When a muscle is relaxed, a few muscle fibres remain contracted to give the muscle a certain amount of firmness but not enough to produce movement. It is this muscle tension that is referred to as muscle tone, which we often describe as either flabby or firm.

Muscle tone is important in maintaining posture, as it assists the body in standing up and keeps the muscles prepared for action. **Extensors** are muscles that straighten out a limb, whereas **flexors** are muscles that bend a limb. Both the extensors and the flexors need to be partially contracted to keep the body upright and the joints steady.

Firm muscle tone can be achieved by exercising. Flaccid muscle tone is usually a result of a lack of use but can also be caused by damage to the nerve supply. Voluntary muscles require regular exercise. When a muscle is not used, it can become flaccid. In extreme circumstances and after a long period of disuse, a muscle will eventually waste away (**atrophy**).

Posture

When the body is balanced, upright and straight and the muscles are not working too hard to hold it up, this is good posture. Poor posture is when the body is not balanced and the muscles have to work much harder to maintain an upright position. As a result they become very tired and usually will start to ache. Poor posture also affects the internal organs by compressing them and this affects their function. Digestive problems often result from poor posture and breathing can also be affected.

Main extensors and flexors
used in posture

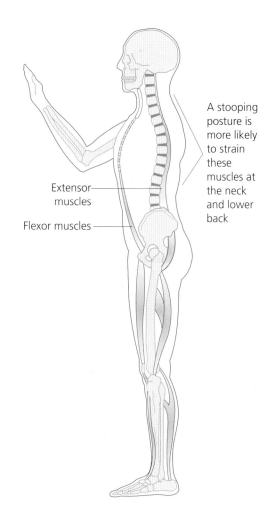

A stooping posture is more likely to strain these muscles at the neck and lower back

Extensor muscles

Flexor muscles

Muscle groups

Muscles of the head and face

The two groups relevant to massage are the muscles of mastication and the muscles of facial expression. The **muscles of mastication**, which are used in chewing, are attached to the bone and are involved in the movement of the lower jaw or mandible. (See Table 4.4.)

Table 4.4 *Muscles of mastication*

Muscles	*Position*	*Action*
Temporalis	At the side of the head, in front of and above the ear, down to the lower jaw	Raises the lower jaw
Pterygoid (lateral and medial)	In the lateral part of the cheek, underneath the masseter	Moves the jaw from side to side
Masseter	In the lateral region of the cheek, between the cheekbone and the angle of the jaw	Raises the lower jaw

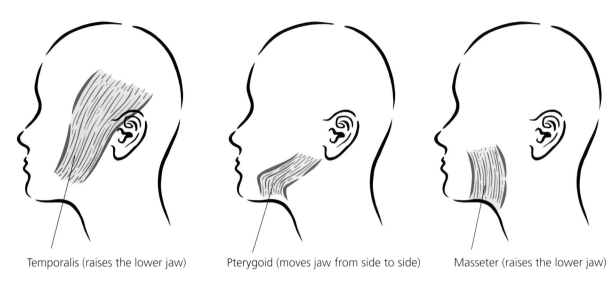

Temporalis (raises the lower jaw)   Pterygoid (moves jaw from side to side)   Masseter (raises the lower jaw)

Muscles of mastication

Table 4.5 *Muscles of facial expression*

Muscles	Position	Action
Frontalis	On the forehead	Raises the eyebrows, creases the forehead
Occipital	At the back of the head	Moves the scalp backwards
Corrugator	Below the eyebrow	Wrinkles between the eyebrows (vertically); frowns
Orbicularis oculi	Around the eye	Closes the eye; winks
Nasalis	At the side of the nose	Dilates the nostrils; expresses anger
Orbicularis oris	Surrounds the mouth	Closes the mouth; puckers the lips; shapes the lips during speech
Mentalis	Extends from the lower lip over the centre of the chin	Lifts the lower lip; protrudes the lip; wrinkles the chin
Triangularis	Radiates laterally from the corners of the mouth	Draws down the corners of the lip
Procerus	On the nasal bone; in the skin between the eyebrows	Causes small horizontal creases at the root of the nose
Caninus	On the skin at the corner of the mouth	Creates an expression of snarling
Risorius	Radiates laterally from the corners of the mouth	Retracts the angle of the mouth; produces a broad grin or smile
Buccinator	At the side of the face	Compresses the cheeks; puffs out the cheeks
Zygomaticus major and minor	Extends from the upper lip	Draws the mouth upwards, as when laughing
Depressor labii	Extends from the lower lip over the chin	Pulls down the bottom lip; creates a sulky expression
Quadratus labii	Radiates from the upper lip	Flares the nostrils; raises the lips, forms a furrow; nasolabial giving a sad expression

The second group are the muscles of facial expression. These may be attached to skin or other muscles rather than bone. (See Table 4.5.)

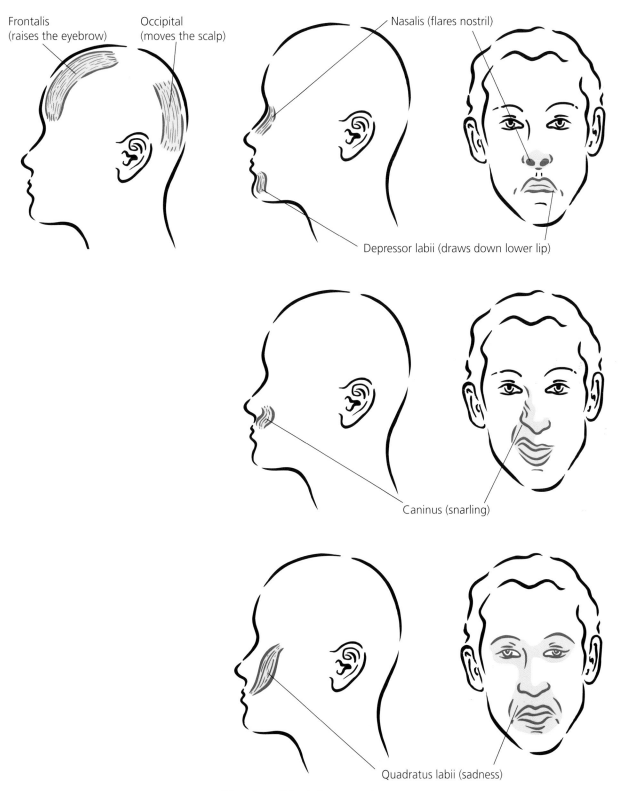

Frontalis (raises the eyebrow)

Occipital (moves the scalp)

Nasalis (flares nostril)

Depressor labii (draws down lower lip)

Caninus (snarling)

Quadratus labii (sadness)

Muscles of facial expression

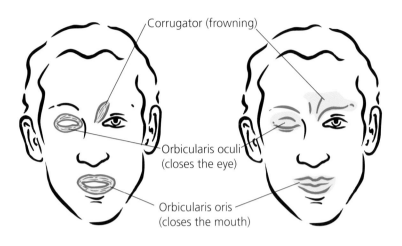

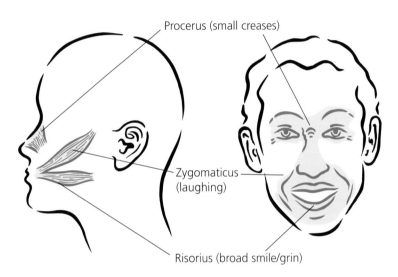

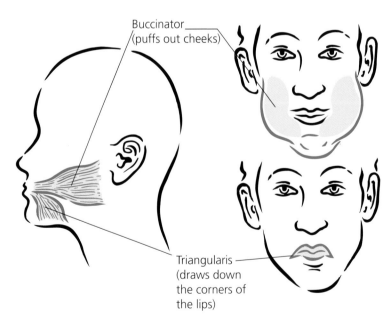

Muscles of facial expression (continued)

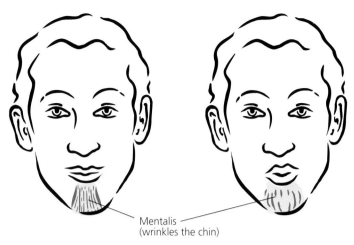

Mentalis
(wrinkles the chin)

Muscles of facial expression (continued)

Muscles of the neck, chest and shoulders

Table 4.6 *Muscles of the neck, chest and shoulders*

Muscle	*Position*	*Action*
Sternocleido-mastoid	Down the side of the neck, from below the ear to the breastbone	Turns and flexes the head
Platysma	At the side of the neck and chin	Helps to draw down lower lip

Sternocleido-mastoid

Sternocleido-mastoid

Platysma

Platysma

Table 4.6 *(continued)*

Muscle	Position	Action	
Pectoralis major	Beneath the breasts and across the front part of the thorax (upper part)	Draws arm forward and rotates it medially	Pectoralis major **Pectoralis major**
Pectoralis minor	Below the pectoralis major, its origin is the third, fourth and fifth rib and it inserts into the outer corner of the scapula	Draws shoulder downwards and forwards	Clavicle / Pectoralis minor / Sternum **Pectoralis minor**
Trapezius	Down the back of the neck, onto the shoulders, down onto the mid-spine	Lifts and raises the shoulder as in shrugging	Trapezius **Trapezius**

Muscles of the thorax

Table 4.7 *Muscles of the thorax*

Muscle	*Position*	*Action*
External intercostals	Muscle fibres run downwards and forward and connect the lower border of one rib to the rib below	Maintain the shape of the thorax wall. Used in breathing, they draw the ribs upwards and outwards, when breathing in
Internal intercostals	Lying between the ribs, they run upwards and forwards to the ribs above	Draw ribs downwards and inwards when breathing out
Serratus anterior	Below axilla, along the sides of the ribcage	Used when punching and pushing. Rotates scapula upwards and draws scapula forwards
Diaphragm	Divides the thorax from the abdomen	Volume of thorax is increased when muscle contracts

Muscles of the thorax

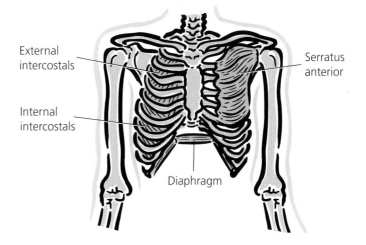

External intercostals

Serratus anterior

Internal intercostals

Diaphragm

Muscles of the back

Table 4.8 *Muscles of the back*

Muscle	Position	Action
Latissimus dorsi	Down the back, in the lumbar and lower thoracic region	Rotates the arm; draws it away from the body body and rotates it inwards (as when climbing with both arms in a fixed position, it helps to pull the body upwards)
Erector spinae	Lies on either side of the spine coming from the neck going down to the pelvis. Three groups overlapping	Keeps the body upright; extends the spine
Gluteals	Situated in the buttocks, they connect the pelvis and femur. Consist of three layers: gluteus maximus, medius and minimus	Used in walking, running and to raise the body into an upright position. Also adduct and rotate the femur

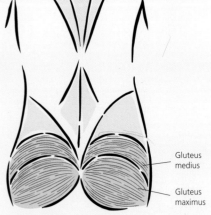

Latissimus dorsi

Latissimus dorsi

Erector spinae

Erector spinae

Gluteus medius

Gluteus maximus

Gluteals

Muscles of the arms and shoulder

Activity

Hold out your arm, palm facing upwards. Ensure you can see your forearm.

Flex all your fingers drawing them towards the forearm.

Can you see the tendons moving?

Table 4.9 *Muscles of the arms and shoulders*

Muscle	*Position*	*Action*
Deltoid	Lies over the top of the shoulder coming from the clavicle and scapula going to the upper humerus	Draws arm backwards and forwards; abducts the arm to a horizontal position
Biceps	Down the anterior surface of the humerus	Turns the palm upwards; flexes the elbow
Triceps	Along the posterior surface of the humerus	Extends elbow
Brachialis	Under the biceps in front of the humerus from halfway down its shaft near the elbow joint to the ulna	Flexes the elbow

Muscles of the arms, shoulders and hands

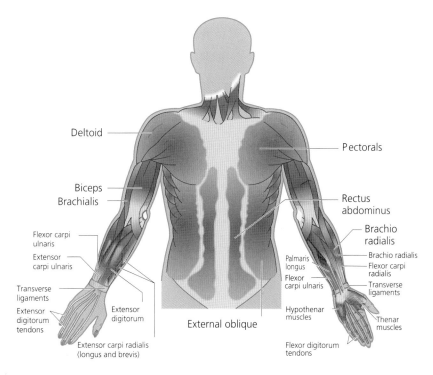

Muscles of the arm and hands

Table 4.10 *Muscles of the lower arm and hands*

Muscle	*Position*	*Action*
Brachio radialis	Situated on thumb side of forearm. Its origin is at the humerus shaft and it inserts at the end of radius bone	Flexes elbow
Flexors	Middle of forearm	Flex and bends the wrist, drawing it towards the forearm
Extensors	Little finger side of forearm	Extends and straightens the wrist and hand
Thenar muscles	Situated below the thumb in the palm of hand	Flexes thumb and moves it inwards and outwards
Hypothenar muscles	Below little finger in palm of hand	Flexes little finger and moves it outwards and inwards

The fingers and hands are moved by muscles and tendons in the forearm.

When these muscles contract they pull on the tendons, which causes the fingers to move.

Flexors bend the wrist drawing it towards the forearm.

Extensors straighten the wrist and hand.

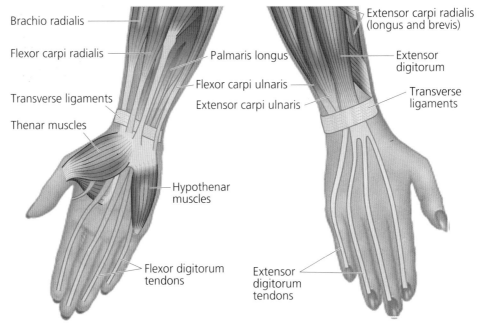

Muscles of the arm and hand

Muscles of the abdomen

Table 4.11 *Muscles of the abdomen*

Muscle	Position	Action
Rectus abdominis	At the front of the abdomen coming from the pelvis to the sternum and the lower ribs	Compresses the abdomen, tilts the pelvis up and flexes the spine
Obliques (internal and external)	Lie to either side of rectus abdominis, run downwards and outwards; external obliques lie on top of the internal obliques, run downwards and forward	Compress the abdomen and twist the trunk

Muscles of the abdomen

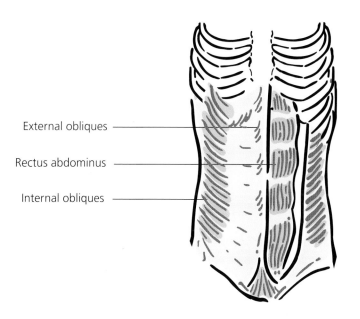

External obliques

Rectus abdominus

Internal obliques

Muscles of the legs and feet

Table 4.12 *Muscles of the legs and feet*

Muscle	Position	Action
Quadriceps Rectus femoris Vastus lateralis Vastus medialis Vastus intermedius	Situated at the front of the thigh, a group of four muscles running from the pelvis and top of the femur to the tibia through the patella and patellar ligament	Extend the knee and help in hip flex
Hamstrings Biceps femoris Semimembranosus Semitendinosus	Three muscles situated at the back of the thigh from the pelvis and top of the femur; femur, down to the bones of the lower leg below the knee	Flex the knee and extend the thigh. Used in walking
Adductors Adductor longus Adductor magnus Adductor brevis Gracilis Pectineus	Situated in the inner thigh	Adduct hip, and flex and rotate femur
Sartorius	Cross the front of the thighs from the outer front rim of the pelvis to the tibia at the inner knee	Abducts and rotates the femur and flexes the knee and hip. Used when sitting cross-legged
Tensor fascia latae	Situated on the lateral side of the thigh	Rotates and abducts the thigh inwardly
Gastrocnemius	Calf of the leg	Plantar-flexes the foot and flexes knee
Soleus	Below the gastrocnemius	Plantar-flexes the foot
Tibialis anterior	Front of the lower leg	Points the foot upwards, dorsiflexion, and allows the soles to face inwards (inversion)

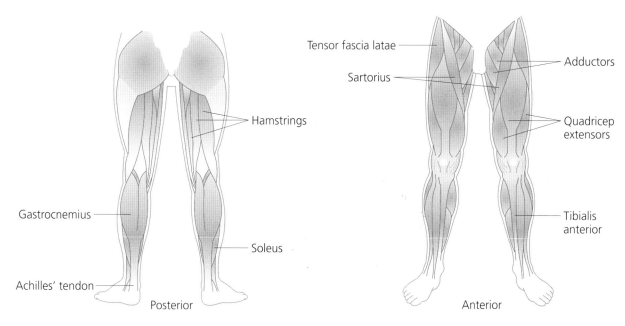

Tensor fascia latae

Sartorius

Adductors

Quadricep extensors

Hamstrings

Gastrocnemius

Soleus

Tibialis anterior

Achilles' tendon

Posterior

Anterior

Muscles of the legs

The muscles in the foot work together to help move the body when walking and running. The foot is moved primarily by muscles in the lower leg, which pull on the tendons and, in turn, move the feet and toes.

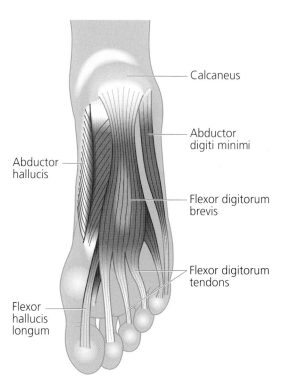

Calcaneus

Abductor digiti minimi

Abductor hallucis

Flexor digitorum brevis

Flexor digitorum tendons

Flexor hallucis longum

Muscles of the foot

Tip

Maintaining muscle fibres: tapotement causes muscles to expand and contract.

Health & safety

Never massage over muscles that are extremely painful.

Tip

Massage has the following effects on muscles:

- Massage increases blood flow, which leads to an increase in oxygen and nutrients to the muscle tissues and speeds up removal of waste products. When muscles are working they need a greater supply of oxygen and produce more waste products. Massage will relieve muscular fatigue by removing the lactic acids that build up in the tissues.
- Muscles that are tense and contracted can become relaxed after a massage. Regular massage will help muscles to function to their fullest capacity.
- Muscles work over joints. If the movement of the joints is impaired by adhesions, for example in the shoulder joint, then the full range of movement will be prevented. Massaging this area can help loosen and release these adhesions, gaining more mobility in the joints, more movement in the muscles and therefore increasing the range of movement.

Circulatory system

The circulatory system, also known as the cardiovascular system, consists of the heart, blood vessels and blood and is also closely related to the lymphatic system and its parts. It provides the main transport system in the body, as blood carries oxygen and required nutrients to various parts of the body and removes waste products such as carbon dioxide.

Blood

Tip

The skin may hold as much as one half of all the blood in the body!

Blood is a liquid tissue. It consists of a fluid component, known as **plasma**, and a solid component that includes **cells**. Plasma constitutes 50 to 60% of blood volume.

Red blood cells (**erythrocytes**) are formed in the bone marrow and account for as much as 98% of the total number of blood cells. The primary function of red blood cells is to carry oxygen from the lungs to the rest of the body and carbon dioxide from the body to the lungs. They can do this because they contain haemoglobin, which combines readily with both of these gases. White blood cells (**leucocytes**) are produced in the spleen, lymph nodes and the bone marrow. The primary function of these cells is to protect the body from infection and disease. **Platelets** are also found in the blood. They are also formed in the bone marrow and play an important role in allowing blood to clot at a wound site.

Plasma provides the fluid in which red blood cells, white blood cells and platelets can be carried around the body. It is derived from food and water taken into the body and about 90% of plasma is water while a further 7% is proteins. Plasma regulates the fluid balance in the body and the pH of blood. The blood also carries fluids and dissolved gases.

Blood protects, regulates and transports materials around the body. Blood transports oxygen from the lungs to the cells of the body, carries carbon dioxide and other waste products from the cells to the lungs, kidneys and sweat glands. It transports nutrients from the digestive system to body cells, carries hormones from the endocrine glands to cells of the body and also transports enzymes around the body. It regulates the pH of the body, helps to regulate body temperature (by **vasoconstriction** and **vasodilation**) and protects the body from disease and infection.

The heart

The heart is the organ at the centre of the circulatory system. It acts as a pump by contracting and forcing the blood through a closed network of blood vessels. It is made up of cardiac muscle tissue and is positioned above the diaphragm, between the lungs, in the thorax. It is a hollow organ about the size of a fist and it has four chambers: the

The heart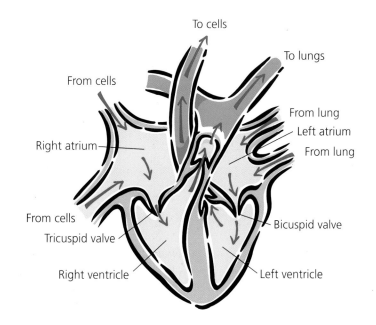

right and left atria and the right and left ventricles. The right and left sides of the heart are divided by the septum and the atria are connected to the corresponding ventricles by a valve.

During diastole, the heart relaxes and it fills with blood from the veins. During systole, the heart contracts and contractions of the atria and the ventricles force blood out of the heart through the arteries.

The heart is made up of three layers:

1 **pericardium** (outer covering). This is a double-layered bag that encloses a cavity filled with pericardial fluid. This reduces friction when the heart beats.
2 **myocardium** (middle covering). This makes up the bulk of the heart and is made of cardiac muscle.
3 **endocardium** (inner covering). This layer covers the heart cavities with blood vessels.

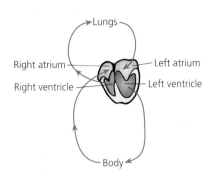

Circulation of blood: overview

Blood vessels

There are three main types of blood vessels: arteries, veins and capillaries. Between them they transport blood around the body and back again.

Arteries

Arteries are thick-walled blood vessels. With the exception of the **pulmonary artery**, arteries carry oxygenated blood away from the heart, transporting oxygen and nutrients to various parts of the body. When the heart contracts, blood is pushed through the arteries and this can be felt as a **pulse**.

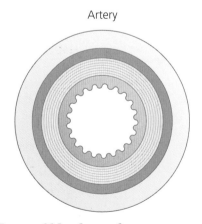
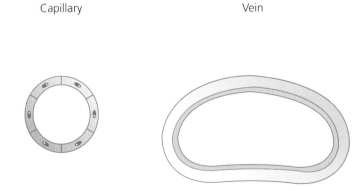

Types of blood vessel

Arteries vary in size from the **aorta**, which is the vessel through which oxygenated blood leaves the heart and is about 2cm in diameter, to microscopic arterioles. These branch into smaller and smaller vessels as they get further away from the heart.

Arteries supply blood to the organs at high pressures, hence their thick, elastic walls, while smaller arterioles control the blood flow through the capillary bed. The smooth muscles in the walls of the arteries and arterioles are richly supplied with nerves, which contract to constrict the size of the **lumen** – the cavity through which the blood flows – and therefore increase blood flow.

Blood flow through the muscles is also controlled by this process. During exercise when muscles are contracting, blood flow is increased as increasing supplies of oxygen and glucose are required and increased waste products – mainly carbon dioxide, heat and lactic acid – are produced and need to be carried away.

Capillaries

From the arterioles, blood flows into the capillaries, which are thin vessels (single cell layer) and do not contain valves. The main function of capillaries is to take nutrients and amino acids from the blood to the tissues and remove waste products from the tissues. Once exchange of oxygen and nutrients has taken place and the blood has picked up any waste products, the capillaries become larger vessels called venules and then veins.

Vasodilation and vasoconstriction

The skin capillaries help to regulate body temperature. If the body temperature begins to rise, the capillaries in the

Vasoconstriction and vasodilation

Blood flow through skin when hot   and when cold

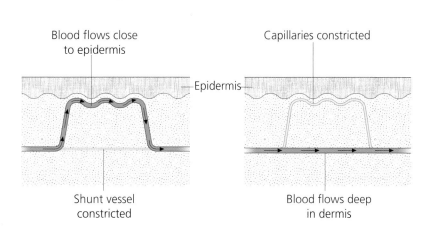

Blood flows close to epidermis

Capillaries constricted

Epidermis

Shunt vessel constricted

Blood flows deep in dermis

skin open up, allowing the blood to flow closer to the skin's surface. This is called **vasoconstriction**. Heat is lost through the skin and the blood and body are cooled. Conversely, if body temperature begins to drop, the blood can flow deeper releasing less heat into the environment and maintaining body temperature more efficiently. This is called **vasodilation**. Vasoconstriction and vasodilation are controlled by the autonomic nervous system – nerves that control the arterioles that feed the capillary network for the skin. Impulses from the vasomotor nerves cause the muscles to contract, reducing the diameter of the vessel. When the nerve impulses are inhibited, the muscles relax and the vessels enlarge. In this way, the nerve impulses control the flow of blood to the tissues in direct proportion to the tissue's needs.

Veins

Veins have much thinner walls than arteries and are less elastic. They are also closer to the skin's surface. With the exception of the aorta, veins carry deoxygenated blood back to the heart along with the waste products of metabolism, which are then passed from the blood to the lungs and exhaled. Venules are the microscopic vessels that continue from the capillaries and merge to form veins. The flow of blood in veins is slower and under less pressure than the flow in arteries. When muscles contract and exert pressure on the veins, the veins tend to collapse. As this happens repeatedly, the blood is forced along towards the heart, valves preventing the blood from flowing backwards.

Varicose veins are the result of valves that are incompetent and allow the blood to flow backwards, which then stretches and weakens the walls of the veins. The veins on the surface of the leg are the most commonly affected as gravity forces the blood back down the leg.

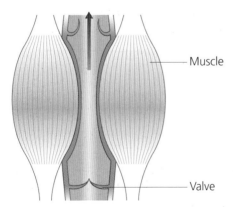

Muscle

Muscles squeeze the blood in the veins back towards the heart

Valve

A varicose vein allows blood to flow backwards

The walls become distended so the valve cannot work

Varicose veins

Blood pressure

Blood pressure is lower in the veins than it is in the arteries. Blood pressure is recorded by two figures: systolic (when the heart contracts) and diastolic (when the heart relaxes). The blood pressure of an average, healthy male adult should be approximately 120 (systolic pressure) over 80 (diastolic pressure) which is written as:

$$\frac{120}{80} \text{ mm/tg}$$

Blood pressure tends to vary with age, weight and sex and is also affected by exercise, stress and anxiety.

Blood circulation

There are two main types of circulation: pulmonary circulation, between the lungs and the heart, and systemic or general circulation, between the heart and the rest of the body.

Oxygenated blood leaves the heart from the left ventricle via the aorta, carrying both nutrients and oxygen to all parts of the body via the vast network of arteries. As the blood delivers oxygen and nutrients, it picks up waste products from the liver and transports them along to the kidneys to be eliminated as urine. As well as supplying oxygen and nutrients, the blood also picks up hormones from the pituitary, adrenal and sex glands and delivers them to their destinations – the skin, hair, heart, muscles and brain.

Circulation of blood: detail

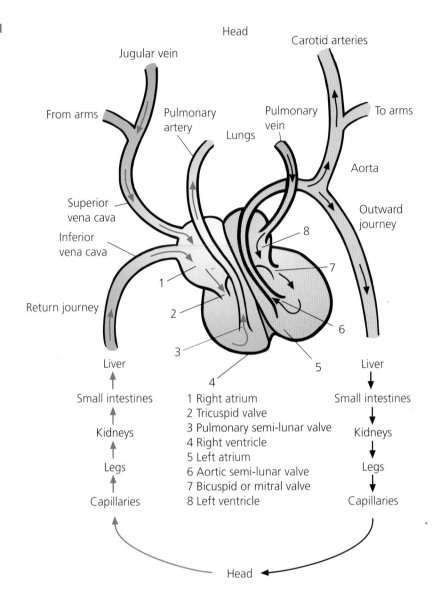

1 Right atrium
2 Tricuspid valve
3 Pulmonary semi-lunar valve
4 Right ventricle
5 Left atrium
6 Aortic semi-lunar valve
7 Bicuspid or mitral valve
8 Left ventricle

Having delivered these vital 'materials', the blood continues to the right atrium via the inferior and superior vena cavae.

The deoxygenated blood, loaded with carbon dioxide, then passes through the tricuspid valve into the right ventricle. It then travels via the pulmonary artery to the lungs where the carbon dioxide from the blood is extracted and exhaled, refuelled with oxygen. The oxygenated blood then leaves the lungs via the pulmonary vein and enters the left atrium where it passes through the bicuspid valve to the left ventricle and embarks on systemic circulation.

Lymphatic system

The lymphatic system consists of the lymph fluid, lymph vessels and lymph glands (or nodes). It is closely related to the blood circulation system but unlike the blood circulation system, it has no muscular pump. The lymph moves through the vessels and around the body when large muscles squeeze the vessels. Lymph travels in one direction only, from body tissue back towards the heart.

The main functions of the lymphatic systems are to:

● remove bacteria and other foreign material
● help prevent infection
● drain away excess fluids that are then eliminated from the body.

Lymph is a clear, colourless watery fluid similar to blood plasma. It contains nutrients, including fatty acids, glucose,

Lymphatic system

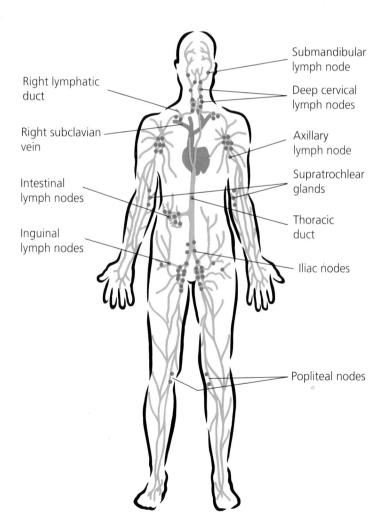

Right lymphatic duct

Right subclavian vein

Intestinal lymph nodes

Inguinal lymph nodes

Submandibular lymph node

Deep cervical lymph nodes

Axillary lymph node

Supratrochlear glands

Thoracic duct

Iliac nodes

Popliteal nodes

Tip

It is extremely important when massaging to ensure the movements are directing the blood and lymph flow back towards the heart.

Lymph

A lymph vessel

Tip

Oedema is the swelling of tissues and can occur when fluids accumulate instead of returning to the bloodstream.

Health & safety

Never massage over swollen lymphatic nodes.

Never massage a client if they have an infection, as this contraindicates the treatment.

amino acids, mineral ions, dissolved oxygen and hormones, all of which are necessary to the health and growth of tissues. Lymph is filtered through the walls of the capillaries. In the spaces between the cells where there are no blood capillaries, lymph provides nourishment. It also removes excess carbon dioxide and nitrogen waste, which cannot be carried by the blood. It also carries a type of white blood cell called **lymphocytes**. A second type of white blood cell, known as a monocyte, is also carried.

Monocytes or **macrophages** line the walls of the lymph nodes and destroy and engulf any debris, bacteria or foreign bodies carried in the lymph. They also manufacture antibodies to fight bacteria, which pass into the bloodstream along with the circulating lymph. When we suffer from an infection, the lymph nodes nearest to the infectious site swell and, as the white cells fight the germs, the area becomes tender.

Lymph vessels

Lymph vessels, like veins, have valves along their length to prevent lymph flowing backwards. The vessels run very close to the veins around the body. The vessels join to form larger lymph vessels and eventually flow into one of two large lymphatic vessels, the **thoracic duct** (or left lymphatic duct) and the **right lymphatic duct**. The right lymphatic duct receives lymph from the right side of the head and upper body; the thoracic duct receives lymph from the left side of the head, the neck, the chest, the abdomen and the lower body. These large lymph vessels empty their contents into a vein at the base of the neck, which in turn empties into the **vena cava**. The lymph is mixed into the venous blood as it returns to the heart.

Lymph nodes

Lymph nodes, usually called glands, are tiny oval structures, usually between 1mm and 25mm in length, that filter the lymph. They extract poisons and bacteria, defending the

Tip

Massage stimulates and increases lymphatic circulation. This leads to faster removal of waste products such as carbon dioxide and lactic acid, which helps prevent fatigue.

A lymph node

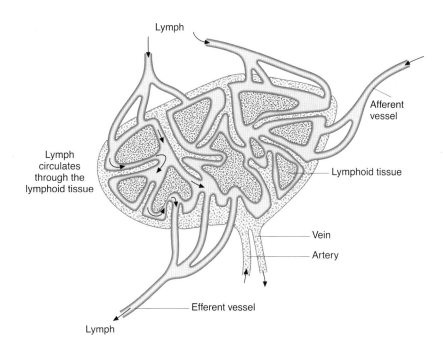

Lymph

Afferent vessel

Lymph circulates through the lymphoid tissue

Lymphoid tissue

Vein

Artery

Efferent vessel

Lymph

body against infection by destroying harmful organisms. **Lymphocytes**, cells found in the lymph glands, produce **antibodies** that fight against the invasion of any micro-organisms.

Nervous system

The nervous system acts as a communication system, carrying messages around the body to control other systems. It enables you to sense any changes inside or outside the body and to respond to them. It works with the endocrine system to maintain homeostasis or a stable condition.

The nervous system includes:

- the **brain**, which is protected by the surrounding bones of the cranium
- the **spinal cord**, which passes through the vertebrae bones of the spinal column
- a large number of **nerves** all over the body.

The brain and the spinal cord make up the **central nervous system** (CNS) and 12 pairs of cranial nerves arising from the brain and 31 pairs of spinal nerves arising from the spinal cord make up the **peripheral nervous system**. All sensations from the body are relayed by the

Table 4.13 *Brain function*

Area of brain	Position	Function
Cerebellum	Present at the back of the brain, it has two lateral wings shaped like a butterfly	Maintains posture and controls motor skills (motor coordinating centre)
Cerebrum	Major part of the brain. Consists of two hemispheres	This is the centre of memory, thought and intelligence. Controls all voluntary muscular movement, receives all sensory information, enabling us to feel, smell, hear, see and taste
Medulla oblongata	This is a continuation of the spinal cord	Controls all the autonomic nervous system, such as the heart rate and movement of food through the body. Also controls involuntary reflexes such as swallowing, coughing and sneezing
Hypothalamus	Positioned above the pituitary gland, to which it is linked	Controls body temperature, hunger and thirst
Ventricle	This contains cerebrospinal fluid and is a cavity in the brain	The fluid removes waste, acts as a shock absorber and delivers nutrients

peripheral nervous system to the central nervous system, where the appropriate reaction is initiated.

The brain is composed of several parts and each performs specific functions. For example, the cerebrum receives sensory information and initiates and controls all muscular movement.

Nerves

A nerve is a collection of nerve fibres that emerge from the central nervous system. Sensory nerves are linked to sensory

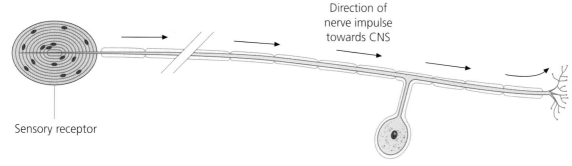

Sensory receptor

Direction of nerve impulse towards CNS

A sensory neurone

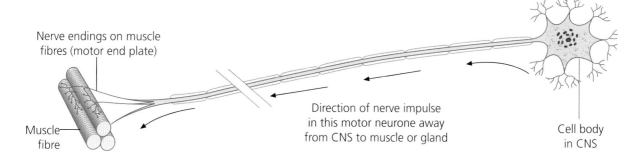

Nerve endings on muscle fibres (motor end plate)

Muscle fibre

Direction of nerve impulse in this motor neurone away from CNS to muscle or gland

Cell body in CNS

A motor neurone

Tip

When massage is applied to the body, effects on the nervous system are usually either relaxing or stimulating.

receptors, while motor nerves end in a gland or muscle. Some nerves contain only sensory nerve fibres which receive information and then relay it to the brain; some nerves contain only motor nerve fibres, that act on information received from the brain, while some nerves contain a combination of the two.

The inside and outside of the membrane of nerve fibres are charged. Messages are passed along the nerve fibres in the form of electrical impulses, that are caused by changes to these charges. When a nerve fibre is resting, that is not conducting any message, there are more positive ions

Conduction of nerve impulses

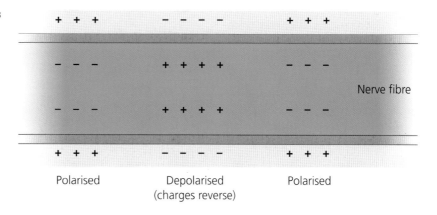

Polarised

Depolarised (charges reverse)

Polarised

Nerve fibre

present on the outer surface and more negative ions present inside the membrane, and it is said to be polarised. When the neurone is stimulated, a wave of depolarisation passes along the fibre as the charges become temporarily reversed. Potassium and sodium ions present in all the body fluids are positively charged, whereas chloride ions are negatively charged.

Relaying messages

Passage from one neurone to another

Neurones (nerve fibres) pass information to and from the central nervous system. Inside the central nervous system, impulses pass from one neurone to another even though they never physically touch. When an impulse reaches the end of the nerve fibre, a chemical called a neurotransmitter is released. This chemical then passes into the gap between one neurone and the next (known as a synapse) before being taken up by an adjacent neurone. This action causes an electrical impulse within the neurone.

Passage of an impulse across a synapse

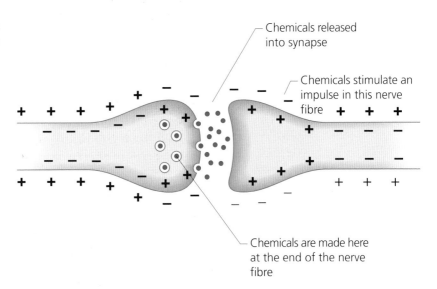

Passage from neurone to muscle fibre

Technical note

The area of contact between the neurone and the muscle fibre is called the **neuromuscular junction** or **motor end plate**.

As the motor nerve enters the muscle at the motor point, the individual neurones of that nerve branch off so that each neurone makes contact with the individual muscle cells. Motor neurones release a chemical transmitter into the muscle that causes all the muscle fibres in its **motor unit** to contract.

Synapse and neuromuscular junction

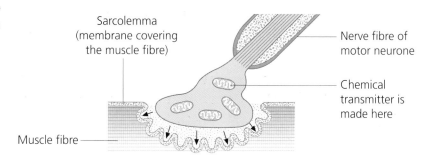

Sarcolemma (membrane covering the muscle fibre)

Nerve fibre of motor neurone

Chemical transmitter is made here

Muscle fibre

Voluntary or reflex

The CNS is involved in both reflex and voluntary actions. Voluntary actions, those which we can control such as speaking and walking, are initiated by the brain. A reflex response is a quick involuntary response to stimuli such as touching a hot plate. In reflex actions, impulses are passed through the sensory nerve fibres to the spinal cord and are then transmitted through relay neurones to motor neurones. This is called a spinal reflex. The message is also passed to the brain (as a result of impulses passing up the spinal cord) and you become aware of what you have done, which may often cause a vocal response!

Autonomic nervous system

The autonomic nervous system controls the involuntary activities of the smooth muscle, cardiac muscle and the glands. It is responsible for a variety of things from regulating the size of the pupil – vasodilation – and vasoconstriction – heart rate, gut movements and secretions from the glands.

There are two divisions within the autonomic system. The first is sympathetic, associated with stress, and the second, parasympathetic, associated with peace. Many organs receive a supply from both of these divisions – fibres from one division will stimulate an organ's fibres while fibres from the other division will inhibit it.

The sympathetic division is stimulated in periods of danger or stress and prepares the body for 'fight or flight'. This causes the heart rate to speed up, the pupils to dilate, sweating to increase, the bronchioles in the lungs to dilate and blood sugar levels to rise, as the blood flow through the muscles is increased. The parasympathetic division is stimulated in times of relaxation. These fibres stimulate digestion and absorption of food.

Tip

If the massage pressure is too light, it can become irritating. If the pressure is too deep, it can be painful.

Tip

Massage can have either a stimulating or relaxing effect on local nerves depending on the movements carried out, for example effleurage can lead to the person calming down through slow, deep manipulation being applied or invigorated by applying brisk, superficial manipulations. Applying pressure to any painful areas, especially around the neck and shoulder region, will lead to temporary numbing and, as a result, pain relief.

Digestive system

The long muscular tube running all the way from the mouth to the anus is called the alimentary tract and is where digestion takes place. Food is taken in through the mouth, broken down and absorbed into the blood. Waste is then eliminated.

Digestive system

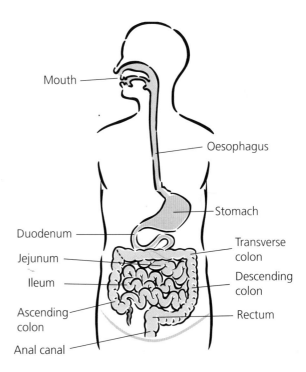

Structure

The digestive system comprises the following parts.

Mouth

In the mouth, food is broken down into smaller pieces by chewing and mixed with saliva from salivary glands. The enzyme ptyglin is contained in the saliva, which works on some of the carbohydrates to turn them into smaller molecules of maltose and glucose.

Pharynx and oesophagus

The bolus of food is pushed to the back of the mouth where the pharynx muscles push it down into the oesophagus. The oesophagus is a long thin tube that leads to the stomach. The bolus moves through the oesophagus by peristalsis, muscle contractions that move food through the tract. We have no conscious control over this muscular action.

Stomach

This is a muscular organ situated on the left side of the abdomen below the diaphragm. In the stomach, food is broken down further, as it mixes with gastric juices and enzymes. Food can stay in the stomach for up to five hours until it turns into a liquid form, chyme. A hormone called gastrin stimulates the cells of the stomach to release hydrochloric acid. This reacts with the enzyme pepsin, which helps break the food down further into peptones. Mucous secretion prevents the stomach from being damaged by the gastrin and acid production. At this point, it goes into the small intestine.

Small intestine

This is about 8m long in total and consists of the duodenum, jejunum and the ileum. Peristalsis continues to help the food move along. Food is further digested with the aid of several juices. These are:

- **Bile** produced in the liver and stored in the gall bladder. Bile helps to break up fat droplets, a process known as **emulsification**, and neutralise the chyme.
- **Pancreatic juice** produced in the pancreas. This contains enzymes that continue to digest the fats, carbohydrates and proteins.
- **Intestinal juice** released by the small intestine. This completes the breakdown of all the nutrients.

From the duodenum, digested food enters the jejunum and ileum. The jejunum absorbs the nutritional elements within the food.

In the ileum there are thousands of minute villi that enable the digested food to be absorbed into the bloodstream. From the small intestine, the food passes into the large intestine.

Absorption of food

Digested food is absorbed by diffusion through the villi of the small intestine. Simple sugars from digested carbohydrates and amino acids from protein pass from the villi and are carried to the liver where they are processed. Vitamins and minerals travel through the villi and are absorbed in the bloodstream to help with the body's normal functions and cell metabolism. Fat molecules from digested fat pass into the intestinal lymphatics and are carried through the lymphatic circulation before they go into the blood and circulate.

The liver

The liver sits on the right side of the abdominal cavity under the diaphragm. It is the largest gland in the body and plays a major part in metabolism by regulating the absorption of nutrients from the small intestine. The liver:

- secretes bile
- regulates blood sugar, amino acids, fat content and plasma proteins
- detoxifies waste and drugs
- stores vitamins A, D, E, K and B12 as well as minerals, iron, potassium and copper.

When the bloodstream has absorbed the nutrients, it transports them to the cells in the body for metabolism. Glucose is used to provide energy for the body's cells. Amino acids are used to provide new tissue and repair any damaged cells. Fatty acids are used to produce heat and energy and some of the fats are used as a layer around vital organs such as the heart. Other fats are stored under the skin.

Large intestine

This is about 1.3m long and consists of the ascending, transverse and descending colons all of which are coiled around the small intestine. The large intestine divides into the **caecum**, **rectum** and **anal canal**. The caecum is where the appendix is attached and the ileum opens. The rectum is a smaller muscular tube that runs through the pelvis and anal canal to its opening where solid waste matter from the body is excreted. This is part of the descending colon.

Tip

Never massage the abdomen after the client has just eaten or if there is any pain present.

The functions of the large intestine are:

● absorption of water from the waste

● the making of waste (bacteria and food that is not digested)

● storage of waste

● elimination of waste through the anus to the outside of the body.

Tip

Massaging the alimentary tract can aid peristalsis and help treat constipation.

Nutrition

A nutritious diet is a major requirement for providing the body with energy and the ability to grow, repair and maintain itself.

The five main groups of nutrients are:

1   carbohydrates
2   fats
3   proteins
4   minerals
5   vitamins.

Water is also essential to the diet. Insufficient water intake leads to dehydration and constipation.

Carbohydrates

Carbohydrates are the main source of energy for the body. Excess carbohydrate is converted into fat and most of it is stored as adipose tissue beneath the skin. There are three types of carbohydrate:

1   monosaccharides, which are simple sugars:
   ● glucose found in fruit, the blood of living animals and plant juices
   ● fructose found in fruits, plant juices and honey
   ● galactose found in the milk of mammals

2   disaccharides, which are double sugars and are made of two monosaccharide units joined together:

- sucrose found in sugarcane
- sugar beet found in fruits and carrots
- maltose formed during digestion of starch
- lactose found only in milk

3   polysaccharides, which are formed from a varying number of monosaccharide units. They are divided into two groups:

- starches found in cereals, pulses, root vegetables, bread, potatoes, pasta and rice
- glycogen made from glucose by animals, small amounts are stored in the liver and muscles for energy.

Fibre

Fibre is a source of carbohydrate that we cannot digest. Fibre helps to keep the digestive system healthy. Fibre is found in all vegetable sources and wholegrain cereals such as wheat, rice, oats, wholemeal bread, breakfast cereals and bran. Many fruits, especially apples and plums, are good sources. Food that is high in fibre contains more bulk but fewer calories. Fibre is made up of non-starch polysaccharides, which can be either soluble or insoluble. Insoluble fibre helps food move through the digestive system by giving the muscles something to grip onto, therefore preventing constipation. An example is cellulose. Soluble fibre can help reduce the amount of cholesterol in the blood. Pectin is an example and is derived from apples, plums, turnips and sweet potatoes.

Fats

Fat provides energy in a concentrated form. It provides us with energy, warmth, and protects the vital organs such as the heart. Excess fat is stored in adipose tissue beneath the skin and this gives the shape and contour of the body. Sources of fat in the diet are butter, margarine, oils, nuts, cream, egg yolk, cheese, lard and meats. Fatty foods are a source of the fat soluble vitamins A, D, E and K. They also supply essential fatty acids. Fatty acids may be saturated or unsaturated. Saturated fats are hard fats such as butter, lard and suet (animal sources). Unsaturated fats are vegetable oils such as corn, soya and sunflower.

Proteins

Protein is essential for major growth, repair, and maintenance of the body. It is a major constituent of all cells and forms antibodies, hormones and enzymes. Proteins are complex molecules that contain the elements carbon, hydrogen, oxygen, nitrogen and sometimes sulphur. Proteins form chains of amino acids which are linked. There are about 20 amino acids found in proteins, of which nine are termed essential:

- animal protein – contains all essential acids; include meat, fish, milk, cheese and eggs
- vegetable proteins – a few essential acids are missing from these. Food sources are cereals, pulses, nuts, vegetables and soya.

Protein is essential for growing children, adolescents, pregnant women and people recovering from sickness.

Minerals

There are about 15 elements required by the body and these must be obtained from food. Major minerals are required in small amounts and they are:

- calcium
- phosphorus
- magnesium
- iron
- sodium
- chlorine
- potassium
- zinc.

Vitamins

Vitamins are a group of chemical compounds that are required by the body in very small amounts. These should be obtained from food. Lack of vitamins will result in specific deficiency diseases. Vitamins are either fat soluble – A, D, E and K – or water soluble – B group and C.

Respiratory and olfactory systems

Respiration is the process by which we inhale oxygen and exhale carbon dioxide, which is a waste product of oxidation. The primary organ used in respiration is the lungs.

Respiratory system

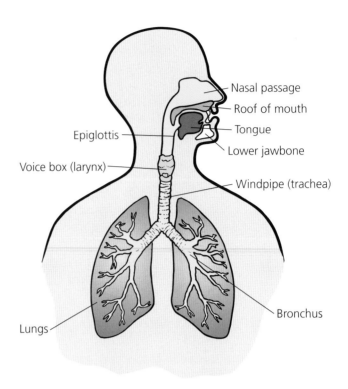

When we breathe, we can breathe in through either the mouth or the nose. Breathing is more effective through the nose because it warms and moistens (with mucus) the air, filters dirt and dust (with the cilia) and alerts us to any potential problems of air quality by the sense of smell.

There are three types of breathing:

1 **Apical (shallow) breathing** occurs when a person is excited, stressed or in danger. It only uses the upper lobe of the lung resulting in shallow breathing.

2 **Lateral costal breathing** is deep, slow breathing that uses the upper and middle lobes of the lungs.

3 **Diaphragmatic breathing** uses the upper, middle and lower lobes of the lungs. It is very deep and calming and is practised by people who play wind instruments.

The nose plays an important part in the olfactory system. Sensory receptors attached to the first cranial or olfactory nerve are present in the upper nasal passage. They are coated with a watery mucus in which certain chemicals dissolve. These then stimulate the sensory receptors and a message is transmitted to the brain's olfactory bulb where the smell is interpreted.

Smells can alter a person's mood and influence their behaviour. A good example of this are the animal

Olfactory system

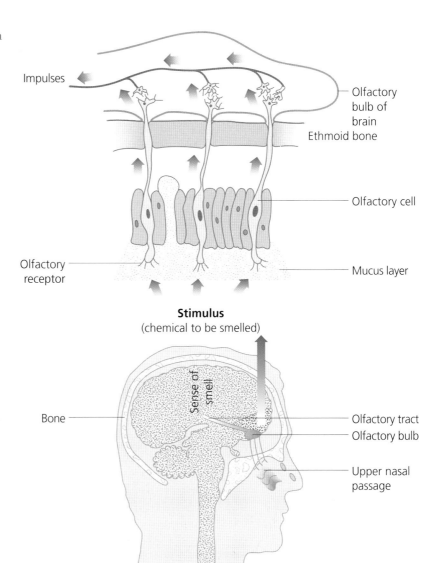

pheromones, which encourage sexual attention. The part of the brain involved in olfaction is very close to the areas of the brain that control emotions, the limbic system. In addition to being absorbed into the bloodstream, essential oils used in aromatherapy take advantage of the limbic responses through olfaction.

The limbic system is the part of the brain that receives messages from the olfactory cells in the nose. It is involved in our emotions and consists of a group of structures that encircle the brainstem. Smells evoke feelings and may take on emotional significance through memory and association. This can be especially important in aromatherapy massage.

The breathing mechanism

At each intake of breath, the **intercostal muscles** situated between the ribs contract: this raises the ribcage and creates a greater space in the thoracic cavity. At the same time, the diaphragm contracts and is pulled down, causing air to be drawn into the lungs. As the diaphragm and intercostal muscles relax and return to their original positions, the air is then pushed out of the lungs.

Respiration refers not only to breathing, but signifies the uptake of oxygen and production and removal of carbon dioxide. This takes place in three contexts:

1   An exchange between the air (from the external environment) and the blood. This exchange takes place in the lungs and is referred to as **external respiration**.
2   An exchange between the blood cells. This occurs throughout the body and is referred to as **internal respiration**.
3   An exchange within the cells of the body, where oxygen is used to 'burn' foodstuffs, releasing energy or synthesising cell materials. This occurs in the body and is referred to as **cellular respiration**.

During a body massage treatment, the rate of external respiration slows down to an even, easy rhythm. It involves mainly the thoracic region of the body, with only very small movements of the intercostal muscles. Internal respiration is increased slightly because the blood and lymph systems are being stimulated to rid the body of toxic waste. Cellular respiration occurs when the body's energies are not needed

Tip

Never massage if the client has any acute respiratory conditions, e.g. bronchitis.

Tip

Certain massage movements, for example tapotement and percussion, affect the lung tissue. Circulation to the bronchioles is increased, which, in turn, nourishes and feeds the tissues. This improves both the elasticity of the lung tissue and gaseous exchange within the lungs.

It is important to encourage clients to breathe correctly, especially during treatments. Correct breathing can:

- help to prevent lung infections by increasing resistance
- help to improve lung elasticity
- encourage good posture
- help to maintain nutrient supply to muscles
- aid relaxation.

to carry out physical or mental activities. Some of this energy is used up by the normal functioning of the cell; the remainder is lost as heat, hence the feeling of warmth often associated with massage treatments.

Renal system

The renal system, or urinary system as it is sometimes known, deals with the elimination of liquid waste from the body. The urinary system is made up of:

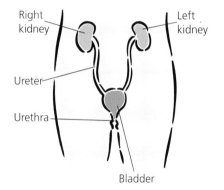

- **two kidneys**, which lie on either side of the spine at the bottom of the thoracic region and the top of the lumbar region, filtering impurities from the blood, regulate the salt and water balance, maintain pH balance, produce urine and control fluid balance
- **two ureters**, which are thin tubes that take the urine from the kidneys to the bladder
- **the bladder**, a pear-shaped bag located in the pelvis; urine is collected and stored here until ready to be released, its size varying depending on how full or empty it is
- **the urethra**, which takes the urine from the bladder to the outside of body. The urethra is longer in males than it is in females.

Renal system

Tip

During massage, the lymphatic system is stimulated. This can increase the urine content passing to the bladder.

Endocrine system

Endocrine glands secrete hormones (chemical messengers) into the bloodstream. They are then circulated around the body affecting their target organs. Most hormones are associated with long-term changes, like the growth hormone, but some bring about fast changes, for instance the adrenaline that prepares the body very quickly when it is suddenly stressed.

Table 4.14 *Endocrine glands and their functions*

Gland	Hormone	Function
Pituitary gland	Follicle stimulating hormone (FSH), luteinizing hormone (LH), anti-diuretic hormone (ADH)	Controls reproduction, affects the water balance. Situated in the brain, the pituitary gland is also known as the master gland because it secretes trophic hormones that act on other endocrine glands
Pineal		Affects growth and also development of sex glands
Thyroid gland	Thyroxine	Controls rate of metabolism
Thymus		Helps immune system
Parathyroid gland	Parathormone	Controls blood calcium levels
Pancreas	Insulin	Controls blood sugar level
Adrenal glands	Adrenalin (medulla)	Prepares the body for action
	Glucocorticoids (cortex)	Reduces stress responses such as inflammation
	Aldosterone (cortex)	Controls potassium and sodium levels in the blood. This hormone can also cause excess oedema (water retention)
	Corticosteroids (cortex)	Help to maintain homeostasis
Ovaries	Oestrogen and progesterone	Control development and function of female sex organs and associated sexual characteristics, e.g. fat being stored in the breasts, hips and thighs
Testes	Testosterone/androgens	Control development and function of male sex organs and associated sexual characteristics, e.g. development of facial and body hair, muscular development

Glands of the endocrine system

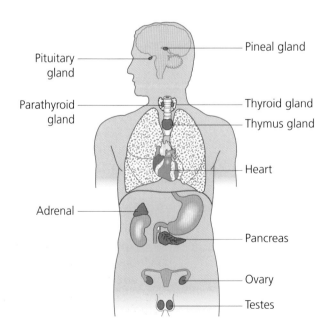

Tip

The onset of menstruation in females is controlled by oestrogen, progesterone and also FSH and LH secreted from the pituitary gland, which bring about changes in the ovaries and the uterus.

The endocrine system maintains homeostasis or constancy within the body. It can do this because the amount of hormone released by the endocrine glands is controlled by the amount of a particular hormone which is needed.

Tip

High stress levels can affect the homeostasis of the body as well as being the root cause for a number of common illnesses such as headaches, digestive problems, high blood pressure and insomnia. Massage can help regulate the body by promoting relaxation, which enables the body to function properly. Certain essential oils used in aromatherapy can also effect certain endocrine glands.

Breasts

The breasts are attached to a layer of connective tissue and strands of connective tissue (suspensory ligaments) run through the breast tissue, attaching the skin to the connective tissue layer that covers the muscles. The hormone oestrogen is responsible for their growth during puberty. The breasts lie over the pectoral and serratus muscles.

The breasts are also known as the mammary glands and their main function is to produce milk after pregnancy (the hormone progesterone causes them to grow when pregnant). Milk is produced by the hormone prolactin and is passed through ducts to the nipple. Milk is then released during breast feeding, when the hormone oxytocin is produced as the baby starts to suckle. Oxytocin helps the uterus return to its normal size more quickly after birth, as it also causes the uterus to contract; therefore, breast feeding is beneficial in helping this to occur.

The glandular tissue that the breasts are composed of is very similar to the tissue found in the sweat glands. The cells that secrete the milk are supported by connective tissue and are divided into lobules that are separated by fat (adipose tissue): it is the fat that determines the size of the breast.

Breast tissue

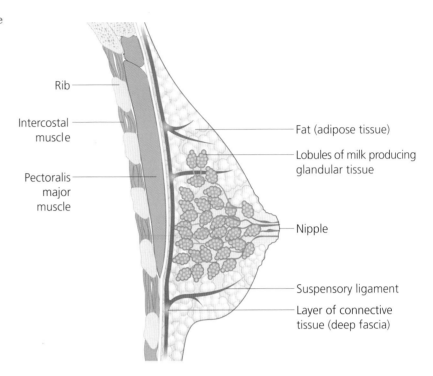

Rib

Intercostal muscle

Pectoralis major muscle

Fat (adipose tissue)

Lobules of milk producing glandular tissue

Nipple

Suspensory ligament

Layer of connective tissue (deep fascia)

The breasts contain:

- **lymphatic vessels** – drainage takes place mainly at the axilla glands (situated under the arm)
- **blood vessels** – the main ones are the axillary and subclavian arteries
- **internal mammary nodes** – when breasts are feeding, these nerves are stimulated and the flow of oxytocin is stimulated, which will promote the flow of milk.

Blood and lymph supply to the breast area

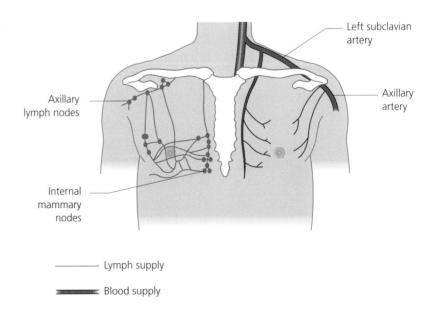

Left subclavian artery

Axillary artery

Axillary lymph nodes

Internal mammary nodes

——— Lymph supply

▬▬▬ Blood supply

Psychological benefits

From headaches and insomnia to digestive problems, high blood pressure and depression, many common illnesses can in, some instances, be stress related. Stress can also depress the body's immune system making it more vulnerable to a number of infections.

However, not all stress is negative. In the right amounts and under the right circumstances it can be very positive. Taking on a new challenge makes life exciting. Everyone has their own stress threshold and a point when challenges and everyday living become too much to cope with. If too much physical or psychological strain is put on us, the normal balances of the body become upset. Combined with other factors such as poor diet and lack of sleep, stress levels can rocket and the results can vary enormously. High blood pressure, migraine, sleeping problems, digestive problems, minor aches and pains, depression, lack of concentration, feeling constantly angry or irritable and skin conditions such as eczema are just some of the conditions that can be caused or exacerbated by stress.

Massage has long been used as a method of counteracting stress and in today's world stress is becoming increasingly common. Massage helps to reeducate the body on how to rest and relax. By rebalancing the body and boosting the immune system, the body should be able to fight off infection and get back on the road of recovery.

A relaxing massage can occasionally induce the client to fall asleep. Most tend to fall into a state of deep relaxation. Clients often feel more refreshed after a massage than after a full night's sleep. It is quite common for a client to return after a massage and announce they had slept much better than they had done for a long time.

The soothing effect of massage encourages:

- an improvement in concentration and alertness due to an increased oxygen supply to the brain
- emotional honesty as the client relaxes and tension is alleviated
- an increase in confidence brought about by physical touch and the uplifting effect of the massage
- an increase in energy levels brought about by the release of tension.

Knowledge review

1   Draw a large labelled diagram to show the structure of the skin.
    Include the following:
    - five layers of the epidermis
    - a hair follicle
    - sweat and sebaceous glands
    - nerve endings
    - capillaries.
2   Which structures are found beneath the dermis?
3   State two effects of massage on the skin.
4   Describe the endocrine system.
5   List all the glands of the endocrine system.
6   What effect do the following hormones have on the body:
    - insulin
    - adrenalin?
7   What effects does massage have on the endocrine system?
8   Name the three main types of blood vessel.
9   Which type of veins have valves and why?
10 Describe two effects of massage on the circulatory system.
11 Why do the cells in the body need a blood supply?
12 Name the lymphatic nodes indicated on the diagram.

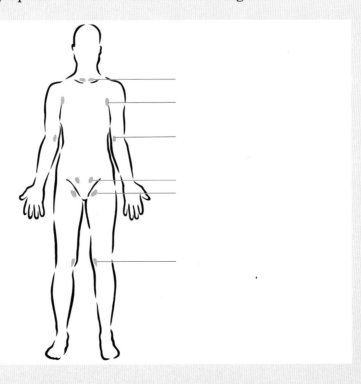

Lymphatic

13 Describe the main functions of the lymphatic system.

14 State the effect of massage on lymphatic circulation.

15 Label the organs indicated on the digestive system diagram.

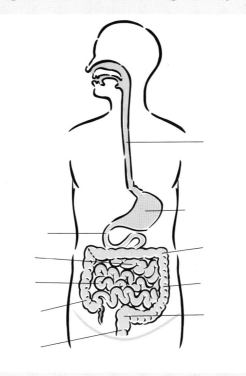

Digestive

16 What is the effect of massaging the alimentary tract?

17 Label the elements indicated on the diagram of the renal system.

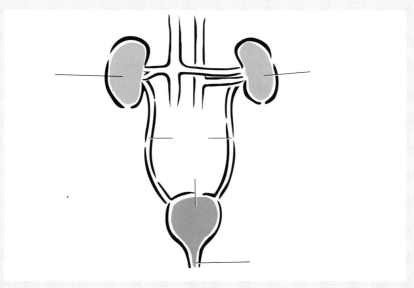

Renal

18   What is the main effect of massage on the renal system?

19   Label the muscles indicated in the diagram of the abdomen.

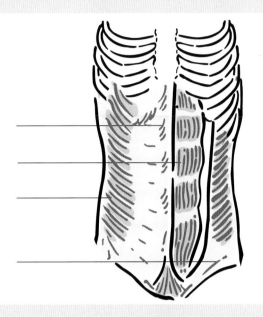

Abdominal

20   In which areas of the body would you find the following:
- metatarsals
- metacarpals
- cervical vertebrae
- humerus
- tibia
- radius
- clavicle?

21   Name the bones that make up the hand.

22   Name the bones that form the foot.

23   State any effects of massage on the bones.

24   In what areas of the body would you find the following muscles and state the main function of each:
- trapezius
- pectoralis major
- deltoid
- tibialis anterior
- gastrocnemius
- quadriceps

- gluteals
- external oblique
- brachio radialis.

25 Describe two effects massage has on muscles.

26 Describe the difference between a tendon and a ligament.

27 Describe the difference between voluntary and involuntary muscle tissue.

28 What is the function of connective tissue?

29 Describe the function of a sensory nerve.

30 How do nerve impulses pass along the nerve fibres?

31 What is meant by the autonomic nervous system?

32 Explain the effect of effleurage movement on the nerves.

33 Describe the type of joint found in the:

- hip
- elbow
- knee.

34 Describe the effect of massage on the joints.

35 What is an erythema and what are its possible causes?

36 What is the function of the olfactory system?

37 What are the benefits of breathing correctly?

38 State the effect massage has on the respiratory system.

Client consultation and contraindications to treatment

5

Learning objectives

This chapter covers the following:

- **client consultation**
- **contraindications**
- **figure diagnosis**
- **keeping records**
- **evaluating treatment**

Client consultation and recognising and acting on contraindications to massage are integral essential knowledge points in the following units:

- **BT17, Provide head and body massage treatments**
- **BT20, Provide Indian head massage treatment**
- **BT21, Provide massage using pre-blended aromatherapy oils**

This chapter explains the importance of and techniques required for client consultation and details the areas that must be covered and recorded on the client's records prior to commencing a massage treatment. It highlights the range of contraindications that could prevent or affect treatment.

Client consultation

Before commencing a massage treatment, the therapist needs to gain a range of information from the client. If the client has not been treated by you or one of your colleagues relatively recently, you should carry out a full consultation. During this consultation, a detailed record card must be completed and it is essential that all personal details are recorded. If they are a regular client, you should begin each treatment with a scaled-down consultation.

Consultations should be carried out in a private area, for example a treatment room or cubicle, as you will need to ask the client a series of questions, many of which may be of a personal or confidential nature, such as their medical history.

Aims of a consultation

The most important reason for carrying out a consultation is to ensure that the client is suitable for treatment and that they are not contraindicated in any way. As a therapist, it is essential that you are familiar with a whole range of conditions that contraindicate massage treatments. The most common are covered later in this chapter.

However, there are number of other things you should aim to achieve during the consultation process:

- Put the client at ease.
- Build a good rapport with the client.
- Ascertain why the client has come for a massage. The client may have an underlying reason for seeking treatment that is not immediately obvious or that they are reluctant to admit, for example they may be suffering from stress and you should try to identify this prior to commencing treatment.
- Build up knowledge about their lifestyle. You can do this by asking open questions.
- Ensure that the client has realistic expectations about the treatment.
- Ensure the treatment they have requested, or the one you have recommended, is the most suitable treatment for their needs.

Throughout the consultation, you should encourage the client to ask any questions that may occur to them. You should answer them all in a professional and honest

Tip

It is very important that you keep this record card up to date. Personal details need to be accurate and you should keep a log of any treatments given together with relevant notes.

Tip

Look at the examples of consultation forms for body massage, Indian head massage and aromatherapy massage that follow. The backs of forms can be used to write treatment notes on.

manner. At the end of the consultation, the client should understand everything that is going to take place and have an idea of what type of massage they will be receiving and what it involves. For example, if it comes to light that they have a lot of tension in the neck and shoulders you can spend more time in this area or if they are menstruating you can omit the abdomen area. Consultations also give the therapist an indication of any areas where the client does not want to be touched. At this stage, the client should be feeling relaxed and ready for their treatment.

If after the consultation you are unsure of the client's suitability for treatment, you should tactfully explain why it is important for them to seek permission from the doctor before treatment can be given.

Client referral

A client may, after consultation, need to seek their doctor's approval in order for the treatment to be carried out. A simple and easy way of getting approval without disturbing the doctor too much is to compose a simple standard letter for which only the doctor's signature is required.

Sample doctor's approval letter

Date:

Clinic address:

Dear Dr Jones

A patient of yours, Jenny Smith, has requested a body massage treatment.

After carrying out a consultation I learned that she is suffering from epilepsy.

I would, therefore, be very grateful if you would indicate, by signing the attached, if you think Jenny is suitable for treatment.

Many thanks,

Therapist

Adele O'Keefe

BODY MASSAGE CONSULTATION

Date	Therapist name

Client name	Date of birth

Address	Postcode

Evening phone number	Day phone number

Name of doctor	Doctor's address and phone number

Related medical history (conditions that may restrict or prohibit treatment application)

Are you taking any medication (this may affect the condition of the skin or skin sensitivity)?

CONTRAINDICATIONS REQUIRING MEDICAL REFERRAL
(preventing head and body massage treatment application)

- ☐ skin disorders – active
- ☐ skin disease
- ☐ high or low blood pressure
- ☐ severe bruising
- ☐ recent head and neck injury
- ☐ severe cuts and abrasions
- ☐ severe varicose veins
- ☐ medical conditions
- ☐ recent scar tissue
- ☐ epilepsy
- ☐ pregnancy
- ☐ diabetes
- ☐ heart disease
- ☐ dysfunction of the nervous system

TREATMENT AREAS
- ☐ neck
- ☐ face
- ☐ head
- ☐ chest and shoulders
- ☐ arms and hands
- ☐ abdomen
- ☐ back
- ☐ legs and feet
- ☐ full body
- ☐ gluteals

LIFESTYLE
- ☐ occupation
- ☐ family situation
- ☐ dietary and fluid intake
- ☐ sleep patterns
- ☐ exercise habits
- ☐ smoking habits
- ☐ hobbies, interests, means of relaxation

MASSAGE TECHNIQUES
- ☐ effleurage
- ☐ petrissage
- ☐ tapotement (percussion)
- ☐ frictions
- ☐ vibrations
- ☐ pressure points

LUBRICANT (IF USED)
- ☐ oil
- ☐ cream
- ☐ powder
- ☐ gel
- ☐ emulsion

CONTRAINDICATIONS THAT RESTRICT TREATMENT
(treatment may require adaptation)

- ☐ skin disorder
- ☐ high or low blood pressure
- ☐ recent scar tissue (avoid area)
- ☐ recent scar tissue
- ☐ cuts and abrasions
- ☐ mild eczema/psoriasis
- ☐ undiagnosed lumps, bumps, swellings
- ☐ asthma
- ☐ product allergies
- ☐ recent injuries to the treatment area
- ☐ certain medication
- ☐ abdomen during menstruation
- ☐ migraine
- ☐ epilepsy

PHYSICAL CHARACTERISTICS
- ☐ weight
- ☐ size
- ☐ muscle tone
- ☐ age
- ☐ health
- ☐ skin condition

OBJECTIVES OF TREATMENT
- ☐ relaxation
- ☐ sense of well-being

EQUIPMENT AND MATERIALS
- ☐ couch/chair/stool
- ☐ gyratory massager
- ☐ towels
- ☐ audio sonic
- ☐ spatulas
- ☐ infrared
- ☐ protective covering
- ☐ consumables
- ☐ oil removal medium

Therapist signature (for reference)

Client signature (confirmation of details)

INDIAN HEAD MASSAGE

Date	Therapist name

Client name	Date of birth

Address	Postcode

Evening phone number	Day phone number

Name of doctor	Doctor's address and phone number

Related medical history (conditions that may restrict or prohibit treatment application)

Are you taking any medication (this may affect the condition of the skin or skin sensitivity)?

CONTRAINDICATIONS REQUIRING MEDICAL REFERRAL
(preventing Indian head massage treatment application)

☐ bacterial infection, e.g. impetigo
☐ viral infection, e.g. herpes simplex
☐ fungal infection, e.g. tine ungium
☐ skin disorders
☐ skin disease
☐ high or low blood pressure
☐ recent head and neck injury
☐ severe bruising
☐ severe cuts and abrasions
☐ hair disorders
☐ medical conditions
☐ recent scar tissue
☐ dysfunction of the nervous system
☐ epilepsy

TREATMENT AREAS
☐ scalp ☐ head ☐ face
☐ neck ☐ shoulders ☐ upper back
☐ arms ☐ hands ☐ primary chakra areas

MASSAGE TECHNIQUES
☐ effleurage ☐ petrissage
☐ tapotement (percussion) ☐ frictions
☐ vibrations ☐ pressure points

LUBRICANT (IF USED)
organic oil – type [_____] ☐ cream

CONTRAINDICATIONS THAT RESTRICT TREATMENT
(treatment may require adaptation)

☐ cuts and abrasions ☐ bruising and swelling
☐ recent injuries to the treatment area
☐ medication ☐ mild eczema/psoriasis
☐ recent scar tissue (avoid area)
☐ undiagnosed lumps, bumps, swellings
☐ migraine ☐ allergies

LIFESTYLE
occupation [_____]
family situation [_____]
dietary and fluid intake [_____]
(including allergies)
hobbies, interests, means of relaxation [_____]
exercise habits [_____]
smoking habits [_____]
sleep patterns [_____]

PHYSICAL CHARACTERISTICS
☐ weight ☐ size
☐ muscle tone ☐ age

OBJECTIVES OF TREATMENT
☐ relaxation ☐ maintenance of health and well-being
☐ improvement of hair and scalp condition

EQUIPMENT AND MATERIALS
☐ towels ☐ comb
☐ spatulas ☐ protective covering
☐ consumables ☐ hairclip
☐ stool

Therapist signature (for reference)

Client signature (confirmation of details)

AROMATHERAPY CONSULTATION

Date	Therapist name

Client name	Date of birth

Address	Postcode

Evening phone number   Day phone number

Name of doctor   Doctor's address and phone number

Related medical history (conditions that may restrict or prohibit treatment application)

Are you taking any medication (this may affect the condition of the skin or skin sensitivity)?

CONTRAINDICATIONS REQUIRING MEDICAL REFERRAL
(preventing aromatherapy massage treatment application)

☐ bacterial infection, e.g. impetigo
☐ viral infection, e.g. herpes simplex
☐ fungal infection, e.g. tinea corporis
☐ systemic medical conditions
☐ severe skin conditions
☐ chemotherapy patients
☐ radiotherapy patients

CLIENT
☐ male
☐ female

PHYSICAL CHARACTERISTICS
weight
height
muscle tone
age
skin condition

CONTRAINDICATIONS THAT RESTRICT TREATMENT
(treatment may require adaptation)

☐ cuts and abrasions
☐ bruising and swelling of known origin
☐ recent scar tissue
☐ pregnancy
☐ during lactation
☐ epilepsy
☐ post-epilation
☐ allergies

LIFESTYLE
occupation
family situation
dietary and fluid intake
(including allergies)
hobbies, interests, means of relaxation
exercise habits
smoking habits
sleep patterns

OBJECTIVES OF TREATMENT
☐ relaxation
☐ sense of well-being
☐ uplifting

Therapist signature (for reference)

Client signature (confirmation of details)

SALON NAME, ADDRESS, PHONE NUMBER

Part 1

Name: _____ Address: _____

Telephone number – Daytime: _____ Evening: _____ _____

Date of birth: _____ Occupation: _____ _____

Part 2: Medical history

Name of doctor: _____ Telephone number: _____

	Yes	No
Any recent illness?	☐	☐
Are you taking any medication at present?	☐	☐	If yes, what are you taking? _____
Are you receiving any medical treatment?	☐	☐	If yes, what treatment? _____

Part 3: Do you suffer from any of the following?

	Yes	No		Yes	No
Heart condition	☐	☐	Dysfunction or disorders to the nervous system	☐	☐
Epilepsy	☐	☐	Cancer	☐	☐
Circulatory problems	☐	☐	Recent operations/scar tissue	☐	☐
Thrombosis/phlebitis	☐	☐	Skin diseases or disorders	☐	☐
Diabetes	☐	☐	Any swellings or inflamed areas	☐	☐
High/low blood pressure	☐	☐	Fractures/recent sprains/muscle strains	☐	☐

Any other: _____

Part 4: Female questions only

Number of pregnancies: ____ Dates: _____ Could you be pregnant? ____ How many months _____

	Yes	No		Yes	No
Could you be menopausal?	☐	☐	Do you suffer from pre-menstrual tension?	☐	☐
Are you menstruating at present?	☐	☐	Do you suffer from period problems?	☐	☐

Part 5: General

Do you suffer from any of the following?

	Yes	No
Skin complaints, e.g. psoriasis/allergies/eczema/dermatitis/other	☐	☐
Muscles, joints conditions, e.g. arthritis/rheumatism/muscular aches and pains/other	☐	☐
Respiratory conditions, e.g. asthma/sore throat/colds/other	☐	☐
Digestive complaints, e.g. indigestion/constipation/other	☐	☐
Urinary problems, e.g. fluid retention/water infection/thrush/other	☐	☐
Do you suffer from migraine/headaches?	☐	☐	If so, how often? _____

Part 6: Overall summary of client's general health

_____

_____

Part 7: Summary

Is GP referral required? _____ GP approval received _____ Date: _____

Part 8: General lifestyle

Do you smoke? ____ If yes, approx. how many per day? _____ On average, how many units of alcohol do you consume per

How many cups of tea/coffee do you drink per day? _____ week? _____

Generally, how would you describe your diet? _____ What are you hobbies? _____

Do you take any vitamin or other supplements? _____ How do you relax? _____

Do you exercise on a regular basis? _____ What is your general sleep pattern? _____

If yes, what type of exercise? _____ How often? _____ On average, how many hours do you sleep per night? _____

How would you describe your energy levels? low ☐ medium ☐ high ☐

At the moment are you feeling: anxious ☐ depressed ☐ stressed ☐

Client declaration

The information I have given is correct, and I am therefore willing to proceed with the treatment that has been discussed.

Treatment agreed: _____

Client signature: _____ Date: _____ Therapist signature: _____

A consultation form

Tip

Dealing with several clients one after another can be very exhausting. Try to 'switch off' between each one. This will help you feel less tired at the end of the day. Listen, but remember not to take on your clients' problems or you will become emotionally and physically drained.

Consent form

The above treatment you have requested, is suitable/unsuitable for the above-named client.

Signed:

Dr Jones

Date:

Once the form has been completed, it is extremely important to get the client to sign it. This indicates proof of accuracy. It the client fails to divulge any information, for example a heart condition, you have the evidence that these questions were asked and the fact that you were unaware of this condition was not a result of negligence. Whenever you treat a client, you should also sign the card on which the treatment has been noted. In a multi-therapist practice, it will then be clear which therapist performed which treatments.

Contraindications

Health & safety

If the client has a small cut or graze that represents a local contraindication, a small adhesive plaster can be apply to the area to avoid the risk of cross-infection.

One of the key things to identify during a client consultation is any condition that contraindicates the proposed treatment. A contraindication is any condition or symptom of the body that prevents a treatment taking place. It is very important that you have a good knowledge of all contraindications to body massage before carrying out a treatment. It is essential that you check thoroughly for these at the consultation as inappropriate treatment could incur risk to the client, therapist and other clients through cross-infection.

Contraindications can be either local or general. A local contraindication is one in which the area surrounding the condition must be avoided, for example if there is a varicose vein on the calf muscle, you should avoid massaging the lower leg. A general contraindication is one in which the client should, on no account, be massaged. Only when the condition clears up or approval is given by the client's doctor in writing can the client receive treatment.

Local or restrictive contraindications

With local contraindications, although the affected areas should be avoided, other areas of the body can usually still be massaged. If you are in any doubt, refer your client to their GP for medical advice.

Avoid massaging over:

- cuts, bruises and recent scar tissue, less than six months old. As well as being painful, there is a risk of infection
- areas affected by skin disorders such as eczema, psoriasis and dermatitis
- skin abrasions – risk of infection
- areas affected by sunburn – painful
- bites and stings – as well as being painful, there is a risk of infection
- abdomen if the client is menstruating or in the early stages of pregnancy
- swellings – medical advice should be sought if the reason for an oedema is unclear
- severe varicose veins – massage can worsen this condition
- local areas affected by thrombosis. This condition is quite common in the deep veins of the calves. Blood tends to clot in the veins and massage may disturb the clot causing it to start moving through the veins and end up causing a blockage in a major organ
- fractures and sprains
- acute joint conditions and tender muscles – unless medical advice has been sought
- areas of inflammation
- moles and warts
- areas of thin, crêpey skin – avoid deep manipulations and tapotement movements.

General or total contraindications

If any of the following conditions are present, medical advice should always be sought prior to treatment. In many cases you will need to exercise special care if given the go-ahead for treatment.

- some long-term medication – check with the client's GP if you are unsure
- asthma – although massage can help alleviate symptoms, medical advice must be sought if the condition is severe
- undiagnosed lumps, bumps and swellings
- loss of skin sensation – medical advice must be sought

Health & safety

Never perform massage on a client whom you suspect is under the influence of alcohol or drugs. Also, do not perform treatments on a client suffering from fever, infectious diseases or who is feeling generally unwell.

Important note

Never diagnose conditions – this is not your professional area. If in any doubt, obtain written consent from the client's GP.

- cancer – massage should only be carried out on people suffering from cancer under medical supervision as it could cause the cancer cells to spread via the lymph
- nervous disorders – medical advice must be sought
- embolism – medical advice must be sought
- spastic conditions – massage could worsen symptoms
- blood pressure problems:
  - high blood pressure – medical approval will usually be given as massage can often help this condition
  - low blood pressure – this can lead to clients feeling faint or dizzy, so if medical permission is granted, you must ensure that the client is supervised when they get up from the massage couch
- heart conditions – massage stimulates the circulation and this may have an effect on any heart condition. Always seek medical consent
- during the active phase of rheumatoid arthritis
- epilepsy – medical permission will usually be given for massage in cases of epilepsy, as in most cases this condition will be controlled with medication. However, you should never leave an epileptic client unattended
- diabetes – many people with this condition are prone to circulation problems and also problems with skin sensation. Take special care when performing massage treatments.

Skin diseases and disorders

The skin is covered by micro-organisms that cannot be seen by the naked eye. Some of these micro-organisms are responsible for some of the skin diseases and disorders that you are likely to come across as you practise body massage. You need to be able to recognise at least the most common ones and understand those that do and that do not contraindicate treatments. For those that do contraindicate treatment, refer the client to their doctor, as there is a risk of cross-infection.

Micro-organisms can be pathogenic – that is, disease-producing – or non-pathogenic. A non-pathogenic organism is not harmful. In fact, many non-pathogenic organisms are beneficial and help contribute to our general health.

A **disease** is an infectious, transferable, pathogenic condition but a **disorder** is a non-infectious, non-pathogenic condition of the skin, hair or scalp. As a general rule, where skin disorders are present, if they contraindicate treatment in any way, it will be local rather than total. Referring or refusing to treat a client who clearly has a non-pathogenic disorder can cause them considerable anguish, while treating someone with an infectious disease can put you and your other clients at risk of cross-infection.

Skin diseases

An infectious disease can be passed on from one person to the other by air droplets, for example when coughing and sneezing. A contagious disease is passed on through direct or indirect contact, for example touching the infected area or using materials that have touched it. A good example of how this can happen is when a towel touched by an infected person is reused.

There are four types of pathogenic micro-organism:

1 bacteria
2 virus
3 fungus
4 infestations.

In this next section, we take a look at some of the most common skin diseases that would contraindicate treatment.

Bacteria

Bacteria are minute, unicellular micro-organisms. They are found almost everywhere and are either pathogenic or non-pathogenic.

Bacteria can enter the body in several ways through:

- direct contact, e.g. touching an infected person
- unhygienic working practices, e.g. the use of unsterilised equipment
- indirect contact, e.g. touching contaminated objects
- consuming contaminated food
- respiration, as many bacteria are airborne.

As a therapist you must not provide treatment to anyone who has any visible signs of bacterial infection. Infections usually present themselves as pus, which is usually present in abscesses, boils and pustules.

Table 5.1 *Common bacterial infections*

Condition	Status	Description	
Impetigo	Infectious and highly contagious	An infection of the epidermis, most commonly found on the face where pus-filled blisters form. When burst, the infection spreads and yellow crusts are formed. Requires medical treatment	**Impetigo**
Boils (furuncle)	Infectious	An infection of the hair follicle caused by the staphylococci bacterium. It usually starts as a small red nodule and gradually increases in size simultaneously becoming inflamed and very painful	
Carbuncle	Infectious	Several boils appear together and these can be found almost anywhere on the body	
Conjunctivitis	Infectious and contagious	Inflammation of the lining of the eyelid and the mucous membrane that covers the eye. The eye becomes red, itchy and exudes pus. Avoid facial massage	
Styes	Infectious	Small pus-filled adhesions on the lash line resulting in an infected hair follicle. Avoid facial massage	**Boils**
Paranychia	Infectious	An infection of the tissue surrounding the nail plate. It is usually red and swollen with pus in the cuticle and in the nail walls. Requires medical treatment	

Viruses

Viruses are smaller micro-organisms than bacteria. They are classed as parasites because they can only live and reproduce within living cells. They spread by multiplying within a healthy tissue cell until they burst the cell wall. They are then free to invade other cells and repeat the process, therefore spreading the infection.

Table 5.2 *Common viral infections*

Condition	Status	Description	
Herpes zoster (shingles)	Infectious	Attacks the nerve pathways causing significant pain. Small blister-like spots on the skin's surface near the nerve endings. Found almost anywhere on the body	
Herpes simplex (cold sore)	Infectious and contagious	Small blisters that burst forming an oozing crust, usually occurring around the mouth area. Tend to be triggered by changes in temperature, ultraviolet light, ill health or stress-related illnesses	**Herpes Simplex**
Warts	Infectious and contagious	Common warts appear on the hands and face as a result of abnormal reproduction of the cells in the germinativum layer of the epidermis. Warts are infectious and should be referred to the doctor	**Warts**
Verrucae (plantar warts)	Infectious and highly contagious	Found on the feet. Round and firm with a rough surface. Client should be referred to a chiropodist	**Verrucae**

Viruses are responsible for diseases as wide ranging as influenza, chicken pox, measles, hepatitis B and AIDS (acquired immune deficiency syndrome), which is caused by HIV (human immunopathic virus).

Fungi

Fungal diseases are spread by direct and indirect contact. Like viruses, they are classed as parasites. Moulds, yeasts and mildew are all fungi. They cannot manufacture their own food and therefore need to obtain food from other living organisms. A good example of this is ringworm.

Table 5.3 *Common fungal infections*

Condition	Status	Description	
Ringworm	Highly infectious and contagious	Starts as small red circular patches. Affects the skin on different parts of the body. Healing takes place from the centre, so appears as single or multi-ringed lesions. The fungus produces enzymes that break down the keratin. These can appear as a mild scaling to more severe areas that are inflamed and extremely itchy. The small maculae – or flat spot – is red and tends to spread outwards	 **Ringworm**
Tinea pedis/ athlete's foot	Very contagious	The name given when ringworm affects the feet. The fungus is usually found in between the toes and then tends to spread to the sides of the feet and the soles. Its appearance is usually flaking, cracking and weeping, accompanied by itchiness	
Tinea unguium	Infectious and contagious	The name given when ringworm affects the nails. The fungus usually invades the free edge and then spreads to the nail root. It can either appear as whitish patches that can be scraped off or as yellow streaks that are in the middle of the nail. The nail plate becomes very spongy, and furrowed and in some cases will become completely detached	
Tinea corporis	Infectious and contagious	The name given when ringworm affects the whole body. When it affects only the upper trunk it is known as tinea versicolor. Red pimples appear and spread at the edges, leaving a red ring with a normal skin colour in the middle. Pustules and scales usually develop over the rings	 **Tinea corporis**

Infestations

Infestations are tiny animal parasites that invade the skin and live off human blood. These are highly contagious.

Table 5.4 *Common infestations*

Condition	Status	Description
Scabies	Contagious	Caused by a female mite that is fertilised on the skin's surface and then burrows into the skin to lay its eggs; this condition is often referred to as 'the itch'. The eggs hatch after four days and 10 days later the mature mite appears on the skin's surface. Scabies tends to invade in between the fingers, on the palms and on the soles. They appear as grey ridges that track the routes of the burrows in the skin. The itch is a result of pimples caused by allergic reaction to the mite, its eggs and larvae. This gets worse as body temperature increases. Constant scratching produces inflammation and causes the skin to become coarser
Pediculosis capis (head lice)	Extremely contagious by direct and indirect contact	Caused by a small animal parasite that lives for approximately 30 days by sucking the blood from the scalp. The lice cling to the hair of the scalp and lay eggs attached to the hair close to the skin. Before laying eggs, lice first inject the site with an anticoagulant that causes irritation. The resultant scratching can cause secondary infection. Although lice lay up to 300 eggs in their lifetime, only a few survive and a typical infestation amounts to about 20 lice Towels and bedding that have been in contact with this condition should be disinfected before being laundered
Pediculosis pubis	Extremely contagious	A condition in which small parasites infest the body hair – usually the pubic hair, eyelashes and eyebrows. The lice cling to the hair of the body, eggs are laid, attached to the hair close to the skin. The lice bite the skin to suck out the blood for nourishment, creating an irritation and leaving small red marks. Itching can lead to secondary bacterial infection
Pediculosis corporis	Very infectious and contagious	Small parasites feed and live on the body skin. The lice cling to the hair of the body, eggs are laid, attached to the hair close to the skin. The lice bite the skin to suck out the blood for nourishment, creating an irritation and leaving small red marks. Itching can lead to secondary bacterial infection

In the Scabies description row:

Scabies

Skin disorders

The following is a list of some of the most common skin disorders that you as a massage therapist might encounter. These skin conditions are neither infectious nor contagious. They can broadly be classified as skin conditions, malignant skin conditions, allergic conditions, pigmentation disorders and sebaceous gland disorders.

Skin conditions

Table 5.5 *Common skin conditions*

Condition	Description
Psoriasis	Normally affects the knees, lower back and scalp although it can also affect other areas of the body. Its appearance is red, itchy flaky skin. The red patches of skin are covered in waxy, silvery scales and secondary infection can occur if bacteria enter skin broken through scratching. No treatment is completely effective, although medication can help relieve the symptoms. *This condition is not infectious and does not contraindicate treatment* **Psoriasis**
Seborrheic (senile) warts	Warts are slightly raised, black or brown in colour, rough patches of skin. They are usually found on the trunk, scalp, and the temples and can be cauterised by a physician. *This condition is not infectious*
Xanthomas	Found on the eyelids. Their appearance is a flat or raised area of skin that is yellow in colour. Their growth is thought to be connected with diabetes and abnormal blood pressure and can sometimes be corrected with a low-fat diet. *They are not infectious and should not interfere with body massage treatments in any way*
Erythema	An area of the skin in which the blood vessels have dilated due to either injury or inflammation. The affected area appears red and erythema may occur locally or generally all over the skin. It is not infectious. The cause of the condition needs to be identified, as it may be an allergic reaction. If the cause is unknown, *the client should be referred to the doctor*
Dandruff (pityriasis simplex)	In its simple form, dandruff is normal shedding of the stratum corneum, the uppermost layer of the epidermis. Specialist shampoo can help to control this condition. Sometimes, if scales are allowed to build up, there is a risk of trapping bacteria on the scalp. Yeast may also grow, resulting in a musty smell from the scalp. *Medical treatment should be advised if this condition is suspected* Indian head massage treatments will help to improve pityriasis simplex but bacterial infections should be cleared first
Alopecia (hair loss)	There are different categories of alopecia (hair loss) ranging from Alopecia universalis, completely hairless, to Alopecia areata, small areas of hair loss on the scalp. This latter condition is sometimes stress related or due to shock, but can also be an after-effect following surgery or illness. The hair almost always grows again as the patient recovers, but it may have lost all colour pigment and now appear white. Indian head massage has been found to help promote healthy hair growth and greatly improve these conditions
Keloids	Keloids occur after a skin injury. They are made up of overgrown abnormal scar tissue that tends to spread and are non-infectious. They are characterised by excess collagen deposits. The skin tends to be red, raised and ridged. The skin must be protected from UV exposure to avoid it from becoming discoloured **Keloid scar**
Verrucae filliforms (skin tags)	These are non-infectious and appear as skin-coloured threads projecting from the skin, which are approximately 3–6mm long They are mainly situated on the eyelids and neck area, but can occur under the arms Treatment can be carried out by the skin tags being removed by a qualified electrologist or a physician using diathermy to cauterise them

Malignant skin conditions

Table 5.6 *Malignant skin conditions*

Condition	Description	
Squamous cell carcinomas or prickle cell cancers	Can occur anywhere on the skin although they originate in the epidermis. When fully formed, the carcinoma appears as a raised area of skin. *This is a medical condition* and is often treated by radiation	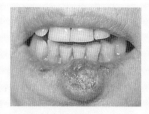 **Squamous cell carcinoma**
Basal cell carcinomas or rodent ulcers	Usually occurs on the face and tends to occur in middle age. These tend to be small shiny waxy nodules with a depressed centre. The disease extends with more nodules appearing on the border of the original ulcer. *This is a medical condition*	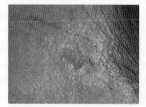 **A basal-cell carcinoma**
Malignant melanomas/ moles	Rapidly growing skin cancer. It is not infectious. If you notice that a client has a mole that is changing in size, structure or colour, bleeds or is itchy, you should recommend that they *seek medical advice* without causing alarm. Melanomas start as a bluish/black mole that starts to get bigger quite quickly, at the same time getting darker in colour and developing a halo of pigmentation around it. Later it becomes raised, ulcerates and bleeds. Secondary growths will develop in the internal organs if the melanoma is not treated. These are usually found on the lower abdomen, legs and feet	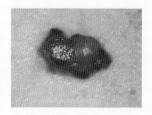 **Malignant melanoma**

Health & safety

If you notice that a mole on a regular client's body is changing shape or size, bleeding or forming a crust, advise them to seek medical attention.

Allergic conditions

An allergic reaction appears as an irritation. The area is usually itchy, red and swollen accompanied by discomfort. The substance causing the reaction is referred to as an allergen. Allergens may be vegetable, animal or chemical substances

Tip

Some essential oils used in aromatherapy massage are contraindicated for certain conditions. If medical consent is given for massage for a client suffering from a certain condition, you should check to see if there are any contraindicated oils associated with that condition. See Chapter 11, page 275.

Tip

The use of hypoallergenic body products minimises the risk of skin contact with any irritants.

and may be eaten, inhaled or absorbed following contact of the skin. Most allergens are proteins that are ingested or chemicals that come into contact with the skin's surface.

Every individual has a different tolerance to the various substances encountered in daily life. What may cause an allergic reaction to one person may well be perfectly harmless to another. You may suddenly become allergic to a substance that you have been using for years and equally you may also cease to be allergic to something to which you have always been allergic.

Health & safety

The type of allergens known to cause an allergic skin reaction are:

- sticking plaster
- nail polish
- hair and lash dyes
- lanolin
- certain foods, especially peanuts, lobster, cow's milk and strawberries
- plants such as chrysanthemums
- metal objects containing nickel.

A number of more specific conditions can result from allergies. (See Table 5.7.)

Table 5.7 *Allergic conditions*

Condition	Description
Dermatitis	There are two types of dermatitis: primary dermatitis is when the skin is irritated by the action of a substance on the skin, which leads to skin inflammation; and allergic dermatitis, which occurs on exposure to a particular substance. The skin quickly becomes irritated, causing an allergic reaction. If the skin reacts to a skin irritant outside the body, the reaction is localised. Repeated contact with the allergen will lead to hypersensitivity. If the irritant gains entry into the body, it will be transported by the bloodstream and cause an overall allergic reaction. Dermatitis is not infectious and the skin appears as red and swollen with the possibility of blisters. The treatment is to *avoid the substance*, use steroid creams to soothe the damaged skin and barrier cream to help avoid contact with the irritant(s)

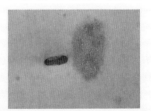

Dermatitis

Table 5.7 *(continued)*

Condition	Description	
Eczema	Eczema normally occurs on the face and neck and areas such as inner creases of the elbow and behind the knee area. The skin is usually red, swollen and blistered. The blisters leak tissue fluid that later hardens producing scabs. It is usually caused by skin contact either internally or externally with an irritant. Treatment is steroid cream. Special diets can help as can avoidance of the irritant	 Eczema
Urticaria (nettle rash)	This is a minor skin disorder caused by contact with an allergen, either external such as insect bites or internal, such as food or drugs. The condition exhibits itself in raised, round whitish skin weals accompanied by erythema. The treatment is antihistamines to reduce the itching and avoidance of the allergen	 Urticaria

Tip

A naevus is any abnormal skin pigmentation. None of these conditions is infectious.

Pigmentation disorders

Pigmentation of the skin tends to vary according to a person's genetic characteristics. Generally, the darker the skin the more pigmentation is present. Abnormal changes in the skin can cause pigmentation to change. **Hypopigmentation** is loss of pigmentation in the skin. **Hyperpigmentation** is increased pigment production.

Table 5.8 *Pigmentation conditions*

Condition	Description
Junction naevi	Non-infectious and can appear anywhere on the body. They are harmless, localised collections of naevoid cells that arise from mass local production of pigment-forming cells. They tend to vary from brown to black in colour
Vascular naevi	Skin condition in which small or large areas of skin pigmentation are caused by the permanent dilation of blood capillaries

Table 5.8 (continued)

Spider naevi (stellate haemangiomas)	Dilated blood vessels forming a star shape or spider pattern. These can occur on the cheek area, upper body, the arms and neck. It is usually caused by an injury to the skin and can be treated by diathermy	**Spider naevus**
Dermal naevi	About 1cm wide, they appear smooth and dome shaped, their colour ranging from normal to a dark brown. Sometimes one or more hairs grow out of them and they are usually situated on the face	
Cellular naevi (moles)	Skin condition in which changes in the cells of the skin result in malformations	
Hairy naevi	Slightly raised moles that vary in size from about 3cm to much larger. Coarse hairs grow from the surface and colour ranges from fawn to dark brown. They can appear anywhere on the skin	
Port wine stains	Dilated capillaries appear in large areas and the naevus is flat and smooth. Usually found on the face and neck area. Camouflage creams are usually effective in disguising these	
Strawberry marks (naevi vasculosis)	Red or purplish raised marks that appear from birth. These can be of any size and located anywhere on the skin. Concealing preparations may be used to cover the condition	**Strawberry naevus**
Chloasma (liver spots)	The result of increased skin pigmentation in specific areas of the body, the most common sites being upper chest, forearms, backs of hands, temples and the forehead. Their appearance is usually flat and smooth with an irregular shape. Colour ranges from light tan to dark brown. They often occur during pregnancy and can also be the result of taking the contraceptive pill, as oestrogen (female hormone) is thought to stimulate melanin production. Chloasma is best kept out of the sun, as the condition will worsen	
Vitiligo (leucoderma)	Characterised by areas of the skin that have lost their pigmentation and are completely white in colour. Their appearance is symmetrically shaped patches of skin, usually situated on the thigh, lower abdomen, face and neck. If vitiligo occurs over hairy areas like eyebrows, the hairs will also lose their pigmentation. Avoid ultraviolet light as the skin does not have the same protection	**Vitiligo**
Albinism	Skin cannot produce the melanin pigment, therefore the hair and skin lack colour. The skin tends to be very pink, the eyes are pink and extremely sensitive to light and the hair is white. This condition can occur on the entire skin. The skin should not be exposed to ultraviolet light and sunglasses should be worn to protect the eyes	
Freckles or ephelids	These are non-infectious. They are small, flat, pigmented areas that are darker than the surrounding skin and tend to be situated on the nose and cheek area of fair-skinned people. They can also occur on the hands, arms, shoulders and back areas. Freckles can be concealed with cosmetics and a sun block is highly recommended to prevent the colour from intensifying. Exposure to ultraviolet light stimulates the production of melanin, which intensifies their appearance	

Table 5.8 *(continued)*

Lentigines	These are non-infectious pigmented areas of skin that tend to be slightly bigger than freckles and do not go any darker in colour when exposed to ultraviolet light. They are slightly raised, brown-pigmented patches of skin and occur on the face and hands. Lentigines can be concealed with concealing products
Dilated capillaries	These are capillaries near the surface of the skin that are permanently dilated. These non-infectious, small, red, visible blood capillaries are usually found on neglected, dry or fine skin such as the cheek area. Dilated capillaries can be treated by using a green corrective camouflage cosmetic or can be removed by a qualified electrologist using diathermy

Table 5.9 *Sebaceous gland disorders*

Condition	**Description**	
Acne rosacea	Tends to occur at puberty, when the hormone imbalance in the body influences the activity of the sebaceous glands, causing an increased production of sebum. The sebum may stay in the sebaceous ducts, causing congestion and bacterial infection of the surrounding tissue. The skin tends to be inflamed accompanied by comedones (blackheads), pustules and papules (pimples). These are usually situated on the face area, but can occur on the chest and back. The client must be referred to seek medical advice	 Acne rosacea
Sebaceous cysts, steatomas or wens	Tend to be semi-globular in shape, either raised or flat, hard or soft. The cysts can be the same colour as the skin or red if there is a secondary bacterial infection. Sacs of sebum form in the hair follicles or under the sebaceous glands in the skin: the sebum becomes blocked, the sebaceous gland becomes distended and a lump forms. Can form anywhere on the skin and medical advice should be sought by the client	
Seborrhoea	Excessive secretion of sebum from the sebaceous glands. Tends to occur in puberty, as a result of the hormonal changes that occur. The skin appears coarse and greasy, comedones, pustules and papules are present. This condition tends to affect the scalp and face, but sometimes also the back and chest area. Medical advice may be sought	
Acne vulgaris	Hormonal imbalance. Tends to occur at puberty due to the increased production of sebum. The sebum may cause congestion as a result of the sebum being retained in the sebaceous ducts and a bacterial infection of the surrounding skin. The area tends to be inflamed and is accompanied with pustules, papules and comedones, which are usually situated on the nose, forehead, chin, chest and back. Medical advice may be sought. Medicated creams and antibiotics are used to treat the condition	 Acne vulgaris

Table 5.9 *(continued)*

Milia	Hard pearly white, small cysts caused by keratinisation of the skin over the hair follicles, which cause sebum to collect in the hair follicle. They are usually situated on the upper face. The milia may be removed by a qualified beauty therapist using a sterile needle to pierce the skin overlying the cuticle and therefore releasing the milia
Comedones (blackheads)	The result of excess sebum and keratinised cells that block the mouth of the hair follicle. Non infectious. This condition tends to affect the nose, chin, forehead, upper back and chest

Comedones

Figure diagnosis

Once all relevant personal details have been completed and any contraindications ruled out, you should undertake a body analysis. It is extremely important to analyse the posture and figure of the client as part of the consultation, to ensure the treatments recommended are going to suit the client's requirements and are going to be the most effective.

There are a number of so-called figure faults. The most common condition found in female clients is a pear-shaped figure characterised by:

- heavy buttocks and thighs
- protruding abdomen
- round shoulders
- a large chest which can sometimes lead to round shoulders.

Many figure faults are due to slack muscles that can be caused by lack of exercise, pregnancy, illness or a sedentary lifestyle.

Body types

There are three main body types that you should learn to recognise as a therapist – endomorph, ectomorph and mesomorph. Being able to recognise these types will help you to distinguish between figure faults that can be changed by posture, diet and exercise and hereditary shapes that, by and large, will remain the same regardless of posture and diet.

Endomorph

Ectomorph

Mesomorph

Endomorph

This type tends to have a higher proportion of fat to muscle. Endomorphs tend to put on weight very easily. Fat deposits around the abdomen, thighs, hips and the shoulders. The hands and feet tend to be small and the neck and limbs short.

Ectomorph

This type tends to be lean and angular with small joints and long limbs. There is practically no body fat or muscle bulk and ectomorphs do not easily gain weight.

Mesomorph

These are athletic body types who tend not to have any weight problems. Mesomorphs tend to have broad shoulders and well-toned muscles with an even distribution of weight.

Being able to diagnose figure type enables you to adapt the massage technique as appropriate. It also enables you to recommend postural exercises to clients who have postural conditions and can be helped in this way. In some instances, you may be the first person to recognise a fault that potentially requires medical attention.

It is important to be able to accurately diagnose figure faults, as incorrect exercises could make a postural condition worse. Very often it is habitual bad posture that creates the postural defects and the use of corrective exercises will eventually improve the condition in most cases. Some people are born with excellent postures, but for those who are not, it can be learnt. Professional models usually glide elegantly along. They practise until it becomes second nature. Good posture is the coordination and interplay of the extensor and flexor muscles of the body. If one group of muscles become weaker or stronger, the whole postural balance gets out of balance. Bad posture not only looks unattractive but can also bring about postural defects.

Carrying out the assessment

The initial figure assessment is visual. It is easy to assess the figure shape even when the client is fully dressed. The next stage is to ask the client to remove their clothes down to the underwear. It is best to check for posture and figure faults in front of a full-length mirror. In this way, the client can observe how their posture may be corrected. Ensure that you observe the client from the front, the back and both sides.

Tip

Don't forget your own posture when you are working.

Inspection from the front

A client who has good posture will stand tall and straight with their weight evenly distributed on both legs. Look for the following:

1 The head should be level, the chin tucked in and the ears level and even.
2 The shoulders should be level, slightly back with the chest and thorax broad and out.
3 The arms and hands should be relaxed and down by the sides of the thigh but not too far forward.
4 The waist should be evenly curved and not more apparent on one side than the other, with hips level not one higher up than the other.
5 The abdomen muscles should be slightly retracted.
6 The legs and knees should be straight, not tightly braced, feet facing forwards, slightly apart and flat feet, knock knees and bandy legs should be noted.

Inspection from the back

1 Check the head, ears and shoulders again from the back view looking out for the same things as before.
2 The medial borders of the scapula should be an even distance from the spine. The inferior angles of the scapula should be lying flat and level against the back of the chest wall.
3 Check the waist and hips as before.

Tip

Remember: while some postural disorders are because of bad posture others are generic postural deformities that cannot be corrected or remedied.

Assessing posture

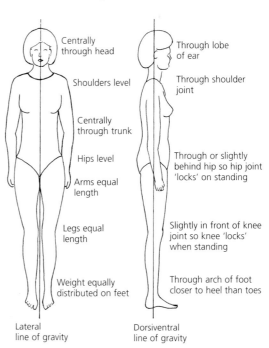

Centrally through head
Shoulders level
Centrally through trunk
Hips level
Arms equal length
Legs equal length
Weight equally distributed on feet
Lateral line of gravity

Through lobe of ear
Through shoulder joint
Through or slightly behind hip so hip joint 'locks' on standing
Slightly in front of knee joint so knee 'locks' when standing
Through arch of foot closer to heel than toes
Dorsiventral line of gravity

Tip

One shoulder being lower than the other in women can be a result of carrying heavy bags on the same side of the body. The dropped or lower shoulder develops shortened muscles, which cause the opposite side of the body to compensate and its muscles to lengthen. The waist will also form an uneven curve.

Tip

The pelvic floor muscles help with excretion and support the organs in the abdomen and pelvis.

4 Check that the spine is straight down the back and not curved in either direction.

5 Check the gluteal folds are even and at the same height.

6 Inspect the legs and feet as before.

Advantages of good posture

Good posture enables more effective breathing, as the chest is not contracted, and more efficient functioning of the digestive organs, as they are not compressed. Muscles will not become as tired if the body weight is evenly distributed, and when bones are in the correct position, postural defects do not occur. Good posture also makes a person's figure much better.

Treating poor posture

Poor posture can cause a slight scoliosis over a period of time. In treating this, the aim is to correct the general poor posture. An appropriate treatment for scoliosis would be static contractions, tensing or tightening muscles without changing their length. These could be given to the muscles of the neck and head, extensors of the back, abdominal muscles, extensors of the hip and knee and the small muscles in the feet in various positions such as lying, sitting and standing. Exercises involving coordination and balance should also be taught. Remember, holding the correct posture during the exercise is of great importance, not just the exercise itself. Each client will have individual requirements depending on their problem.

Common figure faults

The following are types of postural condition that you may encounter as a massage therapist and exercises to tackle them.

Figure faults

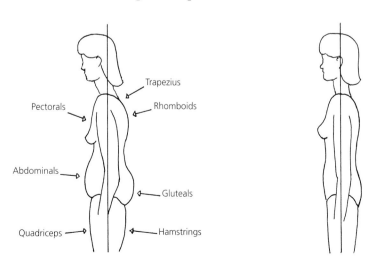

Table 5.10 *Postural conditions*

Condition	Exercise
Flat Back	Characterised by the pelvis being tilted backwards, the lumbar region of the spine being flat and the hamstrings shortened. The client looks very square shouldered and erect as the curves of the spine are almost ironed. Mobility exercises help to mobilise and strengthen the spine and stretch the shortened muscles ● Hump and hollow the spine ● Trunk movements, including forward bends, side flexions in the sitting position and rotations

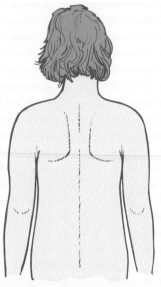

Flat back

| Pelvic tilt | Characterised by the angle made between a horizontal line and a line drawn from the top of the symphysis pubis to the sacral promontory. If the pelvis tilts too far backwards the curve in the lumbar region can become flattened. If it tilts too far forwards, the lumbar vertabrae can become hyperextended

 NB: The angle is greater in the female than in the male and also increases considerably during pregnancy as the ligaments relax and movement is increased

 ● Lie on back, knees bent, arms relaxed at sides. Push the hollow of the back into the floor, hold and relax. Standing with feet slightly apart, knees bent, gently swing pelvis forward, if the tilt is too far backwards, or backwards, if the tilt is too far forward
 ● Kneel on all fours and gently hump and hollow the back |

Pelvic tilt

Table 5.10 *(continued)*

Condition **Exercise**

Kyphosis (round shoulders)

Usually, but not exclusively, caused by habitual bad posture. Characterised by an exaggeration of normal backward curve of the spine in the thoracic region. The client will have a poking chin and round shoulders. The pectoral muscles are tight and shortened with the upper back muscles overstretched and weak. This condition is often accompanied by lordosis

Aim is to loosen the tightened structures and strengthen those which are stretched.

NB: Tight muscles can be stretched when massage is being performed by using the fingers or thumbs and kneading the smaller muscles and on larger muscles using palmar kneading

● Stand with feet slightly apart and shoulders relaxed, rotate the shoulders in a backwards direction

Kyphosis

Lordosis (hollow back)

Characterised by appearance of hollow back in the lumbar region. The pelvis tends to be inclined forward, the abdominal muscles and hamstrings are lengthened and stretched, whereas the lumbar muscles are shortened and the gluteals weakened

Aim is to strengthen and shorten the abdominal muscles and hamstrings, strengthen the gluteal muscles and mobilise the lumbar spine.

● Lie on the floor with knees bent, feet slightly apart and hands resting on the thighs

● Push down the small of the back into the floor until no gap exists. This will move the pelvis forward and tighten the abdominal muscles

● Slowly lift the head and shoulders off the floor and return slowly to the starting position

● Repeat over a period of time

● *Remember to breathe in when raising the head and shoulders and breathe out when lowering back down*

NB: This condition is often accompanied by kyphosis

Kypho-lordosis

Combination of kyphosis and lordosis. When corrective exercises are given, the lumbar spine must be corrected first, so the lordosis is not increased. When carrying out abdominal exercises, the thoracic region and the shoulders must be back and straight so as not to encourage the kyphosis

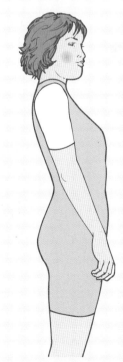

Lordosis

Table 5.10 *(continued)*

Condition	Exercise

Scoliosis

Characterised by a lateral curve of the spine going either to the right or the left side. The curvature tends to either be an 'S' or a 'C' shape. This type of fault causes changes in the muscles, ligaments, bones and joints that can lead to other faults such as one leg shorter than the other, one shoulder higher than the other, uneven scapula and pelvic tilt

Aim with this condition is to restore the balance of the back muscles

- Stride standing – carry out trunk side flexions sliding the hand down the concave side where two muscles are stretched
- Prone lying – keeping the chin in, lift the head and shoulders, then lift the head and shoulders keeping hands clasped pulling down the arms

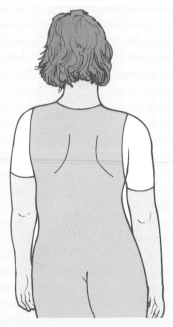

Scoliosis

Winged scapula

Characterised by the inferior angle and the vertebral border of the scapula protruding backwards away from the ribs. This is apparent when the client lifts their arm forwards to shoulder level. The client will tend to have difficulty punching the arm forward, lifting the arm above shoulder level or performing any forward pushing movements. The problem tends to be in the serratus anterior

Aim of these exercises is to strengthen the muscles that hold the scapula to the chest wall

- Stride standing, bending – punch a pillow/punch bag in a forward movement
- Stride standing, arms bent – lean on a wall and push away from it
- Prone lying – press up

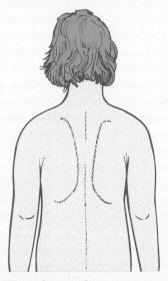

Winged scapula

Weak abdominal muscles (visceroptosis)

Abdominal and pelvic organs are displaced, usually downwards. It is usually caused by weak or overstretched abdominal muscles. Certain body types are prone to a weakness in the abdominal muscles, although certain factors such as pregnancy, operations, poor posture, lack of exercise, obesity and age can also cause weakened abdominal muscles

The therapist should be concerned with the strengthening of these muscles. However, finding out the cause of the weakness is of the utmost importance before commencing any form of treatment

Table 5.10 *(continued)*

Condition	Exercise	
Dowager's hump	Characterised by the head being tilted forward, this condition tends to affect females as they get older, although people can be born with the condition. If this is the case, the person is likely to be under medical supervision in which case you should not treat the client. If the condition has developed, it is probably as a result of fatty deposits accumulating at the back of the neck and over the spine, which then become difficult to correct	

Dowager's hump

Keeping records

Tip

Don't forget, if you keep records on clients you must observe the Data Protection Act 1988, explained in Chapter 1.

Once the consultation is complete, the therapist should ensure that all personal details and treatment recommendations are recorded and ask the client to sign the record card, once they have checked that all the details are correct.

Once a treatment has been carried out, you should record details of how the treatment went, contraindications, etc. Check that all media used are recorded on the form and make a note of any modifications that were needed during the massage. You should also record any points that come out of the evaluation of the treatment and any comments that clients make about the effects of the treatment on subsequent visits.

Evaluating the treatment

Evaluating a treatment is an important part of client consultation. It is important that you evaluate every treatment with feedback from clients wherever possible.

CLIENT FEEDBACK

Client name:

Date of treatment:

Therapist's name:

Date:

	Yes *Please comment*	*No* *Please comment*
Were you made to feel welcome?	_____	_____
Did you discuss your treatment requirements before treatment?	_____	_____
Did you feel comfortable?	_____	_____
Were you happy with the therapist?	_____	_____
Were your needs met?	_____	_____
Did you feel relaxed during the treatment?	_____	_____
Were you happy with the homecare advice?	_____	_____
Would you book another massage?	_____	_____

Thank you for your time. Have you got any further comments that you would like to make?

_____

_____

_____

_____

Client's signature:

Date:

Evaluation form

This can be either formal or informal but whichever method you choose, ensure that it is simple for the client and provides you with all the information you need. You should analyse the results and take appropriate action, and remember to maintain client confidentiality at all times:

- Oral questioning. This can be as simple as asking the client if they have enjoyed and were satisfied with the treatment received.
- Written feedback. This can be achieved by asking the client to fill in a client treatment evaluation. An example is given in this section.

Dealing with client dissatisfaction

Remember that not all client feedback will be positive. However, unless the treatment was a complete disaster or the client is completely unreasonable, giving the client the opportunity to highlight areas where the treatment could be improved not only allows you to improve your treatment, but in most cases will make the client more likely to return. If the client is dealt with in an appropriate manner, you should be able to resolve the problem and retain the client. The following steps should be taken:

- Take the client to a private area and listen to the complaint.
- Try to resolve it immediately.
- Record the complaint and action.
- Inform the insurers if necessary.

It is important to take client complaints seriously, as in some instances they may threaten legal action. Remember, never deal with any issues outside your responsibility.

Knowledge review

1 What is a contraindication?

2 State the details you would list on a client's record card before the following treatments are carried out:
   - aromatherapy massage
   - massage treatment.

3 When carrying out the client's consultation, you recognise treatment is contraindicated as the client has an infectious skin disorder. What action do you take?

4 List the details you would include on a client's record card and explain why they are important.

5 Name eight contraindications to a body massage.

6 Name four infectious skin disorders.

7 Name three non-infectious skin conditions.

8 Explain the condition of pityriasis simplex.

9 How would you recognise alopecia areata?

10 Describe the following conditions:
   - flat back
   - kyphosis
   - lordosis.

11 What are the advantages of good posture?

12 How would you carry out an assessment of your client's posture?

13 List the three body types.

Preparation for massage

6

Learning objectives

This chapter covers the following:

- **preparation of the therapist**
- **preparation of the treatment area**
- **equipment**
- **preparation of the client**

Preparation for treatment is an integral essential knowledge area in the following units:

- **BT17, Provide head and body massage treatments**
- **BT20, Provide Indian head massage treatment**
- **BT21, Provide massage using pre-blended aromatherapy oils**

This chapter covers the necessary preparation stages for massage of the therapist, the client and the treatment area. Before carrying out any massage treatment, it is important to prepare yourself, the treatment area and the client, implementing all hygiene practices.

Preparation of the therapist

Appearance

The appearance of both you and your work environment is a reflection of your professionalism. Remember, first impressions count and your clients will judge you on the basis of these things. Clients will have confidence in you if you always look clean, well groomed and smart.

Personal hygiene

As you are going to work in close proximity with your clients it is essential to clean yourself daily with bathing or showering. This will remove the sweat, dead cells and bacteria that cause body odour. An antiperspirant applied under the arms daily will help reduce perspiration, while a deodorant will mask the smell of sweat. Underwear should be clean and changed daily.

Oral hygiene

Teeth should be cleaned every morning and evening and also after every meal. Dental floss should also be used. Breath fresheners and mouthwashes may be required to freshen the breath. Remember to visit the dentist regularly to maintain healthy teeth.

Hands

It is essential that you wash your hands regularly, as they are covered in germs. Most of them are not harmful, but some can cause ill health and disease. It is essential to wash your hands after you have been to the toilet and before eating, as well as before and after treating each client and, if need be, during the treatment as well. This will minimise the risk of cross-infection and also convey an hygienic and professional image. When washing your hands, it is always more hygienic to use liquid soap (with a detergent containing chlorhexidine) from a sealed, disposable dispenser. Disposable paper towels or warm air dryers should be used to dry the hands.

If you have any cuts or abrasions on your hands, it is important you cover them with a clean dressing to prevent the risk of secondary infection. Nail polish should never be used when treating a client, as the client may be allergic. In addition, it hides any dirt that is present underneath the nails so it is better to present visibly clean, polish-free nails to inspire confidence.

Alexandra

The therapist in overalls

Tip

Every salon/clinic has its own rules on dress, jewellery, etc. to reflect its own professional image. Find out what the dress code is in your place of work and adhere to it.

Feet

To ensure fresh and healthy feet, wash them daily and ensure they are thoroughly dried. Make sure your shoes are comfortable, fit properly and have a low comfortable heel. It is important to remember that you are on your feet all day long. Foot sprays and medicated powders can be used to keep the feet dry and cool.

Hair

If hair is long, it should be tied back securely to ensure it does not fall forwards, either over your own face or the face of the client when working. Hair should always be clean as well as tidy.

Clothing

You must wear a clean and pressed protective overall each day. Fabrics used for overalls are normally lightweight and comfortable to work in. Cotton is ideal as air can circulate, allowing perspiration to evaporate and therefore discourage body odour. The overall should be fairly loosely fitted and not too short. Most overalls are white as this signifies a clean image to clients. An overall may consist of a dress or tunic top with matching trousers.

Overalls should be laundered regularly and a fresh, clean overall worn each day.

Jewellery

Jewellery must be kept to a minimum. A flat wedding ring is acceptable but you should avoid wearing watchstraps or bracelets, which may catch the client's skin during treatment.

Ethics

As a professional therapist, you must adhere to a code of ethical practice. Although this is not a legal requirement, the code may be used in criminal proceedings as evidence of improper practice.

Posture

Posture is the way you hold yourself when walking, sitting and standing. Correct posture will enable you to work for much longer periods without becoming tired and will also prevent stiff joints and muscle fatigue. It is important to stand with:

- the head up and balanced centrally
- shoulders relaxed but slightly back
- abdomen pulled in
- hips level
- bottom tucked in
- knees level
- weight evenly distributed and feet slightly apart.

Your posture should be relaxed, as the arms need to be free and the hands in control. You should not work or stand with a hollow or bent back, rather the body weight should be supported by both feet and be upright. The strain imposed by heavier movements will be less fatiguing if the load is evenly distributed. Use the body weight to relieve any strain in the upper spine and the shoulder area. Once the client is positioned on the couch in a comfortable position, it is important that you can stand near to them, as having to reach will result in a poor massage for the client and strain on your arms and back.

Stance

How you stand when performing the massage is of great importance. Two standing positions are commonly used. These are:

1 **Stride standing**. In this position, the feet are placed two foot lengths apart and the weight is distributed between them.
2 **Walk standing**. In this position, one foot is placed in front of the other, two lengths between the heels and weight is evenly distributed.

You can pivot freely from walk standing to stride standing and vice versa during the massage. When working longitudinally along the length of the muscle fibres, you stand in walk standing and when massaging transversely across the muscle fibres, you can swivel into stride standing.

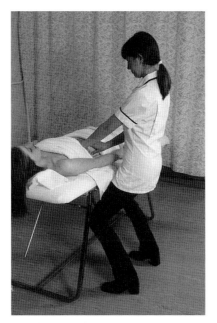

Stride standing

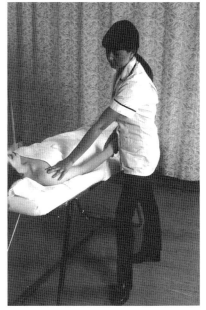

Walk standing

Poor technique results when the feet are in the wrong position because the body weight is thrown out of balance, which affects the rhythm, depth and smoothness. As well as resulting in a poor massage, this can also lead to a bad back. Although you will tend to sway slightly backwards and forwards when completing sweeping movements, to help body rhythm, unnecessary movements should be avoided as they are a waste of energy and can distract the client. Body weight can be used to regulate the pressure and massage movements as they are applied.

Hand exercises

Your hands should be soft and smooth, with both the hands and joints supple and relaxed. In order to achieve this suppleness, you will have to practise the following exercises, in order that both hands work equally well and your joints become mobile and flexible.

1   Make a tight fist, hold it for a few seconds and then quickly unclench, stretching out your fingers as far as possible.
2   Roll the wrists round and round going one way and then the other.
3   Rotate the hands from the wrist, first one way and then the other.
4   Place the index fingers and thumbs together and stretch them as far out as possible.

Tip

Remember, nails should always be well manicured with the nail plate short and unvarnished.

5   Place hands in a prayer position, keeping the fingers together, try and lift out the palms.

6   Still in the prayer position press the fingers against each other one by one, keeping the palms together.

7   Wave the wrist from side to side and then up and down.

8   Place alternate fingers down on hard surface as if playing a piano.

9   Rotate fists in a circular motion.

10 Knead a soft ball.

Hand exercises, step 2

Hand exercises, step 5

Hand exercises, step 6

Hand exercises, step 8

Hand exercises, step 9

Mental preparation

Before starting the massage, you must try and feel calm and relaxed, shut out anything that may distract you and focus only on the client. When dealing with several clients, you need to 'switch off' in between each one. If you can do this, you will not feel as tired at the end of the day.

It is important not to let the client drain you by not taking on board their problems, just listen and then forget once they leave. Otherwise, you will become too involved emotionally and this will leave you physically drained.

Preparation of the treatment area

Hygiene

Hygiene is very important as it prevents cross- and secondary infection. These occur through poor practice such as failing to recognise skin diseases or failing to carry out the correct hygiene procedures. **Cross-infection** occurs when contagious micro-organisms are transferred because sterilisation procedures are not being adhered to. **Secondary infections** can occur as a result of injury to the client during treatment or if the client already has an open wound and bacteria penetrate the skin and cause an infection.

General rules regarding hygiene

- Wherever possible, use disposable products.
- All work surfaces, including trolleys and massage beds, must be wiped with a chlorine preparation. Always follow the manufacturer's instructions. Trolleys and massage beds must be clean and covered with disposable paper tissue.
- Each client should have clean towels and gowns. All dirty laundry must be placed in a covered container.
- All waste must be placed in a suitable container lined with a disposable bag.

Sterilisation and sanitisation can minimise or destroy harmful micro-organisms that could cause an infection. Sterilisation is a complete destruction of all living organisms and sanitisation is the destruction of some but not all the micro-organisms. These techniques are practised in salons and clinics and involve the use of chemical agents – antiseptic, disinfectants, vapour fumigants and physical agents such as heat and radiation.

Radiation (sterilisation)

Ultraviolet (UV) light from a quartz mercury lamp can be used to destroy micro-organisms, although this has limited uses and cannot be totally effective.

The UV bulb is contained in a closed cabinet that can be used to store objects that have been sterilised.

Tip

Remember: never eat or drink in the treatment area.

Activity

Discuss the different ways infection can be transferred in a salon environment. How would you prevent each instance of cross-infection?

UV cabinet

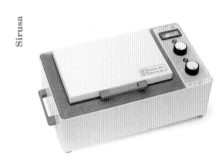

Sirusa

A dry-heat sterilising unit

Heat (sterilisation)

Dry and moist heat can be used to sterilise implements. The most effective method of heat sterilisation is the use of the **autoclave**, which is very similar to a pressure cooker. The temperature reaches 121–134°C when increased pressure is created.

Another method used is a dry hot-air oven. This is similar to a small oven and heats to 150–180°C, although it is seldom used in the workplace.

Yet another method is a **glass bead steriliser**. This is a small unit containing glass beads that are heated electrically. The glass beads transfer heat to the objects they come into contact with and sterilise them.

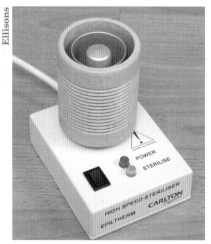

Ellisons

A glass bead steriliser

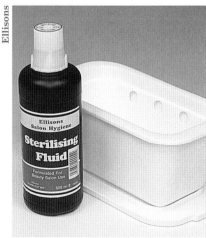

Ellisons

Sterilisation tray with liquid

Autoclave

Not all objects can withstand the heating process and therefore items need to be checked before using this method.

To avoid damaging the autoclave always used distilled deionised water.

Ensure that stainless steel objects are of a good quality before using this form of sterilisation to avoid them rusting.

Disinfectants and antiseptics (sanitisation)

If, for some reason, an object cannot be sterilised, it must be wiped with surgical spirit and placed in a chemical disinfectant solution such as glutaraldehyde or a quaternary ammonium compound. A disinfectant will not, however,

Disinfectant solutions should be changed as recommended by the manufacturers to ensure it is still effective and fit for purpose.

After removing objects from the disinfectant, always rinse with water to remove all traces of the solution to prevent an allergic reaction on the client's skin from occurring.

Checklist

General hygiene

- Always ensure personal hygiene is of the highest standard. Wash hands with a detergent containg chlorhexidine, which is used for skin cleansing
- Cover all cuts on your hands to avoid cross-infection from occurring and never treat a client who is contraindicated
- Use tools that have been sterilised correctly
- Use disposable products whenever possible
- Always ensure working surfaces – trolleys, couches etc. – are cleaned with a chlorine preparation, always following manufacturer's instructions
- Clean gowns and towels must be provided for each client
- All dirty laundry must be placed in a covered container
- All waste products must be disposed of correctly in a suitable container lined with a disposable waste bag
- Waste that is hazardous must be disposed of following COSHH procedures and training by the employer
- Never eat and drink in the treatment room, as it is not only unprofessional but may lead to ingestion of harmful chemicals
- Never smoke in the treatment area
- Never carry out any treatments in the workplace under the influence of alcohol or drugs, as this will put not only you and your clients but also your colleagues at risk

destroy all micro-organisms. After the implements are removed from the disinfectant, they must be rinsed in clean water to remove all traces of the solution and in order to prevent an allergic reaction on the client's skin.

An antiseptic is much milder than a disinfectant and can, therefore, be applied to the skin, but it does have limited effect. Like disinfectants, antiseptics will not kill all the micro-organisms.

Remember from the previous section that infectious diseases that are contagious contraindicate body treatments and, in some cases, clients with non-contagious skin disorders should not receive massage treatment as it could result in a secondary infection. When practising massage, strict hygiene is required in order to prevent the risk of exposure and cross-infection.

Equipment

Everything must be prepared before the client arrives for the massage treatment. You must make sure that you have everything to hand.

It is essential to ensure that you have everything that you might need, as it disrupts the treatment and gives a poor impression if you have to break away because you have forgotten something. It is also extremely important that the trolley is always within reach so that you can turn and reach anything on the trolley, leaving one hand in contact with the client.

Lubricants

Part of the preparation of a treatment room is preparing the massage medium. The choice of massage medium is very important, in order to provide an effective treatment. Sometimes the client may state which medium they prefer, but usually you choose it to complement the skin type. When clients do request a certain cream or oil, this may be because they believe in what the manufacturer claims their preparations can do and the client feels it will give added value to their treatment.

Remember, always apply the lubricant to your hands first, warm it in your palms and then apply it to the client. If, at the end of the massage, there is an excessive amount of lubricant left on the client, you can wipe it off with an eau de cologne or a warm damp towel, according to the client's preference.

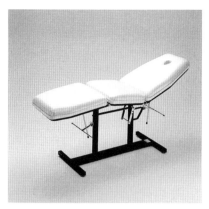

Massage couch

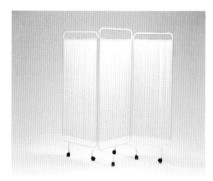

Screen

Stool

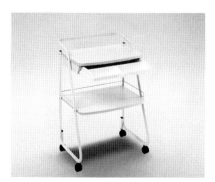

Equipment trolley

 Checklist

Treatment room checklist

✓ Client record card

✓ Massage couch prepared with clean linen and blankets

✓ Spare pillows and towels

✓ Clean gown for the client

✓ Screens to ensure privacy

✓ Comfortable room temperature

✓ Soft lighting

✓ Minimal noise level

✓ Trolley laid out with:

  ✓ massage media

  ✓ tissues

  ✓ bowls

  ✓ cotton wool

  ✓ antiseptic solution

  ✓ any other materials that may be used in the treatment

Health & safety

When using chemical agents always protect your hands with gloves before immersing them in the chemical cleaning agents to minimise the risk of an allergic reaction occurring.

Tip

Sometimes the client may be unclean, particularly their feet. Therefore, it may be appropriate to wash the client discreetly before massaging that area and incorporate this into the treatment, so the client is not offended.

Essential oils

All massage lubricants should be used sparingly and always applied on your hands first and never directly onto the client. There are different types of emollient to choose from.

Powder

Always keep the use of powder to a minimum. If an excessive amount is used, the pores will become clogged. You should always powder your hands rather than the client's body, as powder is of no benefit to the client. Its function is to provide slip for your hands if they are a little sticky. You should only ever use the finest of powders, unscented and unperfumed if possible, to avoid irritation of the skin. Powder is particularly good for oily skin. Remember, if the skin is dry, powder irritates the condition and can sometime make normal skin feel dry.

Oil

Oil is used in a massage to produce a much deeper effect than powder. It enables the therapist to stretch the tissues and increase the depth of the massage, as it enables the hands to glide easily without rubbing or tearing the skin. Oil tends to nourish and soften the skin and it is particularly good for dry skin conditions. If too much oil is used, the tissues will slide away from your hands, producing too much slip and a very superficial massage. The only disadvantage with oil is that it can leave the client with a greasy feeling after the treatment.

Cream

Creams are absorbed more readily into the skin and are excellent for use on very hairy areas. Clients will often choose a cream, as they feel they have a special quality that enhances and softens the skin. The disadvantage with using a cream is that the hands begin to drag and you will need to keep stopping to reapply it. It is particularly good for dry to normal skin type.

Massage emulsion

Massage emulsion is an oil- and water-based preparation. This medium is easily absorbed into the skin, therefore further applications may be necessary to avoid dragging the skin.

Essential oils

Essential oils can also be used as a massage medium. They should always be mixed with a carrier oil and **never** applied undiluted. Most essential oils have therapeutic and curative effects on the body's systems and blends can be made to the specific client's requirements. Essential oils must only be used by a qualified aromatherapist and some are contraindicated for certain conditions. *(See Chapter 11.)*

Preparation of the client

Always greet the client warmly and take them personally along to the treatment room. If it is the client's first treatment, it is essential they are put at ease. It is at this stage that you should carry out the consultation (covered in Chapter 5), making sure you obtain and record all the necessary information. It is important on the first visit to check that that they have no medical conditions that would contraindicate the treatment. In the consultation, you should explain the treatment to the client and make sure that they have an opportunity to ask any questions.

Once the client is ready, you should ask them to change into a gown and unless a preheat treatment is to be carried out first, assist them onto the massage couch. The client should always have use of a footstool in order to get up onto the massage couch. If you feel they need further assistance, it is important to support the client onto the couch.

The client should be settled comfortably and in a position where there will be a minimum amount of disturbance for the full treatment. The position will vary depending on whether the treatment is localised or a full body massage (see Chapter 8). The client must be supported throughout the treatment by pillows and it is important to ensure that only the areas being massaged are exposed. The rest of the body should be covered by clean blankets or towels to ensure warmth and modesty are preserved.

Knowledge review

1 State four basic requirements for maintaining personal hygiene.

2 Why is it important that you wash your hands before carrying out a massage treatment?

3 Define the terms:
   - sterilisation
   - cross-infection
   - secondary infection.

4 List the different types of sterilisation equipment.

5 Explain what is meant by sanitisation.

6 How should the treatment environment be prepared to ensure client comfort? Consider temperature, lighting and sound.

7 Why is it important to have all materials to hand during the treatment?

8 Name the different types of lubricant and state one disadvantage for each.

9 Describe the two different standing positions that should be adopted when massaging a client.

10 What is the purpose of carrying out hand exercises prior to carrying out a massage?

11 List the items that should be prepared before the client arrives for treatment.

12 State how you would prepare your client for the treatment.

Preheat treatments

7

Learning objectives

This chapter covers the following:

- **purpose of preheat treatments**
- **types of preheat treatment**

This chapter covers infrared treatments required in:

- **BT17, Provide head and body massage treatments**

This chapter covers the main types of heat treatment that can be applied to a client before their massage is given. The preheat treatments covered in this chapter are paraffin wax, infrared, steam, sauna, spa, foam and hydro.

Purpose of preheat treatments

Preheat treatments are often applied prior to massage in order to:

- relax the client and warm the body
- soothe any pain the client may suffer
- alleviate any tension.

Heat can be applied to the whole body or to isolated areas such as joints. You will have to ascertain during the consultation whether or not a preheat treatment would be useful/necessary. NB: Case study 2 in Chapter 12 describes a situation where preheat treatment was used.

There are a number of preheat methods and the main ones are examined in turn in the following sections.

Types of preheat treatment

Paraffin wax

Benefits

- Warms the muscles.
- Promotes relaxation.
- Softens the skin and aids desquamation, therefore improving the skin texture.
- Increases circulation.
- Improves conditions such as arthritic joints and any stiffness, helping to increase mobility.
- Relieves pain.

Contraindications

- Skin diseases and disorders.
- Undiagnosed lumps and bumps.
- Severe bruising or swellings.

Procedure

Paraffin wax is suitable as a preheat treatment for either part or all of the body. Once a consultation has taken place and you have ensured that there are no contraindications:

1   Apply a thin coat of nourishing cream to the area.

2   Heat the wax to approximately 37°C and transfer it to a bowl.

3   Test the temperature of the wax by applying a small amount to the back of your wrist.

4   Apply wax to the body with a brush. You should apply about five layers, allowing the previous layer to dry before applying the next.

5   Cover the waxed area with tinfoil and towels to retain the heat and leave to cool.

6   Once the wax has cooled, remove by peeling. The treated area will be warm, relaxed and ready for the massage.

Infrared treatment

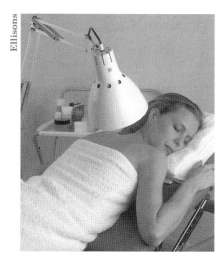

Infrared lamp

Infrared radiation has longer wavelengths than daylight or light from light bulbs, thus its red colour. It can be felt as warmth on the area of the body that is being treated.

The infrared rays penetrate into the epidermis, producing heat that warms and soothes the skin. It can:

- increase circulation
- increase lymphatic flow
- relax muscles in preparation for massage
- relieve muscular and joint pain.

Contraindications

- Skin disorders.
- Diabetes (because circulation is poor as is skin sensation).
- Loss of skin sensation.
- Sunburn.
- Metal plates or pins.
- Circulatory or heart problems.

Procedure

You should always follow the manufacturer's instructions and check for contraindications prior to treatment.

Health & safety

Incorrect infrared treatment can result in:
- headaches
- fainting and burns.

1   A skin test must be carried out prior to the treatment to test the client's sensitivity. Fill two testtubes – one with warm water and the other with cold. Ask the client to close their eyes and test the tubes on the areas that are to be exposed to the heat. If the client can distinguish

Technical tip

Distance and timing are based on the principles of the inverse square law. The inverse square law says that the closer the lamp is to the body, the higher the heat intensity will be and, conversely, the further away the lamp is placed, the less intense, as the rays spread over a much larger area.

between hot and cold, their sensitivity is normal and the treatment may continue. If they cannot tell the difference, you should not use preheat treatment.

2   Ensure that all grease is removed from the client's skin. You can either invite them to take a shower or wipe the skin with a tonic.

3   Position the client covering the areas you do not want to expose to the lamp. Do not forget to protect the client's eyes. The lamp should be warmed up prior to starting the treatment.

4   Position the lamp at the right angle to achieve maximum intensity. Never have the lamp directly over the client. Position the lamp at the correct distance from the client between 40 to 55cm depending on the generator output. If you increase the distance of the lamp from the client, the client will receive the same amount of radiation but it will be more gentle and slow. If the distance from the lamp to the client is doubled, the client will require four times the original amount of time to produce the same effect. If the distance is halved, the intensity becomes four times greater.

5   The infrared treatment can last from 10 to 20 minutes.

6   At the end of the treatment, position the lamp well away from the client for safety reasons.

Wet and dry heat treatments

Steam and sauna are the two main types of wet and dry heat treatment respectively. The following benefits and contraindications apply to both:

- Circulation increases.
- Lactic acid disperses from the muscles via increased circulation.
- Skin colour improves as an erythema is produced.
- Sweat glands are stimulated which helps to eliminate waste products.
- Heart beat quickens and body temperature rises.
- Muscles relax.

Contraindications

- Prescribed medication (obtain medical permission).
- Skin diseases.
- Epilepsy.
- Diabetes.

- High or low blood pressure.
- Thrombosis.
- Coronary thrombosis.
- Lung conditions, asthma, bronchitis, hay fever.
- Pregnancy (later stages).
- Heavy menstruation.
- Heavy meal or excess alcohol consumed just prior to treatment.

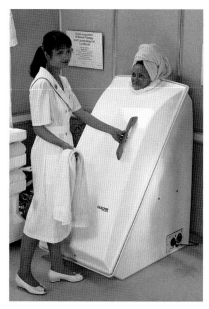

Steam bath

Types of heat therapy

Steam bath

Steam baths produce a moist heat as water is heated to produce the steam. The cabinet has a door and an opening at the top for the head. There is a seat with a tank underneath it, in which the water is heated. Steam baths can be made from metal or fibreglass. Metal steam baths have a tendency to get very hot and, to compensate for this, the client must be protected by towels. This is not necessary with fibreglass steam baths.

Procedure

The steam bath should be cleaned and you should check that there is enough water in the tank prior to the client arriving. You should prepare the seat with towels and switch the bath on approximately 15 minutes before the client arrives. The temperature needs to be between 50 and 55°C.

When the client arrives, you should carry out a consultation and, if everything is okay for the treatment to proceed, you should ask the client to have a shower. Once the bath has reached the correct temperature, you should help the client into the bath, tucking a towel firmly around

Tip

Before adding any spa treatments to the services you provide, think carefully about how worthwhile they will be in terms of usage and profitability. If you do not have facilities for showers, you will be limited in the range of services you can provide.

Tip

Steam alternatives
In a spa environment, clients are likely to use a steam room as an alternative to the cabinet. In a caldarium, the steam in the steam room is infused with natural herbal essences to increase the therapeutic effect, while a hammam is a communal steam bath with a dome-shaped central space and a number of rooms of varying temperature leading off it.

Sauna (traditional wood)

Tip

Alternating heat and cold treatments stimulate a sluggish circulation and improve non-medical fluid retention.

Tip

Sauna coals should be replaced every six months depending on use, as they lose their capacity to absorb and retain heat. Larger coals should be placed underneath smaller ones.

the neck to prevent steam from escaping. You should demonstrate how the client can leave the cabinet if they wish to do so before their treatment time has finished. (They may begin to feel claustrophobic.) Treatment time is between 10 and 20 minutes depending on the individual, but this maximum should never be exceeded. After the treatment has finished, the client should have a warm shower prior to their massage. The cabinet must be cleaned thoroughly with a disinfectant solution.

Sauna baths

The sauna is another form of heat treatment. It has similar effects to the steam bath but uses dry rather than moist heat. Saunas are usually made from panels of log with insulating material between them to prevent heat from escaping. The floor is also pine so it does not become too hot to stand on. Pine is ideal as it keeps dry and absorbs condensation, as well as absorbing the heat and radiating it back into the sauna.

Inside the sauna are resting benches, duckboards, a bucket and ladle, an electric stove and a rail for the stove. The heat is produced from the electric stove, which is controlled by a thermostat positioned as near to the ceiling as possible in order to give an accurate reading.

Benefits

These are largely the same as the steam baths, although there is more sweating. This evaporates quickly leaving the skin dry.

Procedure

The sauna must be switched on at least 30 minutes prior to treatment. The temperature is normally set at 70°C. Towels should be placed on the benches and the bucket filled with water.

Tip

Laconium sauna
An alternative to the traditional sauna is the Laconium sauna, which provides an evenly distributed dry heat at a milder temperature, around 55°C, and usually uses under-floor heating rather than coals on an electric stove. Some people may prefer this type of sauna because the heat is less intense.

Prior to treatment you should carry out a full consultation, during which you should explain the treatment fully to the client. It is beneficial to advise the client to start on a lower bench before moving up to a higher one where it is hotter. Treatment time is usually from 15 to 20 minutes and water should be poured onto the coals occasionally, as this will produce more heat. You should let the client know that they can take cool showers at intervals throughout the treatment.

The sauna should be cleaned on a regular basis with disinfectant and at the end of the day it is advisable to leave the sauna door open to eliminate any smells.

Other preheat treatments

Other preheat treatments include spa baths, foam baths and hydro-oxygen baths:

- **Spa baths** are large baths that can accommodate a number of people at the same time. A gentle overall massage is produced by bubbles that come through air channels underneath and from the sides of the bath.
- **Foam baths** are more frequently found on health farms. They are similar to ordinary baths but produce foam heated to about 40°C. The client semi-reclines in the bath, with only the head visible. This treatment relaxes the muscles and induces perspiring.
- **Hydro-oxygen baths** are cabinets in which the client reclines while hot water jets squirt the body. It is important to check the client for contraindications prior to the treatment and never to leave them unsupervised.

Spa bath

Knowledge review

1 Explain the benefits of preheating treatments before a body massage treatment is performed.

2 Describe the different preheat treatments available to a client.

3 What are the benefits of each treatment?

4 Give the main contraindications for:
   ● paraffin wax
   ● infrared
   ● wet and dry heat treatments.

5 What skin tests should be carried out prior to an infrared treatment?

6 State two effects of an incorrect infrared treatment.

Massage techniques and procedures

Learning objectives

This chapter covers the following:

- **massage movements**
- **massage routines and duration**
- **aftercare**

The massage techniques and procedures covered in this chapter are integral essential knowledge areas in the following units:

- **BT17, Provide head and body massage treatments**
- **BT20, Provide Indian head massage treatment**
- **BT21, Provide massage using pre-blended aromatherapy oils**

This chapter describes basic massage techniques and procedures, including the commercially accepted timings for treatments.

Massage movements

There are five classifications of massage movement. These are:

1 effleurage (including stroking movements)
2 petrissage (or compressions)
3 tapotement (or percussions)
4 frictions
5 vibrations.

Effleurage (stroking)

Effleurage is a sweeping, stroking movement. Its main uses are at the beginning and the end of the massage sequence and as a connecting or link movement that can be used at any point during the massage procedure. Effleurage introduces the client to massage. It allows them to get used to the therapist's touch, to become sensitised to the underlying muscles and tissues while at the same time enabling a massage medium to be applied to the area. This movement has a soothing and relaxing effect.

Effleurage is performed with the palm of the hand or pads of the fingers, depending on the size of the area to be massaged and the amount of pressure to be applied. Effleurage movements can be either superficial or deep. Effleurage should be performed with relaxed hands moulding to the body's contours. The fingers should be relaxed and held closely together and the thumbs should also be relaxed and abducted. Effleurage movements follow the direction of the venous blood return to the heart, applying more pressure on the upward movement than on the return.

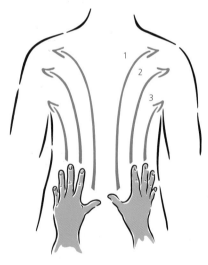

Effleurage

Benefits

The benefits of the effleurage movement are:

- soothing effect on the nerves, inducing relaxation
- increasing both blood and lymphatic circulation
- aiding tension relief, by relaxing contracted, tense muscles
- aiding desquamation, the removal of dead cells

When carrying out any massage treatment, remember to maintain the correct posture yourself. Details of this are covered in Chapter 6. It is important to stand with:

- the head up and balanced centrally
- shoulders relaxed but slightly back
- abdomen pulled in
- hips level
- bottom tucked in
- knees level
- weight evenly distributed and feet slightly apart.

Technical tip

Reinforced movements
Any technique where one hand [ironing] or the fingers are placed over the corresponding hand or fingers will give a deeper pressure. This is known as a reinforced movement.

- helping to reduce non-medical oedema, which is a result of poor circulation and tiredness.

Petrissage

These strokes are deeper than those of effleurage and usually applied with the thumbs, fingers or heels of hands. These movements are characterised by firmly picking up and lifting the tissues from the underlying structures and then releasing, resulting in an intermittent pressure. All these movements relieve muscular tension, fatigue and stiffness. Petrissage manipulations include kneading, picking up, wringing and rolling.

Kneading

Kneading movements may be performed in several ways. The technique can be achieved using both hands, one hand or just part of the hand – palmar, double-handed or single-handed kneading. Pressure is applied firmly then released. The movement is then repeated in an adjacent area. The pressure must always be applied towards the heart. Care must be taken to avoid pinching the skin at the end of the strokes.

Picking up

This movement can be performed with one or both hands, depending on the area to be massaged. For example, if movement is to be carried out on the deltoid muscle, then one hand is used and the muscle can be massaged either side. The technique is to grasp the muscle with the whole hand with the thumb abducted. The muscle is lifted away from the underlying structure, squeezed and then released

Palmar kneading

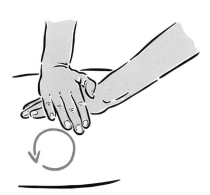

Double-handed kneading

Single-handed kneading

again. On relaxation the other hand picks up a different part and the movement is repeated along the length of the muscle. It is important to ensure that contact is not broken between movements.

Wringing

The muscle is lifted from the underlying structures and then moved from side to side across the muscle length with the fingers of one hand working with the thumb of the opposite hand. The tissue is grasped and stretched.

Rolling

Hands are placed firmly on the area. The superficial tissues are grasped between the fingers and thumbs and gently rolled backwards and forwards against the thumbs and fingers.

Benefits

- Increases blood and lymph circulation bringing fresh nutrients to the organs and speeding up the removal of waste products.
- Increases venous return.
- Breaks down tension nodules in the muscles and therefore helps to prevent the formation of fibrosis in the muscle. This is especially the case for the trapezius muscle of the upper back.
- Speeds up the removal of waste products built up in the tissues aiding the absorption of fluid, particularly around the joints.
- Aids relaxation.

Picking up

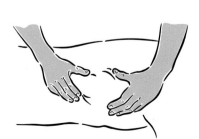

Wringing

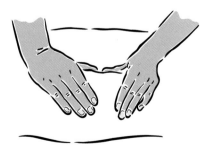

Rolling

Tapotement (percussion)

These movements are used for stimulating and toning the area where they are used. Tapotement movements include cupping (clapping), hacking, beating and pounding. The client must have sufficient muscle bulk or mass to perform this movement, otherwise it could be very painful and lead to bruising. Consequently, these movements should not be used on the thin or elderly. These types of movement should be light and springy and should not cause any discomfort to the client. Wrists need to be loose and flexible. Tapotement movements increase the circulation, which can create a healthy glow, thereby improving appearance.

Cupping

Cupping

Cupping is performed with the hands forming loose cups, which then strike the area being massaged making a very distinctive clapping sound. An **erythema** (reddening) is produced quickly due to the vacuum that is formed in the **palmar** surfaces as they contact the tissues.

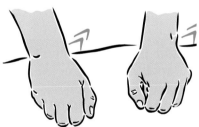

Hacking

Hacking

Hacking is a very fast and light movement. The hands face each other but do not touch and the hands tend to be at right angles to the wrists. The fingers flick against the skin very quickly in rapid succession. The outer three fingers tend to do all the striking. Hacking is a very stimulating movement, stimulating both the circulation and the sensory nerve endings.

Beating

Beating

Beating can be performed slowly or quickly, depending on the type of effect you want to achieve. The hands form a loose fist with the arms relaxed and from shoulder level they strike the client's body. The colour of the skin changes, producing an erythema as the temperature of the skin rises.

Pounding

Pounding

Pounding is performed with the outer borders of the hands, with the hands held loosely but closed. The movement comes from the therapist's elbows and forearms. This movement is very rapid and is as stimulating as the beating movements.

The tapotement movements increase the circulation, improve muscle tone and stimulate sensory nerve endings.

Benefits

- Aids sluggish circulation.
- Helps loosen mucus in chest conditions, when performed over the thoracic region.
- Tones and strengthens muscles.
- Produces local erythema due to a localised rise in skin temperature.
- Stimulates sensory nerve endings, therefore bringing about vasodilation of blood vessels.

Thumb and finger frictions

Tapotement movements are particularly good for cellulite conditions, as they stimulate the skin's surface and the underlying tissues, which then improves their appearance, often likened to orange peel. Cellulite conditions can affect any type of client regardless of their age, body shape or weight. Cellulite usually occurs around the tensor fascia latea muscle (lateral aspect of the thigh), the rectus abdominus muscle (abdomen), the gluteals (buttocks) and the tricep muscles (back of the arm).

Frictions

Frictions are usually applied in small areas of the surface tissue. They are rubbing movements where the skin is rubbed against deeper underlying structures. The movements are applied with a circular technique using the tips of the thumbs and fingers and applying a degree of stretch to the underlying structures. These types of movement help to break down fibrous thickenings, fatty deposits and aid the removal of any non-medical oedema.

Benefits

- Help to break down tight nodules.
- Aid in relaxation.
- Increase lymph and blood circulation.

Vibrations

These movements are used to relieve fatigue. They also relieve pain by stimulating the nerves, which produces a sedative effect on the area. Vibrations are fine trembling

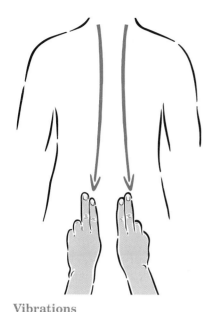

Vibrations

movements that can be performed with either one or both hands. Vibration movements can be **static**, that is, performed in one place, or **running**, that is, moving up or down. Using the palmar surface of the hand, the pads of the fingers or the distal phalanx of the thumbs (this is the smallest bone in the thumb and forms the tip of the thumb), the muscles of the forearm are contracted continually and then relaxed to produce the vibration movements.

Benefits

- Clear and stimulate the nerve pathways.
- Relieve tension in the neck and back, inducing relaxation.
- Can help increase the action of the lungs.
- Helps to increase peristalsis in the colon.

Massage routines and duration

Tip

A massage treatment should include a full range of movements, chosen to suit the client. If the client is especially tense in the upper neck and shoulder region, the therapist should adapt the manipulations and spend more time concentrating on this area and less time on other areas of the body.

The commercially acceptable timing for a full Swedish body massage is approximately 60 minutes. The only areas that are not usually massaged are the face and scalp. The time spent on individual body parts, unless it is decided otherwise during the consultation, is as follows:

- neck and chest – 5 minutes
- arms – 5 minutes each
- abdomen – 5 minutes
- legs – 10 minutes each
- buttocks – 5 minutes (optional)
- back – 15 minutes.

Often a client will book for just a partial massage, so you can use these timings as a guide.

Once the technique has been grasped, the basic procedures outlined in the following can be adapted to suit anyone's needs. You should have established your client's requirements in the consultation and adapted the massage appropriately. The massage technique should always be performed throughout by moulding your hands to the contours of the client's body, smoothly and rhythmically. No break in the continuity should ever occur; contact with the client must be maintained *at all times*.

The massage technique should generally be deep (unless there is any reason why this is contraindicated); using your

body weight in the movements on the back and lower limbs is essential. The rate of the massage should be moderate, unless the client requests it to be slower or faster.

For a full body massage, the client will usually lie in the supine (face upwards) position at the start of the massage to have the front of their body massaged first, turning over to the prone position later, so the massage concludes with their back. The client should be in a position that requires minimal movement throughout the treatment, but when the client needs to move or turn over, you must support the client's body to help them. The reason for working in this order is that, in most cases, massaging the back will be the most relaxing. Finishing on this area maximises the effect of the massage, as the client should become progressively more relaxed. In addition, if clients want to talk to you, they will usually do this at the beginning of the massage, and this is easier if they are supine.

Procedure

- Assist the client to lie on the couch in a supine position, using pillows to support the head, back of neck and under the knee. Massage the body parts in the following order:

  1 right arm

  2 left arm

  3 neck and chest

  4 abdomen

  5 right leg

  6 left leg.

- Turn the client over into the prone position (face down), again using pillows to support the face, neck and shoulders, under the front of the abdomen and hips, and under the front of the ankles. Massage the body parts in the following order:

  7 gluteals and buttocks

  8 back.

The massage technique is always adapted to suit the client's needs. For example, if the client does not wish their gluteals to be included in the massage and complains of tension in the upper shoulders, more time could be spent on that area. You will have found this out during your pre-treatment consultation.

If the client is male, the massage is usually performed with greater depth using all your body weight. (See Chapter 9 for the adaptations you might need.)

Tip

When only one hand is massaging, the other should be supporting the limb that is being worked on.

Arm massage

The client can either be lying on their back or with their head and back supported with pillows. The client's arm should be supported by a pillow. You should be in the walk standing position outlined on page 168.

1   Effleurage to cover the whole arm from finger tips up towards the axilla glands. Supporting the client's arm, your left hand works on the back of the arm and the right hand on the front of the arm. Each hand works alternately until the client is relaxed. (9 times)

2   Continue to support the client's arm and apply deep effleurage to the deltoid muscle, contouring the hand around the muscle. Rotate the movement clockwise and repeat anticlockwise. (3 times)

3   Perform single-handed kneading, alternating, to the bicep and tricep muscles, working upwards with the movement and then sliding back down to the elbow. (3 times)

4   Stand in the stride position and perform picking up to the deltoid muscle. (3 times)

5   Apply picking up to the tricep and bicep muscles. (3 times)

6   Apply wringing to deltoid, tricep and bicep muscles. (3 times)

7   Apply finger kneading to the elbow. Back to walk standing. (3 times)

8   Kneading to forearm and hand. (3 times)

9   Picking up to forearm. Pick up the extensors and flexors working from the elbow to the wrist and slide back up to the elbow. In stride standing. (3 times)

10   Thumb kneading to interosseous membrane (the gap between the radius and ulna bones), working up to the elbow with small controlled movements and then sliding back down to the wrist. In walk standing. (3 times)

11   Thumb kneading to the wrist and tendons of the hand joint, fingers and palm of hand, adapting the pressure so as not to cause discomfort. (3 times)

12   If the client has sufficient tissue present, perform hacking to the whole arm in the stride standing position. Support the client's arm placing the hand of the opposite shoulder on the lateral aspect of the upper arm and perform hacking up and down the arm from the shoulder to elbow. (3 times)

13   Change to walk standing position and complete work on this area by performing effleurage as before. (9 times)

14   Place the client's arm back on the couch and cover with the blanket before repeating the procedure with the other arm.

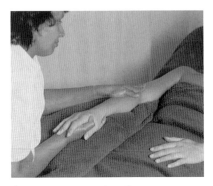

Arm massage, step 1

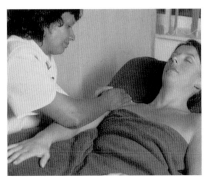

Arm massage, step 2

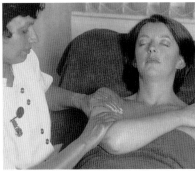

Arm massage, step 4

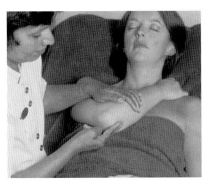

Arm massage, step 7

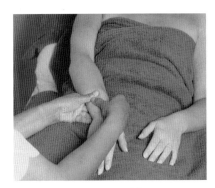

Arm massage, step 10

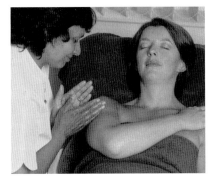

Arm massage, step 12

Tip

Remember not to touch the breast tissue when massaging this area.

Neck and chest massage

The client can be either lying on their back or sitting, with pillows placed behind the head to ensure the neck and chest muscles are relaxed. Start the routine in walk standing position:

1 Facing the client, effleurage across the clavicle, around the shoulders and up behind the neck, adapting the pressure to suit the client. Your hands should keep in contact with the client. As your hands slide back to the sternum, cross them over and effleurage to the deltoids. Keeping the hands on the deltoid, hold for a few seconds, and apply a slight stretch to the area. (6 times)

2 In the stride standing position, apply alternate stroking to the chest from axilla to axilla, ensuring one hand starts as the other is leaving the body. (6 times)

3 Perform double handed kneading over the chest, adapting the pressure to suit the client. (3 times)

4 Keeping the hands in contact with the client, walk round to the top of the couch and thumb knead the trapezius muscle working inwards from the shoulders up the occiput and sliding back round. (6 times)

5 Go back to walk standing and, facing the client, finger knead the clavicle using the index and middle finger. (3 times)

6 In the stride standing position, apply light hacking over the pectoral muscles, if appropriate.

7 In the walk standing position, conclude the neck and chest massage with effleurage. (6 times)

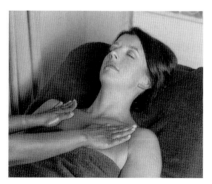

Neck and chest, step 1

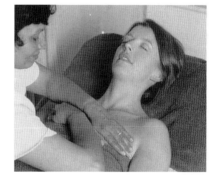

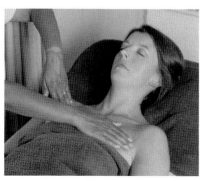

Neck and chest, step 2

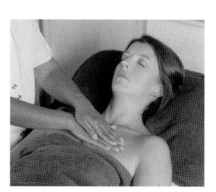

Neck and chest, step 3

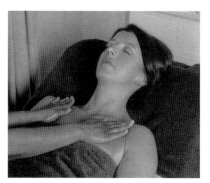

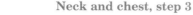

Tip

It is more comfortable for the client if the bladder is empty.

Tip

Never massage on a full stomach.

Tip

Maintain the client's modesty by placing a towel over the chest area and pulling it down to the hips.

Abdominal massage

The client should be lying on their back, with their knees flexed and well supported.

1 In the walk standing position, carry out diamond effleurage by placing the hands on the waist. Effleurage up to the sternum, back to the waist and then down to the pubic symphysis. (3 times)

2 Apply alternate kneading to the lateral walls of the abdomen. (3 times)

3 In the stride standing position, apply wringing to the lateral walls if the client has sufficient subcutaneous tissue. If there is insufficient tissue, wringing will be uncomfortable for the client. (3 times)

4 Apply skin rolling to the lateral walls. Place the palms of the hands underneath the posterior aspect of the abdomen and the thumbs on the anterior aspect. Roll the thumbs down towards the palms of the hands with visible skin underneath the thumbs.

5 In the walk standing position, apply finger kneading to the colon starting from the right-hand side of the client's pelvis. Work up over the ascending colon to waist level. Swing into the stride standing position and continue to knead across the transverse colon. At the left side, swing back into walk standing position and continue to knead down over the descending colon, towards the left groin. This to stimulate peristalsis and aids constipation.

   If the client prefers, this movement can be carried out with a stroking movement with one hand starting as the other one is leaving the body.

6 In the walk standing position, conclude the abdominal massage with effleurage.

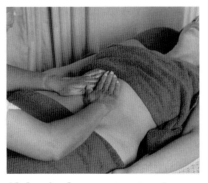

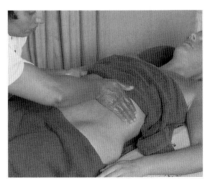

Abdominal massage, step 1   Abdominal massage, step 2

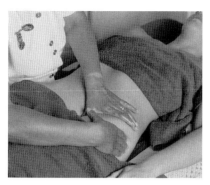

Abdominal massage, step 3

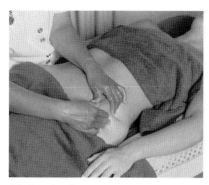

Abdominal massage, step 4

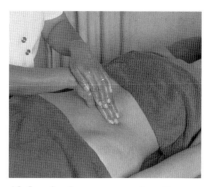

Abdominal massage, step 5

Leg massage

The client is massaged either in a lying position or in the 'long' sitting position. The leg being treated should rest on a pillow in a relaxed outward rotation, knee and hip flexed slightly and the ankle and foot free. Ensure the client's modesty is maintained by placing a towel in the middle of the legs and only having uncovered the leg that is to be worked on. Full support is required for the heavy lower limbs, which means frequent changing of pillow positions. This should on no account affect the rhythm and continuity of the massage procedure:

1 Standing in the walk standing position at the client's ankle, effleurage the whole leg from the toes up to the femoral triangle, covering the anterior, medial and lateral walls. Apply pressure upwards, and ease pressure when returning to the tarsals. (3 times)

2 Starting at the lateral aspect of the thigh, with one hand apply hand kneading from the hip to the patella. Place the other hand on the medial aspect of the thigh below the femoral triangle and when both hands are parallel, knead together down to the patella. This movement can be repeated using alternate kneading movements. (3 times)

3 Slide the palms around the anterior and posterior aspect of the legs so they are placed on the hamstrings and quadriceps and alternately knead the muscles. If the client is large, placing a bolster underneath the patella will make this movement easier. (3 times)

4 In the stride standing position, carry out hacking and clapping movements from the patella to the groin area and back down. This is particularly good to stimulate circulation and therefore aids conditions such as cellulite and poor circulation.

5   In the walk standing position, perform effleurage to the upper thigh. (3 times)

6   Perform finger kneading around the patella in slow rhythmical movements. (3 times)

7   In the walk standing position, flex and support the client's knee with one hand and with the other knead up and down the gastrocnemus and the lateral side of the lower leg. (3 times)

8   Stand at the bottom of the couch in the walk standing position and working upwards, thumb knead the tibialis anterior on the outer shin. (3 times)

9   Working on the feet, place hands on either side of the toes and press gently together. Rotate all the toes clockwise and anticlockwise. (3 times)

10   Effleurage the foot. (3 times)

11   In the walk standing position at the client's ankle, conclude the leg massage by applying effleurage to the whole leg. (3 times)

Leg massage, step 1

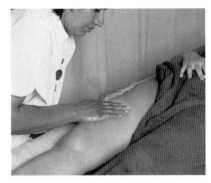
Leg massage, step 2

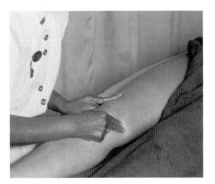
Leg massage, step 6

Leg massage, step 7

Gluteals and buttocks massage

The gluteals are worked on one side at a time, keeping a towel over the area not being massaged to avoid over-exposure of the area. Stand on the opposite side to the gluteal being massaged as this enables you to work inwards with the massage movements:

1   In the walk standing position, support the nearside gluteal with one hand and apply effleurage to the farside gluteal with the other hand. Work inwards to cover the area. (3 times)

2   Knead the gluteals using deep movements. (3 times)

3   Move to the stride standing position and perform double-handed kneading. (3 times)

4   With hands placed at right angles to the wrist and palms both facing each other, apply hacking to the area with fast, light finger movements that flick the skin.

5   Apply beating to the gluteals, clenching the hands into tight fists and hitting the area rhythmically. This can be performed slowly or quickly depending on the response required. Move the hands from shoulder height and place them alternately on the gluteal and back at the starting position. The area is usually covered with a towel to take some of the blows.

6   Pound the gluteals, with the hands held loosely closed, each hand strikes the area alternately in rapid succession. This is a very stimulating movement usually used over adipose tissue.

7   Apply clapping to the gluteals. Form cup shapes with the hands and strike the area rhythmically causing a hollow sound. Again, this movement is used over adipose tissue.

8   To complete the massage of the buttocks and gluteals, perform effleurage over the area.

9   Move to the other side of the client and repeat the routine on that side.

Tip

In some cases the massage may be performed on top of fabric. For example, tapotement manipulations may be performed on the buttock region, with briefs still on, for modesty reasons, if the client is embarrassed. Or a towel can be placed there to receive some of the pressure if the client is not too well built but wants the movements to be carried out.

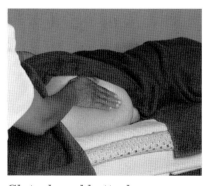

Gluteals and buttocks massage, step 1

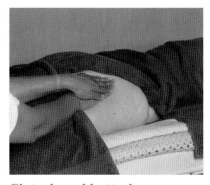

Gluteals and buttocks massage, step 2

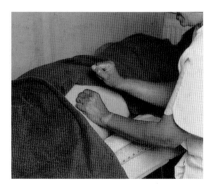

Gluteals and buttocks massage, step 5

Back massage

The client should be lying in the prone position with pillows under the abdomen and the front of the ankles. The client can either rest their forehead on a rolled-up towel or turn their head sideways, with their arms tucked down by their sides:

1   In the walk standing position, effleurage up the back from the sacrum, splitting the hands at the scapula and massaging as far as the deltoid muscles. Slide your hands back down the same route to the starting position. Repeat the effleurage movement covering the trapezius muscle, with the movement ending firmly in the supra-clavicular glands. Slide hands back down the same route. Commence the final movements from the sacrum on the medial borders massaging into the axilla glands before returning. This movement should cover the whole of the back region. (6 times)

2   Working from the scapula to the sacrum in three channels on either side of the spine, perform alternate kneading. (3 times)

3   Again working in three channels down either side of the spine, this time perform reinforced kneading (ironing). (3 times)

4   Place the thumbs in the posterior aspect of the shoulders and thumb knead along the trapezius muscle to the base of the neck. (6 times)

5   Finger knead down both sides of the spine. (3 times)

6   Perform thumb frictions down either side of the spine and then around the scapula. (3 times)

7   In the stride standing position, perform wringing to lateral walls around the back. (3 times)

8   Carry out picking up to the lateral walls around the back. (3 times)

9   Apply skin rolling to the lateral walls around the back. (3 times)

10 In the walk standing position, perform hacking to the back. Always ensure that there is sufficient tissue for this manipulation and take care to avoid the spine and any other bony areas. (3 times)

11 Perform cupping/clapping. (3 times)

12 Complete the massage with effleurage.

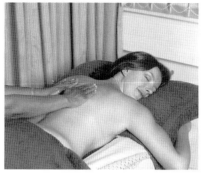

Back massage, step 1

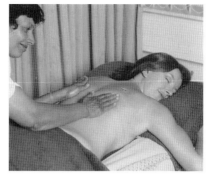

Back massage, step 2

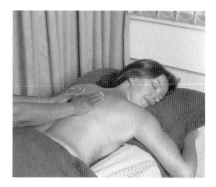

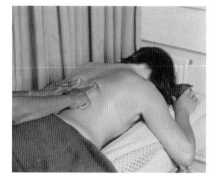

Back massage, step 5

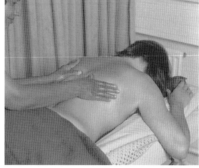

Back massage, step 6

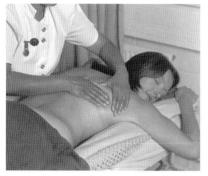

Back massage, step 7

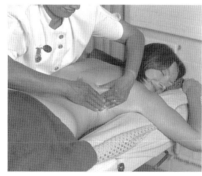

Back massage, step 8

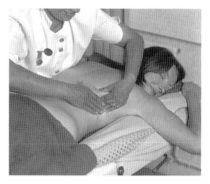

Back massage, step 9

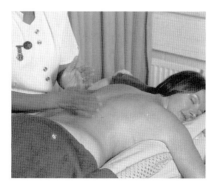

Back massage, step 10

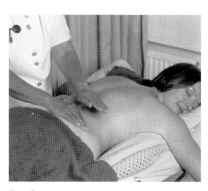

Back massage, step 11

Head massage

A scalp massage may follow the body massage treatment; allow approximately 10 minutes to carry out the head massage. Treatment oil may be applied to the hair and scalp, which will nourish the hair and skin. Always discuss with the client during consultation whether they would like oil to be applied to the scalp area, in order not to disturb the client with questions during the treatment.

1   Effleurage the scalp – place both hands on the hairline above the forehead and start to firmly effleurage over the scalp, moving out a little further out each time to ensure the entire scalp is covered.

2   Finger kneading the scalp – starting at the temple, use the finger tips to slowly but firmly knead the scalp all over. This movement is similar to that made when shampooing the hair but is carried out very slowly.

3   Place the thumbs on the scalp at the hairline and gently apply pressure point techniques. This movement stimulates the nerve pathways, and helps to balance the body by freeing the blockages on the meridian lines of the body.

4   Place one thumb above the other. Each thumb applies alternative pressure in a 'C' shape moving from the hairline to the crown area.

5   Place the knuckles of each hand against the scalp and gently apply pressure, rotating the knuckles of each finger to cover the scalp.

6   Place both thumbs at the crown area; rotate both thumbs simultaneously in a clockwise direction, slightly increasing the pressure with each rotation.

7   Alternate the fingers of each hand and use the fingers to slowly comb through the hair from the scalp, covering all the scalp area.

8   Repeat massage movement as in 1.

9   To finish off the massage, apply gentle pressure to the temples.

Very quietly inform the client that the treatment has now ended, advise them to rest and then in their own time get up slowly to avoid feeling dizzy.

Tip

After a head massage, it is recommended that the client leaves the treatment oil on the hair for the remainder of the day for its conditioning effect to continue.

Aftercare

Once you have completed the body massage, you should take care to ensure that any remaining massage medium is removed with a clean towel or soft tissues before the client gets off the massage couch. You should pay particular attention to the feet, because if there is any excess oil remaining, the client could slip.

You should cover the client with a towel and allow them to rest for a few minutes to allow the circulation to return to normal. This should prevent the client from feeling faint or light headed. Either while they are resting or once they have rested, you should discuss any aftercare that will complement the massage. This can include healthy eating and exercise tips, in particular any exercise that could help to improve any postural problems the client may have.

It is important to advise the client to rest for a few hours once they get home. They should be advised not to eat a large or heavy meal but to drink plenty of fluids. The reason for this is that, as their circulation continues to return to normal, the blood vessels will constrict resulting in the need to pass water more frequently. An increase in fluid intake is important to avoid dehydration.

Tip

Treatment can be recommended as follows:

body massage – 1–2 times/week

mechanical massage – 2–3 times/week

audio sonic – 1–2 times/week

These treatments will vary according to individual treatment plans and the aims of the massage.

Contra-actions

The contra-actions that a client may experience are:

- sickness, sometimes due to the increased circulation of the waste products transported by the lymphatic system
- fainting, due to the blood pressure altering caused by the blood capillaries dilating
- skin reactions due to an allergic reaction to the massage medium
- in some cases, the client may bruise due to excessive pressure applied when tapotement movements are applied.

If the client does suffer from any of these contra-actions you must ensure the room is well ventilated:

Offer the client a glass of water.

Apply a cold compress if a skin reaction occurs.

If symptoms persist, advise the client to seek medical advice.

It is important to note any reactions on the client's record card so that any adverse reactions are noted for future treatments and that continuation of the treatment can be tracked.

Knowledge review

1 How would you prevent cross-infection when carrying out a body massage treatment?

2 Why is it important to maintain posture when carrying out a body massage treatment?

3 Explain the contra-actions that may occur during a body massage treatment.

4 Why is it important to discuss contra-actions with the client at consultation?

5 How should the following be prepared to ensure that the client experiences maximum comfort and benefit from the body massage treatment:
- lighting
- sound
- temperature?

6 Which massage media would be most suitable to the following skin types/conditions:
- dry
- aged
- oily
- sensitive?

7 Why is it important to refer a client to their GP if you identify a contraindication?

8 What do you understand by the term erythema?

9 How would you recognise an allergic reaction to a massage medium?

10 In what direction should the body massage application be sustained?

11 Why is it important to gain feedback from the client after treatment?

12 Give two contra-actions that may occur during or following massage.

13 What aftercare products may be recommended to your client?

14 How often would you recommend a client receive a body massage treatment?

15 What recommendations to the client's lifestyle would you advise for the benefit of treatment to continue for:
- sense of well-being
- relaxation?

Modifications to massage treatments

9

Learning objectives

This chapter covers the following:

- **reasons for adapting massage treatments**
- **mechanical treatments**

Adapting the treatment to meet individual client needs is an integral area of knowledge and understanding in the following units:

- **BT17, Provide head and body massage treatments**
- **BT20, Provide Indian head massage treatment**
- **BT21, Provide massage using pre-blended aromatherapy oils**

This chapter details various ways in which massage techniques can be adapted in response to client requirements and limitations. There are many reasons why you may wish to adapt your massage and these will usually become evident during the course of the pre-treatment consultation. This chapter also introduces basic sports massage and mechanical treatments.

Reasons for adapting massage treatments

Throughout this book it has been stressed that massage should be adapted according to the client's needs and requirements. You should try to gain as much information as possible during the pre-treatment consultation, but you should also continue to solicit feedback throughout the massage in terms of depth of massage and so on. Massage should be adapted because of the physical characteristics or abilities of the client or because of the purpose of the massage.

Adapting massage to various clients

Certain groups of clients will present different problems that will cause you to adapt the usual massage routine.

Physical ability

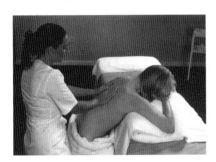

Adapting back massage for a client who can't lie down

The client usually lies on a couch when being massaged, but in some instances this may not be possible. This does not mean that massage cannot be performed but rather the massage procedure would need to be adapted to suit the client's ability.

If a client cannot manage to get onto the massage couch or has problems lying down, for example due to infirmity, it is possible to perform massage on most areas with the client in a chair supported by pillows. From a sitting position, the client's hands and arms, neck, shoulders and chest area, and feet and legs can be massaged easily. The feet and legs can additionally be supported by a stool and pillows.

Clients who are wheelchair bound may be able to be transferred onto a hydraulically controlled couch. If this is not possible, they can be still treated in their wheelchair as just described.

Tip

Watch your posture! If the client is significantly lower than your hip level, try to sit whenever possible.

Many heavily pregnant women do not feel secure being massaged on a couch. If she sits in a low-backed chair or stool, her hands and arms, feet and legs and neck, shoulders and chest can all be massaged from the sitting position. A full back massage can also be carried out if she remains sitting in the chair but leans in over a couch onto pillows for support.

If a pregnant woman has a massage on the couch, but is too heavily pregnant to lie in the prone position, a back massage can be carried out either as just described, or she can lie on her side on the couch, with her top leg bent at a right angle and with her top arm, elbow bent, palm down, placed near the cheek area. She should be supported by pillows so she will not feel she could roll off.

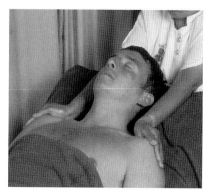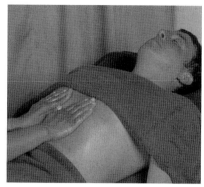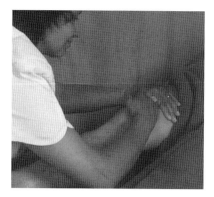

Massage for men

Massage for male clients

If the client is male, massage is usually performed with greater depth, using all of your body weight. This is because male skin tends to be thicker and tougher, the subcutaneous layers contain little fat, the tissues tend to be firmer and the muscles are often resilient and toned. It is also advisable to avoid massaging the lower stomach and the upper inner thigh area (femoral triangle).

Usually an oil lubricant is needed to massage male clients, because they tend to be hairier. This ensures that your hands glide over the body without causing any pain. If the client is very hairy, it may be better to use talc.

Obese clients

When carried out on an obese client, massage movements should be heavy, deep and quite vigorous and applied in a brisk fashion. The main manipulations applied are deep kneading, wringing, picking up, hacking, clapping and, where there is plenty adipose tissue, pounding and beating. This helps to mobilise the fat deposits. However, you should be careful because it is more difficult to assess the muscle tone and sensitivity in obese clients and excessively heavy movements can cause pain in fatty areas.

Purposes of massage

To relieve gravitational oedema

It is extremely important to ensure that any oedema is non-medical before carrying out a massage treatment. A good way to test this is to press the swollen area. If the oedema is non-medical, the indentation from the pressure will slowly fill with fluid again, leaving the skin cool and pale. If the oedema is medical, do not give a massage and advise the client to seek medical advice. If you are unsure of the cause of the oedema, ask the client to seek medical advice.

Clients susceptible to this condition are those who are on their feet for long periods of time and also those who drink a lot of tea and coffee. The aim of this massage is to direct the movement of fluid to the lymph glands for dispersal. Often clients with oedema tend to have swollen hands, and their feet and ankles also appear puffy.

The best way to massage a client with this type of condition is to ensure the affected area that is being massaged is slightly raised. For example, if the condition affects the leg, it should be raised above the groin area and supported by pillows. If it is the arm, it should be raised higher than the axillae. The most effective manipulations are effleurage and kneading movements. Start to massage the area from the proximal end of the limb and using the two manipulations, effleurage and kneading, squeeze up the whole length of the limb, working slowly and covering all of the area, section by section, working towards the lymph gland.

Female clients may find that their abdomen, legs, hands, and, in some instances, their face swell before menstruating. This is usually caused by abnormal water retention that tends to grossly distend the thighs, hips and abdomen. Where the navel distends, the skin appears shiny and in some instances the fluid in the tissue ripples when the client moves. This condition would contraindicate massage and you should advise the client to seek medical advice.

To relieve aches and pains

The client will normally identify where they have a particular ache or pain, and providing there is no medical condition, the therapist can concentrate on that particular area by applying lots of deep pressure while applying effleurage, deep frictions, petrissage and ironing movements.

To relieve stiff joints

As with aches and pains, it is advisable to check that there is no medical reason why the joint is stiff before commencing the massage. The muscles around the stiff joint should be massaged quite vigorously, with effleurage, deep frictions and finger kneading applied to the joint itself.

To relieve contracted muscles

For this type of condition, you should perform deep, slow movements such as stroking, kneading and petrissage. This will help to stretch and relax the muscles. On no account should any percussion movements be applied.

To aid muscle tone

Untoned and flabby muscles may be a result of ageing or weight loss. These type of muscles have usually lost their elasticity. Brisk manipulations are required to stimulate and nourish the muscles that require toning. This can be performed by applying kneading, vibrations, clapping and hacking movements to the area.

To benefit cellulite

This condition is difficult to reduce or remove even when the client is dieting and exercising. The aim of massage is to try and soften and reduce the fatty adipose tissue. Heavier manipulations such as kneading, picking up, hacking, cupping, beating and pounding are required. They should be applied deeply and briskly.

To improve scarring

It is only advisable to massage scar tissue once it is more than nine months old. If it is 'younger' than this, although it may appear healed, the healing process continues in the underlying structures. Massage to this area should consist of manipulations that lift the scar tissue away from the structures underneath. Oil is the best lubricant to use as it allows the skin to stretch more.

To promote relaxation

Achieving a relaxing massage simply involves avoiding/omitting all stimulating movements, such as percussion. You should concentrate on effleurage, stroking, kneading and ironing. These should be performed slowly, rhythmically and firmly with deep pressure being applied. The most beneficial areas to work on are the back and neck areas.

Neuromuscular technique

This technique is usually incorporated into a general massage and is applied to tension nodules/areas of tension. It is important to ensure that the muscles are warmed up first.

Using the fingers or thumbs, identify the tense and nodular areas. Using the thumbs (knuckles or elbows), hold the point with deep pressure for up to 90 seconds until the area starts to become less painful. Once the pain starts to ease off, repeat the process. It is better if the client can relax as much as possible while the technique is carried out. This may be difficult due to the pain so the client should be encouraged to do some deep breathing.

To aid stimulation

When the primary aim of a massage is to invigorate the client, you should use quick light manipulations. These will mainly be percussion movements with some petrissage movements such as wringing, picking up and rolling, together with very brisk stroking movements. Stimulating massages are beneficial for clients who complain of a lack of energy and a feeling of debilitation. This type of massage should leave them feeling refreshed and revitalised.

Different massage techniques can be employed depending on the situation, for example pre-event massage is usually carried out prior to some form of exercise, post-event massage is carried out after exercise has taken place and neuromuscular massage techniques are used to disperse tension nodules.

Pre-event massage (sports massage)

The aim of this type of massage is to:

- help the body to respond well to the demands brought about by increased activity
- facilitate maximum performance.

When muscles are working, an increased supply of oxygen and nutrients are required as muscular activity requires a great deal of energy. It is essential that warm-up and stretching exercises are performed prior to any form of exercise as the body systems are slowly brought up to a peak level and therefore maximum performance can be obtained. Massage will help to obtain these effects, but under no account must it be used as a substitute for exercise. Massage improves the flexibility and extensibility of muscles, increases blood and nutrient supply to the muscles and helps to maintain and increase joint mobility.

This type of massage, which usually lasts about 10 minutes in each area, is performed lightly and quite briskly. It is a stimulating massage applied to parts of the body that are

Tip

Pre-event massage should not take the place of an adequate warm-up.

Did you know

As a result of massage, the brain can be stimulated to release endorphins, the body's own morphine-like painkilling chemicals, into the nervous system.

Tip

Sports massage is designed to help improve athletic performance. It can be adapted to:

- enhance the pre-event preparation and warm-up
- offer assistance and recovery during an event
- aid recovery immediately post-event
- provide maintenance between events
- treat sporting injuries.

Tip

Athletes whose sports involve much strength and power training will have a greater proportion of bulkier muscle fibres. These athletes will benefit from deeper, more concentrated work on the affected major muscle groups.

Tip

Preheat treatments can be used to prepare the client for massage before the main treatment. Mechanical preheat treatments include infrared radiation, described in Chapter 7.

going to be exercised. The types of movement are effleurage, kneading, wringing and picking up to the main muscles; muscle rolling and light hacking and cupping to the large muscles. You should always start with brisk effleurage working towards the heart.

Post-event massage (sports massage)

This type of massage must be given as soon as possible after exercise. The muscles can be painful, tender and sore due to the accumulation of waste products in the muscles, and as a result of any injuries incurred during exercise. Post-event massage is used to remove metabolic waste by speeding up the venous and lymphatic supply. This helps to prevent stiffness, relieve tension and increase nutrients and oxygen to the muscles, helping to prevent fatigue.

1. Start post-event massage with light, gentle stroking movements over the muscles to get a feel for the condition of the tissues. For example, areas of tension and tightness, and also to allow the client to identify any painful areas.
2. Perform effleurage, increasing the depth as the muscles relax.
3. Shake the muscles using the flat of the hand.
4. Perform muscle rolling.
5. Once the muscles have started to soften, continue massage using kneading, wringing and picking up.
6. Finish the massage with deep stroking and effleurage.

Mechanical treatments

Mechanical massage can be used either to complement manual massage or as a treatment on its own. There are three main types of mechanical treatment according to the equipment used:

1. gyratory vibrator (G5)
2. audio sonic vibrator
3. percussion vibrator

Gyratory vibrator

The gyratory vibrator is usually used in general body work. As it is quite a heavy treatment, it is more suitable for use

Tip

Remember that under the Electricity at Work Act, it is your responsibility to ensure that electrical equipment is tested every 12 months by a qualified electrician.

Hand-held gyratory vibrator

on large, bulky and muscular areas. This mechanical massage is usually combined with manual massage.

Gyratory vibrators can be either hand held or floor standing. **Hand-held gyratory vibrators** can be quite heavy to hold so often a floor-standing model is preferred unless the therapist needs to carry it to their clients. Another disadvantage is that there are not many head applicators to choose from. Hand-held vibrators have variable speed control to produce either a deep/relaxing or superficial/stimulating effect.

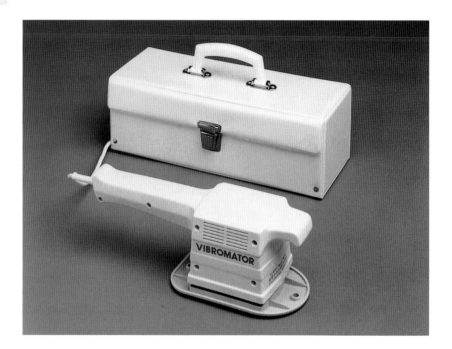

Hand-held gyratory vibrator applicators

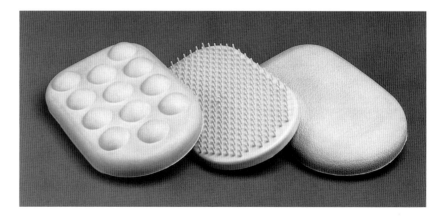

Floor-standing gyratory vibrators are large pieces of machinery supported by a stand. The head is held by the therapist and applied to the client's body. The vibrator operates on a vertical and horizontal plane in a circular movement while vibrating up and down, producing a deep massage. This creates the following effects:

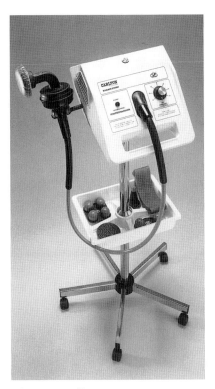

Floor-standing gyratory
vibrator

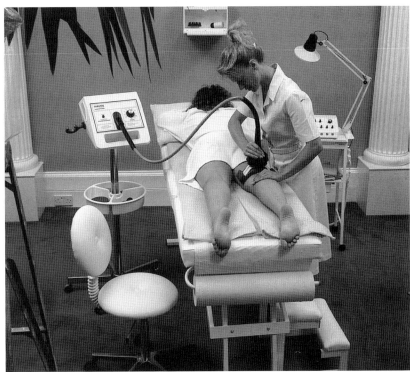

Floor-standing gyratory vibrator treatment

- warmth
- increased blood flow, producing an erythema
- relaxed muscles
- increased skin temperature, stimulating the sweat and sebaceous, glands.

Benefits

This is a popular treatment and the benefits include:

- relaxing tense muscles
- relieving muscular pain and tension
- increasing circulation bringing fresh nutrients to the area
- increasing lymphatic circulation, which speeds up the removal of toxins and waste materials
- improving skin texture by removing the surface dead cells (desquamation)
- stimulating the skin's functions and increasing sebaceous activity, therefore improving dry skin conditions.

The gyratory vibrator gives a heavy treatment and therefore can assist in improving cellulite as well as helping to disperse fatty deposits, especially if the client is trying to lose weight.

A variety of applicator heads designed to give different effects are available. These are summarised in Table 9.1.

Table 9.1 *Gyratory vibrator heads and their purposes*

Applicator	Illustration	Use	Effect
Round sponge applicator		Used at the beginning and end of G5 massage on the trunk	Effleurage
Curved sponge applicator		Designed to massage arms and legs	Effleurage
Round smooth rubber applicator		Used on sensitive skin that might be irritated by the sponge	Effleurage and petrissage effects
Round smooth water massage head		Used with either warm or cold water for relaxing or stimulating effects	Effleurage and petrissage effects
'Eggbox' rubber applicator		Generally used on bulky muscular areas and fatty tissues such as thighs and buttocks	Petrissage
'Pronged' rubber applicator		Generally used on bulky muscular areas and fatty tissues such as thighs and buttocks	Petrissage
'Football' rubber applicator		Can be used over the colon to promote peristalsis	Petrissage
'Spiky' rubber applicator		Stimulates nerve endings and creates a rapid hyperemia. Removes surface dead skin cells therefore improving dry skin conditions	Tapotement
'Lighthouse' rubber applicator		Excellent for nodules on upper trapezius, either side of the spine and around the knees	Friction

Tip

It is important to demonstrate the noise and explain the sensation of any mechanical massage equipment to the client before the treatment so that they are relaxed and know what to expect.

Checklist

Carry out a mechanical massage treatment in this order:

- arms
- abdomen
- fronts of legs
- backs of legs
- gluteals
- back.

Preparation and procedure

- Attachments should be washed before and after treatment in warm soapy water to remove any talc, dead skin cells and sebum. They should be dried and sanitised in an ultraviolet cabinet. Disposable protective attachment coverings can be used.

- When preparing the treatment area you should cover the couch with clean towels, check all general electrical safety precautions and select applicator attachments.

- Prior to treatment you should ensure that a full consultation, including identifying any possible contraindications, has been carried out and an appropriate treatment plan has been agreed. Ensure that the client has removed all jewellery and check that they are well supported on the treatment couch. Explain the sensation and demonstrate the noise from the machine to the client.

- Sanitise your own hands and clean and apply talcum powder to the client's skin over the area to be treated.

- The order of treatment is usually: arms, abdomen, fronts of legs, backs of legs, gluteals, back.

- Select the appropriate heads and secure the attachments. Switch the machine on at the mains and then on the machine itself. Test and demonstrate the machine to the client on your forearm.

- Commence the treatment with effleurage applicators. Always use long sweeping strokes in the direction of the lymphatic and venous flow. When massaging the limbs, apply effleurage strokes towards the trunk in one direction. Pressure should be adapted according to muscle bulk. Apply 4–6 strokes to cover the whole area being treated. Always use one hand to lead or follow the applicator head to soothe the skin.

- When changing applicator heads always switch off the machine. Always keep parts of the client's body that are not being treated covered with clean towels.

- Commence petrissage application at the upper treatment part and descend in a circular kneading motion. Lift and glide the tissues under the applicator head with your free hand. A mild erythema can usually be seen on the skin.

Application to body

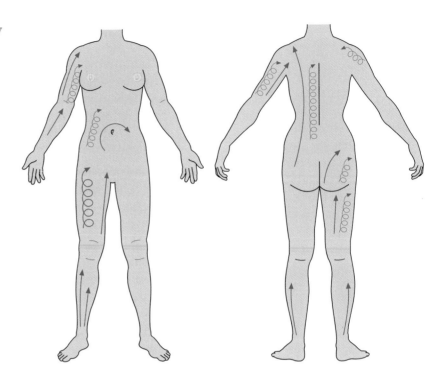

↑ Gliding strokes towards the venous return lymphatic nodes	Rotary movements along muscle length or localised area
Round smooth sponge applicator	Round smooth applicator
Round smooth massage head	Eggbox rubber applicator
Curved sponge applicator	Pronged rubber applicator
Spiky rubber applicator	Football rubber applicator
	Lighthouse rubber applicator (used on upper fibres of trapezius muscle)

Tip

Bruising can result from a too-heavy application or an incorrect choice of applicator head for the treatment area.

- Friction applications are usually applied to small localised areas such as the upper fibres of the trapezius (to relieve tension), either side of the spine (to induce relaxation) and around the knees (to alleviate stiffness). The application is in one direction, in a flowing stroke similar to effleurage.
- Always finish the massage with the effleurage applicators.
- Switch the machine off.
- Complete the client's record card.
- Wash applicators and sanitise.
- Manual massage may be applied to soothe the skin following treatment.

All the following conditions contraindicate use of the gyratory vibrator:

- skin inflammation/broken skin
- highly vascular skin
- varicose veins
- excessively hairy areas
- bony areas/thin clients
- hypersensitive skin
- recent fractures
- senile skin
- skin tags and moles
- treatment over abdomen during pregnancy and menstruation
- thrombosis or phlebitis
- crêpey skin
- acute back problems.

Aftercare

The use of skincare preparations specially designed to increase the skin's tone or firmness in a localised area should be encouraged to support the treatment. These preparations include gels and creams that are applied in light circular movements, working in an inwards direction. When required, advice should also be given on nutrition and weight-reducing diets as well as supportive exercises for the body.

Contra-actions

Bruising may occur due to the application being too heavy, incorrect choice of the applicator head for the body area or if the treatment is too lengthy.

Skin irritation can be caused by the incorrect choice of applicator head and application. This usually tends to be the sponge and spiky applicator heads.

Audio sonic vibrator

This is a small piece of hand-held machinery suitable for localised areas. This treatment is less stimulating to the skin surface, as it penetrates more deeply into the tissues, making it more suitable for sensitive areas.

Audio sonic vibrator

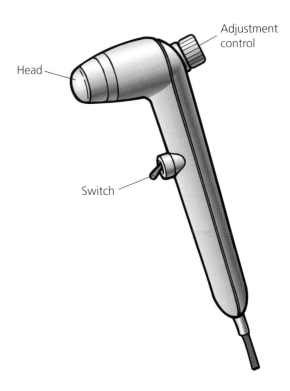

The audio sonic vibrator is particularly effective for relaxing tension nodules. When applied to the body, the sensation is very slight, although it penetrates very deeply into the tissues. This is because it uses sound waves created by an electromagnet. When the current is passing forward, the coil in the machine moves forward; when the current passes backward, the coil passes backward. The applicator head is therefore passing forward and backward as the coil compresses and decompresses the skin tissues alternately.

Benefits

- increasing circulation, bringing fresh nutrients and removing waste products;
- produces an erythema improving the skin's colour;
- raises skin temperature promoting relaxation and relieving tension;
- relieves pain;
- aids desquamation improving skin condition.

Attachments

Flat plate or disc

Used for both the face and body. Used over large areas.

Hard ball

Fibrositis nodules and deep body treatments. Used over smaller areas for more intense treatment.

Preparation and procedure

- The applicator heads should be washed in warm water with a detergent and disinfected with antiseptic and then sanitised in the ultra-violet cabinet.
- Ensure the client is well-supported on the massage couch.
- Explain the treatment to the client and ask the client to remove all jewellery.
- Check for contraindications.
- Cleanse area to be treated.
- Apply lubricant to the area – talc for oily skin, cream for dry to normal skin.
- Select the appropriate head and switch the machine on.
- Test the machine on yourself (forearm).
- Using a circular motion or straight lines cover all the area.
- Apply for 5 to 15 minutes until erythema is present.
- Remove the massage medium from the skin.
- Complete the client's record card.
- Wash applicator heads and sanitise.
- Manual massage may be applied to soothe the skin following treatment.

All the following conditions contraindicate use of the audio sonic vibrator:

- skin disorders and diseases
- infected skin
- bony areas
- migraines/headaches if applying to face and neck area.

Aftercare

Advice on correct posture and exercises is recommended when the client's problem is tension nodules in the muscles.

If the aim of the treatment is relaxation, relaxing baths and massage techniques would be recommended for use at home.

Contra-actions

● Discomfort caused by incorrect frequency and insufficient protection when treating bony areas.

● Erythema caused by the treatment being too lengthy.

● Skin irritation caused by excessive pressure during treatment.

Health & safety

Percussion vibrator
Never apply pressure as this can result in skin irritation.

Percussion vibrator

This piece of machinery is hand held. The applicator head taps up and down on the skin and the force can be increased and decreased. A variety of heads can be used, for example sponge applicator for effleurage effects and spike for tapotement effects. Percussion vibrators are used mainly on the face, neck and shoulder area. Treatment times vary from 5 to 15 minutes.

Percussion vibrator

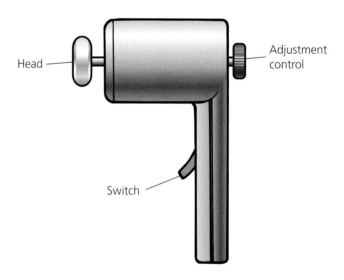

Head

Adjustment control

Switch

Knowledge review

1 What areas should be avoided when massaging a male client?

2 How would you adapt the massage routine for the following conditions:
- gravitational oedema
- obese clients?

3 What massage manipulations would you use to produce:
- relaxing massage
- stimulating massage?

4 How would you adapt a back massage for a pregnant woman, if she could not lie on her tummy?

5 When using electrical equipment such as gyratory massage, what are your responsibilities under the Electricity at Work Act?

6 State three effects of G5.

7 List six contraindications to G5 treatment.

8 What are the effects of the following application heads?
- 'eggbox' rubber application
- spiky rubber application
- lighthouse rubber application?

9 State two effects of the audio sonic vibrator.

10 List two contraindications to audio sonic treatments.

Indian head massage

10

Introduction

Checklist

Objectives of Indian head massage

- Relaxation
- Increases sense of well-being
- Improves the condition of the hair and scalp

Indian head massage helps to relieve stress and tension and creates a great sense of well-being. This type of massage was developed 3000 years ago, at the same time as the beginning of Hinduism, the main Indian religion. Suitable for all ages, it is an Indian family tradition, known as 'champissage' and is part of the ayurveda system, a science of life over 4000 years old and a form of medical treatment. Ayurveda is a method of healing and relieving pain through balancing the body. Ayurveda (or art of life) is based on body, mind and spirit and the fact that each person is different.

Knowledge of massage came to India from China and was based on discovering the various points of the body where rubbing, pressure and manipulations were most effective. By restoring the balance of the body, mind and spirit the person's health is improved.

Indian head massage is one of the most enjoyable and relaxing types of massage one can experience. It can be carried out almost anywhere; the client does not need to undress and it does not require a massage couch. It is both physically and mentally relaxing, the therapeutic touch relieves stress and the tensions of everyday life and leaves a feeling of well-being as well as increasing energy levels.

If too many physical or psychological strains are put on us the balances of the body become upset.

Physiological effects

Indian head massage concentrates on the treatment of the upper back, shoulders, arms, hands, neck, scalp and face. It can have the following physiological benefits:

- general relaxation
- improved blood circulation – warms the tissues, inducing a feeling of relaxation, which helps relieve muscle tension
- improved skin colour – the blood capillaries dilate and bring blood to the skin's surface
- improved lymphatic flow – this helps aid the removal of waste products and toxins, therefore improving the appearance of puffy oedematous skin
- reduced muscular tension – improved supply of oxygenated blood to the area will improve the tone

and strength of the muscles; massage will help to break down adhesions and modules in the muscles helping to eliminate toxins from the tense muscles

- nerve endings soothed and stimulated – depending on the massage movements, the nerve endings can either be soothed or stimulated to help relieve muscular pain and fatigue
- skin regeneration – the skin's layers are stimulated, which helps improve the skin's cellular functions
- softer skin – the sebaceous and suderiferous glands are stimulated, which increases the production of sweat and sebum, increasing the skin's moisture and oil balance
- desquamation – removal of dead skin is accelerated therefore keeping the skin soft and improving its appearance.

Tip

When applied to the scalp, Indian head massage encourages hair growth. The facial massage can help relieve sinus problems, eyestrain, headache and insomnia.

Psychological effects

- Reduces stress levels.
- Relieves tension.
- Induces relaxation.
- Increases energy levels.
- Improves sleep patterns.
- Alleviates feelings of depression and low self-esteem.

Massage movements

Tip

Always adapt massage movements to meet the needs of the client, which you've established during the consultation stage, by adapting either the depth of pressure or the speed of the application.

The movements used in the Indian head massage are:

- effleurage
- petrissage or compressions
- tapotement or percussion
- frictions
- vibrations
- pressure points.

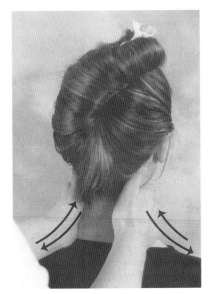

Effleurage

Effleurage

Key characteristics:

- a sweeping, stroking movement
- mainly used at the beginning and end of the massage or as a connecting link
- has a soothing and relaxing effect
- performed with palm of hand or pads of the fingers.

Benefits

- Induces relaxation.
- Increases blood circulation.
- Increases lymphatic flow improving the absorption of waste products.
- Relieves tension.
- Aids desquamation.
- Relaxes muscle fibres.

Tip

Effleurage
A full description of this technique is given in 'Massage procedures' in Chapter 8 page 188.

Stroking movements

This type of movement is used to link other movements, can be applied in any direction, and is usually performed with the whole hand or the fingers.

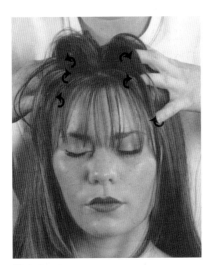

Petrissage

Petrissage

Key characteristics:

- deeper strokes applied with thumbs, fingers or heels of the hands
- includes kneading, picking up, rolling and wringing
- tissue is firmly picked up and lifted from the underlying structure and then released
- care must be taken to avoid pinching at the end of strokes
- kneading – pressure is applied firmly then released; the movement is then repeated in an adjacent area
- picking up – the muscle is grasped with the whole hand with the thumb abducted, the muscle is lifted away from the underlying structure then released. On relaxation, the other hand, without breaking contact picks up a different part. The movement is repeated along the length of the muscle

Tip

Petrissage
A full description of this technique is given in 'Massage procedures' in Chapter 8, page 189.

Tip

Petrissage movements help prevent the formation of fibrosis in the muscle, especially in the trapezius muscle of the upper back.

Tapotement

Tip

Tapotement
A full description of this technique is given in 'Massage procedures' in Chapter 8, page 191.

- rolling – hands are placed firmly on the area, the superficial tissue is grasped between fingers and thumbs and gently rolled backwards and forwards against the thumbs and fingers
- wringing – muscle is lifted from the underlying structure then moved from side to side along the muscle length with the fingers of one hand working with the thumb of the opposite hand
- reinforced kneading – any technique where one hand (ironing), or fingers are placed over the corresponding hand or fingers, will give a deeper pressure is known as reinforced movement.

Benefits

- Relieves muscular tension, fatigue and stiffness.
- Increases blood and lymph circulation.
- Increases sebaceous activity.
- Improves muscle tone.
- Speeds up elimination of waste products.
- Aids relaxation.

Tapotement

Key characteristics:

- used for stimulating and toning the area
- tapotement includes tapping and hacking
- movements should be light and spring with wrists loose and flexible to avoid discomfort to the client
- when performed on the scalp, only light pressure should be used
- on the face, only light tapping should be used
- not to be used on the very thin or the elderly – can be painful and lead to bruising
- tapping – performed rhythmically with the fingertips, very similar to playing the piano
- hacking – a fast, light, stimulating movement. Hands face each other, but do not touch. Fingers flick against the skin very quickly in rapid succession.

Health & safety

Tapotement movements should not be performed directly over the spine. Always ensure the hands are loose and relaxed to avoid any discomfort or bruising occurring.

Benefits

- Increases circulation which can create a healthy glow.
- Improves the appearance and tones areas of loose skin.
- Tones and strengthens muscles.
- Gives local rise in skin temperature.
- Sensory nerve endings stimulated bringing about vasodilation of blood vessels.

Frictions

Key characteristics:

- applied in small areas of the surface tissue
- rubbing movements – skin is rubbed against deeper underlying structures
- applied in a circular movement
- applied with tips of thumbs and fingers applying slight stretch on the underlying structures.

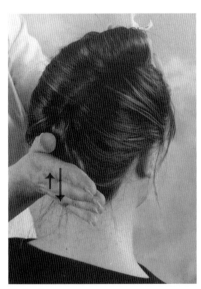

Frictions

Tip

Frictions
A full description of this technique is given in 'Massage procedures' in Chapter 8, page 192.

Benefits

- Break down fibrous thickenings, fatty deposits.
- Aid in the removal of non-medical oedema.
- Stimulate and improve dry skin conditions.
- Increase lymph and blood circulation.
- Aid relaxation.

Tip

In areas that feel any tension, frictions will free adhesions, thereby preventing the formation of fibrosis in the muscular tissue, especially in the trapezius muscle.

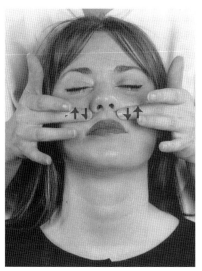

Vibrations – static

Tip

Vibrations
A full description of this technique is given in 'Massage procedures' in Chapter 8, page 192.

Tip

Treatment frequency and timings
It is recommended that Indian head massage is carried out once or twice a week, although it can be carried out as required. The frequency of the treatment depends on the client's time constraints and financial position. Allow 45 minutes for the client's first treatment, including a consultation, the treatment and aftercare advice. The treatment itself will take 30 minutes.

Vibrations

Key characteristics:

- performed with fine trembling movements with one or both hands
- can be 'static' – performed in one place or 'running' – moving up and down
- uses palmar surface, pads of the fingers or the tip (distal phalanx) of the thumb
- muscles of the forearm are contracted continually then relaxed to produce vibration movements.

Benefits

- Relieve fatigue.
- Alleviate pain by stimulating nerves and producing sedative effect on the area.
- Can stimulate sensitive skin without irritating surface blood vessels.
- Clear and stimulate the nerve pathways.
- Relieve tension in the neck and back, bringing about relaxation.

Pressure points

The pressure point technique is based on the principles of Marma, in which pressure on the nerve junctions stimulates vital energy points on the face, ears and head.

Benefits

- Relieve tiredness.
- Induce relaxation.
- Improve circulation.
- Marma pressure point technique balances the body.

Tip

A massage treatment should include a full range of movements, chosen and adapted to suit the client. For example, if the client is especially tense in the upper neck and shoulder region, the therapist should spend more time concentrating on this area and less time on others.

Contraindications

Local and general contraindications
If in any doubt about a client's suitability for massage, advise the client to seek medical advice. Ensure that you have written consent from the doctor before carrying out the treatment. Never diagnose conditions as this is not your professional area.

Contraindications are conditions of the body that prevent a treatment taking place. A contraindication can be either local or general.

A local contraindication is one in which the area surrounding the condition must be avoided, for example this could be recent scar tissue, in which case you would avoid the area during the massage. A general contraindication is one in which the client may *on no account* be massaged. Only when the condition clears up, or written approval is given by the doctor, can the client receive treatment.

The following contraindications are relevant to Indian head massage.

Local contraindications

These usually indicate that other areas of the face, neck, shoulders, back and arms can be massaged while the affected area is avoided:

- bruises
- recent scar tissue (up to nine months old)
- cuts
- skin disorders (e.g. eczema, psoriasis, dermatitis etc.)
- skin abrasions
- sunburn
- bites and stings
- swelling – medical advice needs to be sought if the therapist is unsure why oedema is present
- fractures and sprains
- acute joint conditions
- medication – (long-term) permission from the doctor must be given.

General contraindications

If you suspect any of the following general contraindications, always seek medical advice:

- asthma
- undiagnosed lumps, bumps and swellings
- loss of skin sensation
- cancer – may spread via the lymph
- nervous disorders

- embolism – a blood clot that circulates in the blood stream
- epilepsy – usually this condition will be controlled with medication – if medical permission is given NEVER leave the client unattended
- spastic conditions – massage in some cases may increase spasticity
- diabetes – in some cases the circulation is poor and skin can become very thin (healing process can also be slow)
- blood pressure problems
- high blood pressure – massage can usually help this condition, but always seek medical approval
- low blood pressure
- feeling faint or dizzy – when the client gets up from the massage couch after massage they MUST always be supervised. Never leave them
- heart conditions – massage stimulates the circulation and this may have an effect on any heart condition. Always seek medical consent.

 Checklist

Equipment and materials

Before you carry out the treatment it is important that you have all the necessary equipment and materials to hand:

- ✓ Stool or chair with adjustable height and a low back with an armrest
- ✓ Trolley to place all materials required on
- ✓ Clean towels for every client
- ✓ Disposable paper bedroll
- ✓ Cotton wool and tissues
- ✓ Choice of massage oil
- ✓ Skin cleansing agent, for example eau de cologne or witch hazel
- ✓ Lined bowls or a lined pedalbin
- ✓ Hairclip to secure client's hair away from the neck and a sanitised comb for the client to use after the treatment finishes
- ✓ Client record card

Tip

Make sure you practise hand exercises to keep your joints mobile and flexible. Hand exercises are covered fully in Chapter 6, page 169.

Health & safety

Sterilisation and sanitisation

Ensure that the work area is clean and follows all hygienic practices (see Chapter 6, page 171 Preparation of the treatment area). Clean bedroll and towels must be used for each client to prevent cross-

Checklist

Preparing the treatment area
- Treatment room clean and warm (between 18 and 21°C)
- Adequate ventilation
- Low soothing music
- Soft lighting and subtle décor
- Massage couch or chair covered with clean towels and disposable paper
- All equipment ready on the trolley before the treatment

Tip

See Chapter 6 for more detailed descriptions of preparation for massage.

Client consultation

Tip

Client consultation is covered in full in Chapter 5.

This is all about finding out about the client and completing the client record card. Make sure you carry out a full consultation when the client comes along for the first time for a treatment.

The consultation needs to be carried out in a private area, for example the treatment room or cubicle. The main aims of the consultation process will be:

- to put the client at ease
- to build a good rapport with the client
- to ascertain why the client has come for massage
- to build up picture of their lifestyle (do this by asking open questions)
- to ensure the client has realistic expectations about the treatment
- to ensure the treatment they have requested, or the treatment you have recommended, is the most suitable for their needs.

Tip

The client may have an underlying reason for seeking treatment that is not immediately obvious or that they are reluctant to admit, for example if they are suffering from stress – you should try gently and tactfully to identify these reasons before starting any treatment.

Tip

Ask open questions 'how, what, where, when' – to encourage the client to give more than a one-word response of 'yes' or 'no'.

At the end of the consultation, the client should understand everything that is going to take place, have an idea of what type of massage they will be receiving, feel relaxed, at ease and ready for their treatment.

Record card

During the consultation a record card should be completed and signed by the therapist and the client. The record card should include:

- *Personal details:* name, address and telephone number. These will enable you to contact the client in the event of their treatment being cancelled due to the therapist's being ill.
- *Date of birth:* this will give some indication towards the diagnosis, for example a female client may be menopausal, which may explain some of the symptoms she is be experiencing.
- *Medical history,* including: doctor's details, past medical history (treatment may need to be medical), any medical conditions (treatment may be contraindicated), any medication they may be on (this may contraindicate the treatment, or the treatment may need to be modified), recent operations (again this may contraindicate the treatment or the massage may just needed to be adapted) and number and ages of any children.
- *Lifestyle,* including weight/height, age (the female client may be menopausal), eating habits, regularity of exercise, occupation (for example, does it entail sitting for long periods of time, is it a stressful job?), whether they smoke, number of units of alcohol drunk in a week, sleep pattern, stress levels – need to recognise any underlying factors of stress.

Health & safety

It is essential that you check thoroughly for local and general contraindications at the consultation stage. Inappropriate treatment could incur risk to the client, therapists and other clients. The most common risk is cross-infection. (See Chapter 5.)

INDIAN HEAD MASSAGE CONSULTATION FORM

Date	Therapist name

Client name	Date of birth (identifying client age group)

Address	Postcode

Evening phone number	Day phone number

Name of doctor	Doctor's address and phone number

Related medical history (conditions that may restrict or prohibit treatment application)

Are you taking any medication (this may affect the condition of the skin or skin sensitivity)?

CONTRAINDICATIONS REQUIRING MEDICAL REFERRAL
(preventing Indian head massage treatment application)

- ☐ bacterial infection, e.g. impetigo
- ☐ viral infection, e.g. herpes simplex
- ☐ fungal infection, e.g. tine ungium
- ☐ skin disorders
- ☐ skin disease
- ☐ high or low blood pressure
- ☐ recent head and neck injury
- ☐ severe bruising
- ☐ severe cuts and abrasions
- ☐ hair disorders
- ☐ medical conditions
- ☐ recent scar iessue
- ☐ dysfunction of the nervous system
- ☐ epilepsy

TREATMENT AREAS
- ☐ scalp
- ☐ neck
- ☐ arms
- ☐ head
- ☐ shoulders
- ☐ hands
- ☐ face
- ☐ upper back
- ☐ primary chakra areas

MASSAGE TECHNIQUES
- ☐ effleurage
- ☐ tapotement (percussion)
- ☐ vibrations
- ☐ petrissage
- ☐ frictions
- ☐ pressure points

LUBRICANT (IF USED)
organic oil – type [＿＿＿＿] ☐ cream

CONTRAINDICATIONS THAT RESTRICT TREATMENT
(treatment may require adaptation)

- ☐ cuts and abrasions
- ☐ bruising and swelling
- ☐ recent injuries to the treatment area
- ☐ medication
- ☐ mild eczema/psoriasis
- ☐ recent scar tissue (avoid area)
- ☐ undiagnosed lumps, bumps, swellings
- ☐ migraine
- ☐ allergies

LIFESTYLE
occupation [＿＿＿＿＿＿]
family situation [＿＿＿＿＿＿]
dietary and fluid intake [＿＿＿＿＿＿]
(including allergies)
hobbies, interests, means of relaxation [＿＿＿＿＿＿]
exercise habits [＿＿＿＿＿＿]
smoking habits [＿＿＿＿＿＿]
sleep patterns [＿＿＿＿＿＿]

PHYSICAL CHARACTERISTICS
- ☐ weight
- ☐ size
- ☐ muscle tone
- ☐ age

OBJECTIVES OF TREATMENT
- ☐ relaxation
- ☐ maintenance of health and well-being
- ☐ improvement of hair and scalp condition

EQUIPMENT AND MATERIALS
- ☐ towels
- ☐ comb
- ☐ spatulas
- ☐ protective covering
- ☐ consumables
- ☐ hairclip
- ☐ stool

Therapist signature (for reference)

Client signature (confirmation of details)

Consultation form for Indian head massage

Remember that client feedback will not always be positive. It is essential you take this seriously as, albeit in rare cases, the client may wish to take legal action. Always:

- Take the client to a private area and listen to the complaint.
- Try to resolve it immediately.
- Record the complaint and action.
- Inform the insurers if necessary.

Remember – never try to deal with any issue outside your responsibility.

Tip

When dealing with several clients one after another, you may need to 'switch off' between each one. You will then feel less tired at the end of the day. Remember not to take on your clients' problems. Be gentle and listen, but once the client has gone, try to forget what they have told you otherwise you will become too involved and eventually you will become emotionally as well as physically drained.

Evaluating the treatment: client feedback

It is also very important to evaluate the treatment. This is done effectively by gaining client feedback either orally (simply by asking if they've enjoyed the treatment at the end of the Indian head massage) or by using written feedback through a feedback form. (See Chapter 5.)

Selecting the oils

The best oils to use when massaging the scalp are organic oils. Organic oils are high in polyunsaturated fats and become soft and liquid at room temperature.

Organic oils absorb easily through the skin and take effect on both the inside and outside of the body. Depending on the length of the client's hair and the condition of their scalp, approximately 2–5ml is required for each Indian head massage treatment. The choice of oil depends on its specific properties, texture and smell.

Health & safety

Allergies
Before using any oils you must check with the client that they have no allergy to particular oils. If in any doubt about using an oil, choose an alternative, such as olive oil.

Name of oil		*Uses in Indian head massage*
Almond oil		Particularly good to moisturise dry, sensitive hair and skin Light texture oil High in unsaturated fatty acids, protein and vitamins A, B, D and E
Coconut oil		Medium to light oil suitable for dry skin and dry brittle and chemically treated hair. Good to use in the summer as it has a cooling effect on the scalp
Mustard oil		Strong smelling oil, which produces an intense heating invigorating action. As heat is created it is particularly recommended for use in winter, but the warmth created is also beneficial to clients with arthritis The skin pores open and a cleansing action is created Mustard oil is a particularly invigorating oil and is used extensively for men. It is not suitable on sensitive skin and scalps as it may cause irritation. Mustard oil is hot and sharp and is effective in increasing body heat, relieving pains and swellings and helping to relax stiff muscles
Sesame oil		Highly recommended as a good general oil, due to its high lecithin content, sesame oil helps to relieve swelling and muscular pain and also to strengthen and moisturise the skin Sesame oil is a good balancing oil Rather strong smelling and may irritate sensitive skin and scalps

Posture

The therapist's posture should be very relaxed, as the arms need to be free and hands in control. Avoid standing with a hollow or bent back, but ensure that the body weight is supported by both feet and that the body is upright, so the strain of the heavier movements is less fatiguing. (See Chapter 6.)

Tip

If the therapist's posture is incorrect she could develop back problems. As well as this, a poor posture leads to poor technique – when the feet are in the wrong position, the body weight is thrown off balance, which in turn affects the rhythm, depth and smoothness of the treatment.

Massage procedure

Activity

To experience your own energy field, open and close your hands making a loose fist. Do this several times, then bring your hands towards each other with the palms facing. You should feel a slight resistance or tingling sensation. Try this with a friend – you should be able to detect a response from their energy field.

The first stage of the Indian head massage consists of the grounding or levelling stage. During this stage the therapist begins the massage by balancing the body's chakras. Chakras are invisible, non-physical energy centres located about an inch from the physical body. When energy levels are blocked, negative energy is stored in the chakras, which can lead to a general imbalance of the body. This can manifest itself in mental or physical illness. The chakras work interdependently so an imbalance of one chakra may affect another.

During this first stage of the massage, the therapist is aiming to open up the energy channels in order to prepare the way for the healing properties of the massage to follow. The Indian head massage concentrates on balancing the higher chakras: the throat, brow and crown.

Chakras

There are seven major chakra centres each with an individual function, but all work together in balance with each other. Chakras are associated with flowers (different chakras are represented by flowers with different numbers of petals), elements and colours.

Chakra	*Element*	*Colour*	*Effect*
Base charka known as the root Pelvis/coccyx	Earth	Red	Concerned with connections to the earth, health and survival
Sacral Abdomen	Water	Orange	Concerned with relationships, especially sexual ones
Solar plexis Stomach	Fire	Yellow	Concerned with personal harmony and energy
Heart Chest	Air	Green	Concerned with empathy towards others
Throat	Ether/sound	Blue	Concerned with expressions and communications
Brow Forehead	Mind	Indigo	Concerned with inner vision
Crown Very top of the head	Spirit	White/violet	Concerned with imagination and thought

Tip

A therapist may sometimes feel tired after carrying out an Indian head massage treatment. When energy channels are created, energy is drawn from the therapist to the client.

The seven chakras

Sitting position

The client should be seated in an upright position on a low backed chair, with the chair no higher than the base of the client's shoulder blades.

Levelling or grounding

The spine should be straight, legs uncrossed and feet flat on the ground. The arms should be relaxed and hands resting comfortably in the lap. If practical, the client's shoes should be removed.

Wash your hands.

If oil has been selected to be used on the scalp and hair it is applied at this stage, by gently parting the hair and applying oil to the partings:

Centring

Head rock stress detector

- The therapist's feet should be firmly on the floor and their hands placed on the client's shoulders. Ask the client to relax and close their eyes. The outside energies should pass through the therapist's body to the client.

- The therapist then places both hands on the client's scalp on the crown area and holds for 10 seconds.

- Move to stand at one side of the client.

- Place one hand on the forehead and one on the nape of the neck, hold, then gently move the head forwards and backwards, returning it to its upright position.

- Ask the client to take three deep breaths with you, breathing in through the nose and out through the mouth.

- The head should move more easily now.

- One more movement, then three breaths and then two more movements.

Tip

Breathing should be very slow and deep, breathing through the nose and out through the mouth.

Shoulder massage

Thumb sweeps

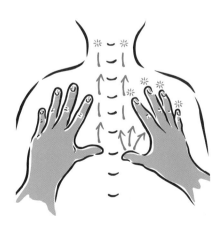

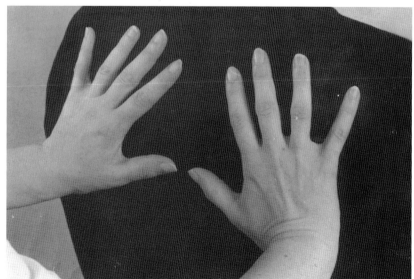

Thumb sweeps

- Place the little fingers of both hands on the outer corners of shoulders, fan out the fingers and reach down the back as far as you can with the thumbs.
- Draw up your thumbs to the little fingers drawing a semi-circle. Repeat this action sweeping to the ring finger, then the index finger. As you make the three sweeps start to work towards the base of the neck.
- Then place the thumbs on either side of the spine, opposite the base of the scapula, and start to push upwards, ending at the occipital bone.
- Carry out each of these movements three times using both hands at the same time, gradually moving towards the spine and finishing off at the occipital bone.

Heel rub

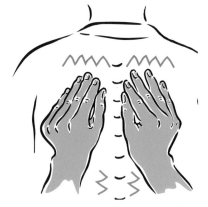

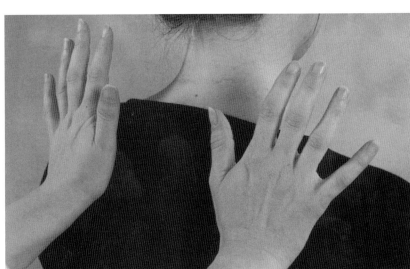

Heel rub

- Using the heels of the hands, start at the base of the scapula and zigzag between the spine and scapula, changing to vertical zigzags above the scapula and working out towards the shoulders.
- Relax your hands and glide down to the starting point. Do this movement three times covering the whole movement.

Thumb pushes

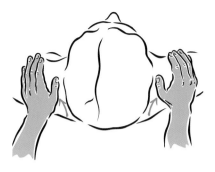

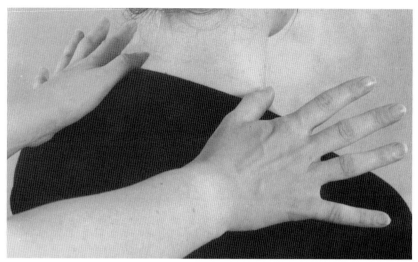

Thumb pushes

- Work over the top of the shoulders from back to front.
- Place your thumbs above the scapula at the shoulder corners and push gently forwards over the ridge of the trapezius muscle.

Carry out each of these movements three times before moving on to a mid-point, followed by the last movements at the base of the neck area:

- Use only the thumbs, with both hands together, working from the shoulder to the base of the neck area. Carry out each movement three times and then move on.

Finger pulls

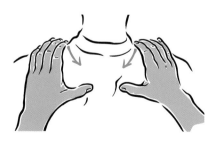

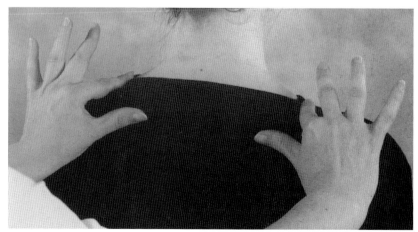

Finger pulls

- Using the index finger perform the opposite movement to the thumb pushes, drawing the finger over the top of the shoulder, keeping your thumb behind the shoulder using it as an anchor, drawing the finger towards it.
- Continue along in three stages, working towards the shoulder corners.
- Starting at the base of the neck, work in three stages towards the shoulder corners.

Hacking

Champissage (hacking)

- Hold your hands in the prayer position. Keeping them relaxed, use the heel of the hands and fingers to strike, remembering to keep the wrist loose at all times.
- Starting at the base of the scapula, follow its shape along to the shoulder corner, then progress along the top of the shoulder to the base of the neck.
- Return along this path to the start position.
- Glide across the spine and follow the same pattern on the opposite side.

Carry out each pattern three times on each side.

Picking up and holding

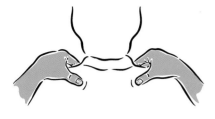

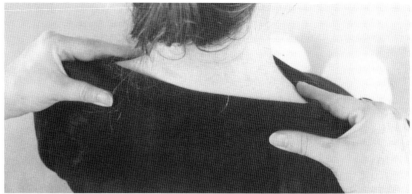

Picking up and holding

Care must be taken not to nip the skin. This movement is carried out along the trapezius:

- Pick up the muscle at the outer corners, hold, then release and move along towards the neck to a mid-point between the outer corner and the base of the neck. Pick up the muscle and hold.
- Move to the base of the neck to perform the last movement.

Carry this out three times.

Smoothing down

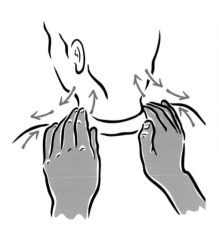

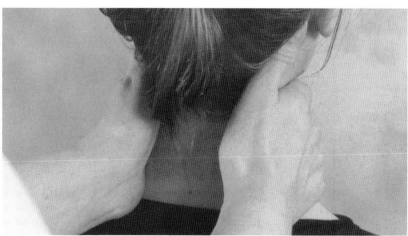

Smoothing down

- Starting at the shoulder tips, use the whole of the palmar surface to make a long sweeping movement along the shoulder and up the neck, until you reach the occipital bone and then back again to the starting point. Use gentle pressure on the upward sweep, releasing it on the way down, ensuring the movement flows.

Carry out this movement three times.

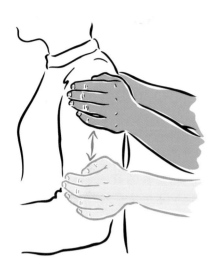

Arm massage

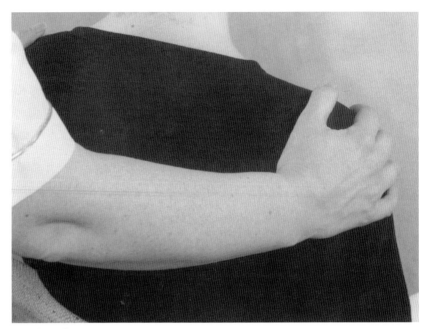

Ironing down

- Place your hands flat on the upper shoulders, then swiftly draw the hands down the length of the upper arm and flick off at the client's elbow.

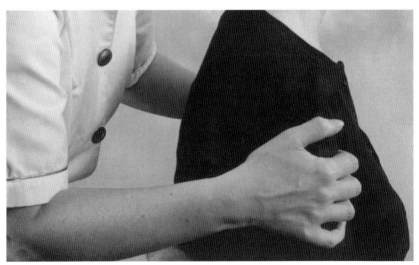

Heel roll

- Knead the upper arm.
- Clasp your hands, interlocking the fingers turning your wrist so that the palms face the client.

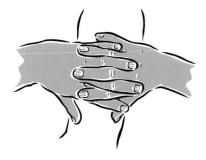

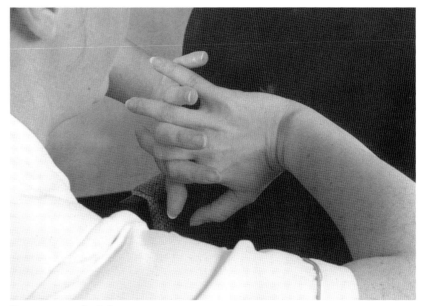

Squeeze and pick away

● Stand at the side of the client and facing the forearm pick up the deltoid between heels of the hands, squeeze and lift away letting the muscle slip out of your grasp.

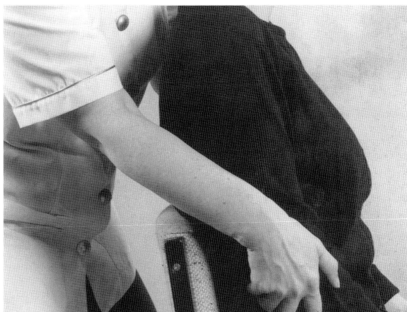

Shoulder lift

● Slide your hands down the upper arms and hold the forearms under the elbows.

● Turn the arms close to the side, lift up the arms as far as is comfortable, gently return them to the resting position.

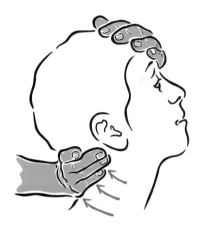

Neck massage

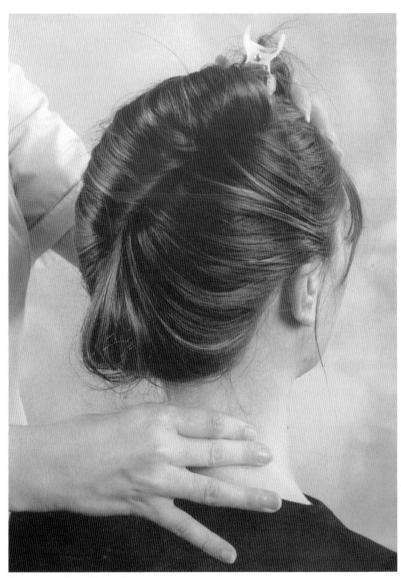

Grasp and pull back

● Pick up the skin and muscle at the back of the neck. Gently lift the tissue with each hand alternately, ensuring that the head is supported at the forehead.

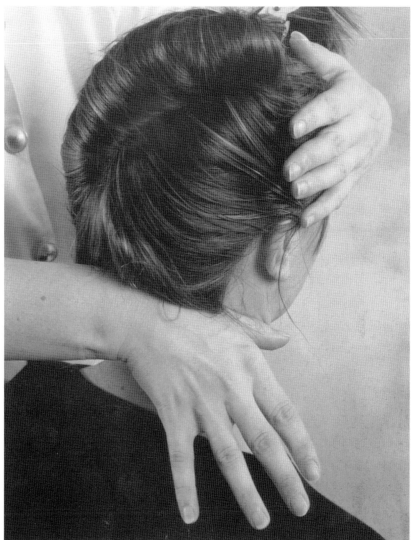

Thumb pushes

● Support the client's forehead; using the pad of the thumb firmly stroke across the side of the neck, starting from the ear, then move to the mid-point and then the base of the neck.

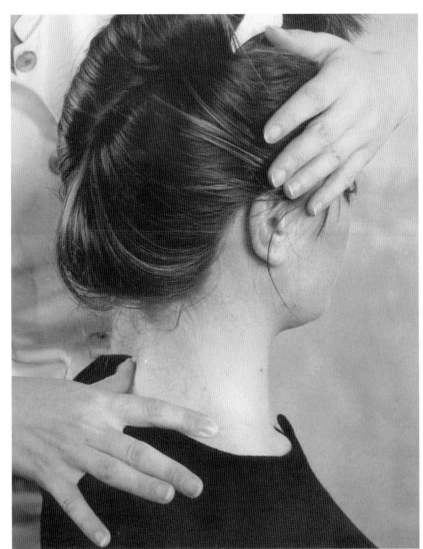

Finger pulls

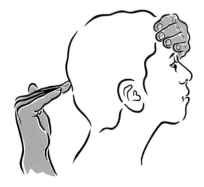

● Repeat the same movement, only using your index finger.

● Repeat both thumb and finger pulls on the opposite side.

● Support the head using the opposite hand, apply horizontal friction movements working across the back of the neck on the occipital bone, moving from ear to ear.

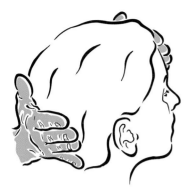

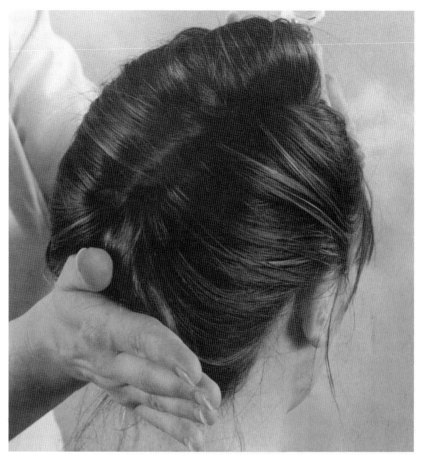

Heel-of-hand rub

● Support the forehead, then, using the heel of the hand, apply a vertical friction movement along the base of the occipital bone.

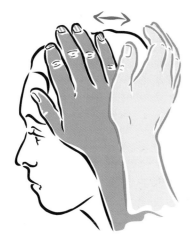

Windscreen wiper

● Support one side of the head.
● Using the heel of the hand, apply a short quick wiping friction movement to the other side of the head, start around the ear and making a zigzag movement around the hairline to the nape and back again, gradually moving up the scalp towards the centre of the head.

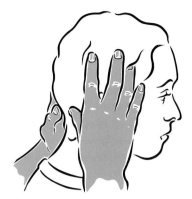

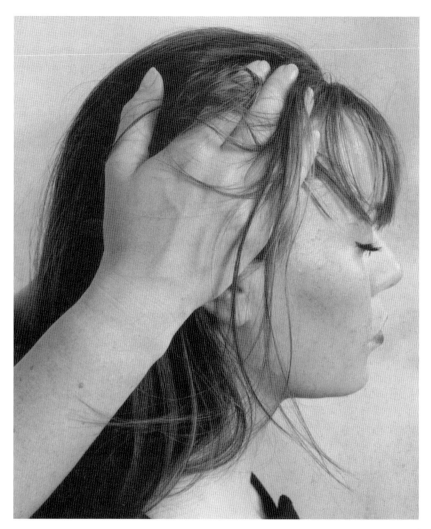

Whole-hand friction

- Stand behind the client resting one hand over the temple area.
- With the other hand, thread the fingers through the hair just above the ears, ensuring that all the palmar surface is in contact with the scalp.
- Using firm but gentle pressure, move your hand quickly up and down, working towards the temple area.
- Repeat on the opposite side.

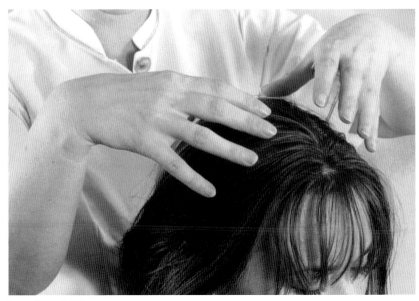

Land and lift

- Standing behind your client, use the pads of your fingers and gently land on the scalp and quickly lift away.
- Cover all the scalp area.

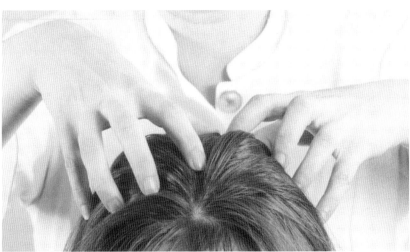

Raking the scalp

- Using both hands, rake your fingers through the hair covering all the scalp area.

Tabla playing

- Using the fingertips in a drumming action, cover the whole scalp.

Squeeze and lift

- Place both hands on either side of the head just below the ears and thread your fingers through the hair, ensuring your hands are resting on the scalp. Using both hands gently squeeze the head and move the scalp upwards then release.
- Repeat the same movement at the temple area and behind the ear.

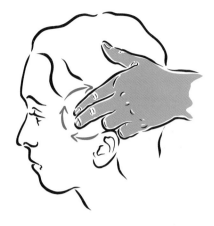

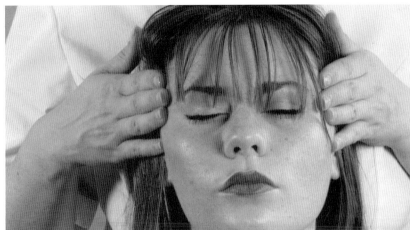

Circular temple frictions

- Using the pads of the index, middle and ring fingers, apply pressure in circular movements to the temple area.

Petrissage to the scalp

- Using the pads of the fingers, apply circular movements to all the scalp area, applying medium pressure.

Pressure points

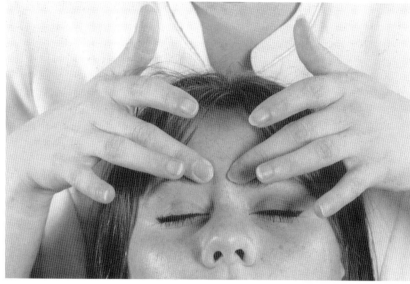

Pressure points – forehead

Pressure points – eye sockets

- Apply pressure points using the pads of the index or middle fingers. Start at the inner eyebrow, apply pressure, hold and release, move up the forehead to a mid-point between the eyebrow and hairline. Apply pressure, hold and release.

- Repeat the pressure and release up to the hairline. Then move along the hairline and work back down to the eyebrows in the same three stages.

- Move on to just under the inner end of the eyebrow, onto the inside of the eye socket and following its shape. Carry on with the pressure, release and glide movements.

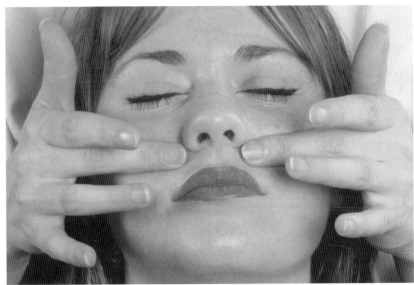

Pressure points – cheekbones

- Glide your fingers down the sides of the nose to the indent at the sides of the nostrils.

- Feel for the point at the end of the cheekbone and slightly under it. Continue with the pressure points using the pads of the index or middle finger. Perform very small, quick friction movements, using both hands at the same time.

- Complete by using a sweeping movement lightly across the cheekbone to the ear.

- Make the final friction where the cheekbone hinges with the lower jaw.

- Gently sweep over the ears.

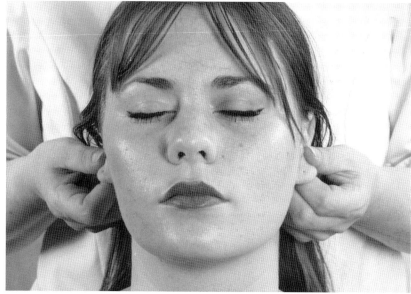

Ear massage

- With small circular movements, use the thumb and fingers to work your way around the ears.

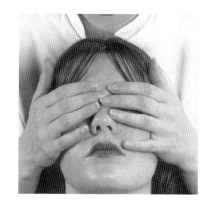

Palmar placing

- Place the heel of your hand gently over the ears, cupping the lower jaw with the rest of your hand. Fingertips should be touching the centre of the chin.
- Swivel your hands gently round until the fingers lie over the closed eyes. Your fingertips should now be touching at the bridge of the nose.
- Move your hands upwards to cover the temples and the forehead area.
- Move up again, covering the parietal and upper frontal area.

Feather fingertip stroking

- Using your finger pads apply light tapping movements, working from the mid-line of the face towards the ears, then from the forehead down to the chin area.
- Repeat twice more.
- Apply circular pressure to the temples simultaneously using the fingertips.

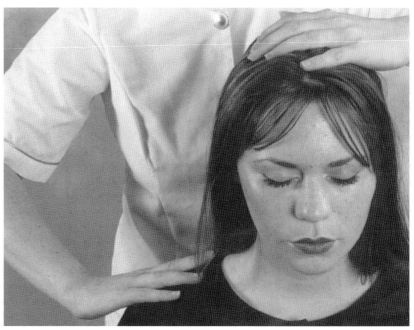

Brushing down

- Stand behind the client. Using your fingers, start with the right hand placed on the scalp above the client's left eye.
- Apply a long, flowing movement over the top of the head down the neck along the top of the shoulder.
- Repeat with the other hand.
- Finish off by stroking both hands off the shoulders at the same time.

Wash your hands.

Adapting the massage

The massage technique will sometimes need to be adapted to suit individual client's requirements.

Massage for male clients

Their muscles tend to be firmer, larger and a lot thicker and their skin tends to be thicker and have less fatty tissue. Male massage tends therefore to be firmer, with the therapist using more of their body weight.

Obese clients

More pressure is required as well as deeper stimulating movements over the fatty areas to help mobilise the fatty tissue.

Thin and bony clients

Pressure needs to be alleviated. Avoid all tapotement movements, otherwise the massage will become very painful and uncomfortable.

Relaxing massage

Avoid all stimulating movements and incorporate more effleurage and light petrissage movements. Pressure should be firm and the rhythm slower.

Tense and tight muscles

All percussion movements should be avoided. Massage should be slow and rhythmical applying slight pressure in order to stretch the muscles.

Slack muscles

Stimulating percussion massage movements should be used to increase circulation and help to tone and firm the area being treated.

Contra-actions

Although the reactions after the massage are usually positive, in some cases clients may experience a negative reaction due to the increased circulation of waste products being transported in the lymphatic system. This is often termed a 'healing crisis'. These reactions include:

- sickness or nausea caused by the increased circulation of toxins
- light-headedness or headaches, depending on what oils have been used
- fainting may be experienced due to the blood capillaries dilating and altering the blood pressure
- skin reactions due to an allergy caused by the massage oil
- a heightened emotional state, with a tendency to tearfulness
- disrupted sleep patterns
- increased secretions from the mucous membranes in the nose and mouth
- aching muscles due to the release of toxins.

The client should be made aware that some of these reactions may occur and be reassured that if they do, they will only be temporary, until the body's natural balance has been restored.

It is important that the therapist asks the client to report any adverse effects to them immediately, so that notes can be added to the client's record card to prevent the same contra-actions occurring in the future.

Health & safety

After their treatment, some clients may feel extremely sleepy and relaxed, due to the release of toxins and increased body channels. Clients reacting this way must not drive home or operate any dangerous machinery, until they feel more alert.

Aftercare and advice

At the end of the massage, advise the client to rest for a few minutes before getting up. A very relaxing massage can leave a client feeling light-headed and any sudden movements can lead to the client feeling dizzy or fainting, as the brain is temporary starved of blood. A few minutes relaxing will enable the blood circulation to return to normal. A glass of water after the treatment will help prevent any feelings of dizziness.

After the treatment it is essential that aftercare advice is given to the client, as this will ensure that they get the maximum benefit from their treatment.

Tip

When oil has been used it is best to avoid shampooing the hair for several hours to allow the oils to benefit the condition of the hair and scalp.

This advice for the following 24 hours should include:

● Rest and avoid any strenuous activities.
● Avoid heavy or highly spiced meals; just eat a light diet.
● Drink plenty of fluids, in particular water, to prevent dehydration.
● Avoid alcohol and caffeine.

If the Indian head massage treatment was for relaxation, your advice should focus on relaxing bath products and self-massage techniques for use at home.

On following the therapist's advice, the client should experience the maximum benefits of the massage treatment. Clients can expect to experience a good night's sleep and to have a greater alertness the following day, as their concentration and thinking will be much improved.

Explain to your clients all the benefits of regular Indian head massage treatments in order to achieve the maximum benefits.

Knowledge review

1   Give an example of what you understand by the following:
    ● questioning skills
    ● listening skills.

2   Give three psychological benefits of an Indian head massage.

3   Give three physiological benefits of an Indian head massage.

4   Give three contraindications that could be identified at consultation that would prevent the treatment being carried out.

5   Give three contraindications that could be identified at consultation that could restrict the treatment being carried out.

6   Why would you need to refer a client to their general practitioner before treatment could be recommended?

7   Why is it important to discuss the client's lifestyle prior to treatment being carried out?

8   Describe the sitting position of the client that will allow them to gain maximum benefit from their treatment.

9   How long should be allowed for an Indian head massage treatment?

10 How should the following be prepared for the treatment:

    ● therapist
    ● client
    ● treatment area?

11 How should the treatment be adapted for the following clients:

    ● male
    ● thin clients
    ● overweight clients?

12 Oils may be incorporated into the Indian head massage treatment. List three oils that can be used as a medium and give a brief description of each.

13 Name the main massage techniques that are performed in the Indian head massage treatment and describe their effects.

14 List the three primary chakra areas treated when performing the Indian head massage treatment.

15 Give two ways in which cross-infection can be avoided when carrying out an Indian head massage treatment.

16 Explain how you would advise the client to breathe to induce relaxation.

17 Why is it necessary that the client rests after the treatment has finished? How long would you recommend?

18 What is meant by the healing crisis?

19 Explain what the client may experience during the healing crisis.

20 List three contra-actions the client may experience after treatment has finished.

21 Why is it important to record the contra-actions on the client's record card?

22 What advice would you give to the client at the end of the treatment?

23 How often would you recommend a client receive Indian head massage treatment?

Aromatherapy

11

Learning objectives

This chapter covers the following:

- **history**
- **essential oils**
- **carrier or fixed oils**
- **aromatherapy massage**

This chapter covers essential knowledge and understanding for the following unit:

- **BT21, Provide massage using pre-blended aromatherapy oils**

It also covers elements of the core mandatory units in relation to aromatherapy massage (these units are covered in full in Chapter 1 and Chapter 2):

- **G1, Ensure your own actions reduce risks to health and safety**
- **G6, Promote additional products or services to clients**

This chapter introduces both the theory and practical techniques of aromatherapy so that you can provide accurate advice and guidance and carry out suitable treatments.

History

Aromatherapy is a natural therapy using essences of plants. The use of essential oils helps to restore, revive and balance both the mind and the body resulting in a feeling of well-being. Aromatherapy has been used for thousands of years.

Egyptians used aromatic essences to embalm – frankincense, myrrh and cedar wood – and mummify – cinnamon and clove – their dead. They also used 'essential oils' in their religious ceremonies and were the first to use the oils for cosmetic purposes. The ancient Greeks used essences as perfumes, to cure illnesses and in massage. Hippocrates fought the Athens plague with aromatic fumigations and herbal medicine! The Romans used 'essential oils' for their healing properties, particularly on battle wounds, and the use of aromatic oils is also reported in the Bible, e.g. Jesus is said to have used aromatic oils in healing and Mary Magdalene anointed Jesus' feet with them at the Last Supper.

The Arabs discovered the art of distilling essential oils in AD10. The Crusaders brought this knowledge and recipes back to their own country between AD10 and 12, and by AD13 the distillation of plants started and chemical products ensued. Knowledge of aromatics and herbs increased throughout medieval history and was studied by many physicians. By the 18th century essential oils were being used in medicine and by the 19th century they were popularly used in the perfume industry.

It is, in fact, a French chemist named Gattefosse who may be credited as being the real founder of aromatherapy in the early 20th century. While working in the laboratory, he burnt himself badly with a bunsen burner. He immediately plunged his burnt hand into a vat of lavender oil and inadvertently discovered how quickly the burn healed without leaving a scar or becoming infected. Following this incident, Gattefosse conducted more research into essential oils and published his first book on aromatherapy in 1928.

During the Second World War, a French doctor, Dr Jean Valnet, began to use essential oils on wounded soldiers. Marguerite Maurey, a biochemist working for a perfumery, introduced massage as a way of getting the oils into the body. And in the 1950s she introduced aromatherapy to England, when she travelled to London and opened a clinic where the art of aromatherapy was both practised and taught.

Today many people are looking for alternative methods to help relieve some of the stresses and tensions of modern life. Given that stress is one of the main contributory factors to many diseases and disorders such as high blood pressure and heart disease, aromatherapy has become particularly popular.

Aromatherapists are now found working in hospitals and doctors' surgeries, as well as alternative centres and beauty clinics.

The oils can be used in many ways:

Tip

See later in chapter for aspects of consultation in aromatherapy in relation to the use of essential oils.

- massage
- inhalation
- steamer
- compresses
- air sprays
- burners
- baths
- lotions/oils
- candles
- foot spas
- hair/skin products
- potpourris.

Essential oils

An essential oil is an oil present in a flower, fruit, root, leaf, seed, bark or an aromatic plant. Oils are in the form of tiny odoriferous droplets and it is these droplets that are always changing their chemical composition according to the change of season or time of day. Essential oils have a large range of aromas and colours including red, brown, blue, yellow and green. As well as being used in aromatherapy, essential oils are also found in perfumes, pharmaceuticals and food flavourings. They are largely made up of three elements – carbon, hydrogen and oxygen.

The molecules in essential oils are very small and this is how they are able to penetrate the skin and enter the bloodstream. Even though the components are individually relatively simple in structure, an oil can be made up of hundreds of components, some being present in minute amounts. It could be that it is these trace components that have the therapeutic properties and that helps to explain why chemically reproduced oils may smell very similar but do not have the same therapeutic properties.

Tip

Oils from the same botanical family group blend well together.

Although essential oils have a very simple molecular structure, the active constituents that make up the oil make it complex. These active constituents work **synergistically**, that is, they work much more powerfully and effectively when combined with other oils.

Properties of essential oils

Essential oils:

- mix with mineral oil and vegetable oil
- do not mix with water or alcohol
- have an odour
- evaporate
- are not greasy to touch
- are volatile, although the extent of the volatility varies according to whether the essential oils are **top**, **middle** or **base** note.

Activity

On three pieces of blotting paper, put a few drops of a top note oil, a middle note oil and a base note oil and put away in a dark place. Check each day to see which oils still keep their aroma. How many days did each oil keep its aroma?

Top note

Top note essential oils are the most volatile. They have a sharp aroma and a highly stimulating effect. They are absorbed into the skin very quickly, last on the skin for about 24 hours and are used to stimulate the mind and body.

Top notes are obtained from citrus fruits:

- basil
- bergamot
- clary sage
- eucalyptus
- grapefruit
- lemon
- lemongrass
- orange
- petitgrain
- sage
- tea tree.

Middle note

Middle note essential oils are moderately volatile and last on the skin for about two to three days. They are used to help bodily functions. Middle notes are usually obtained from flowers and herbs:

- black pepper
- camomile
- cypress
- fennel
- geranium
- juniper
- lavender
- marjoram
- melissa
- pine
- rosemary.

Base note

Base note essential oils are known as fixatives as they 'hold back' the fast evaporation of the top note essential oils. They have the slowest evaporation rate and last for about seven days, as they are absorbed very slowly into the skin. Their effect is soothing on the mind and body.

Base notes are obtained from woods and resins that have a rich, heavy aroma with a relaxing and sedating effect:

- frankincense
- myrrh
- sandalwood
- ginger
- patchouli
- ylang ylang.
- jasmine
- rose

Storing essential oils

Essential oils all have different shelf lives and some last longer than others. However, if oils are not stored correctly, they will lose their therapeutic properties. Essential oils should always be stored in a cool, dark place away from direct sunlight. Exposure to light and extremes of temperature can damage the oil's properties. The storage bottles should be dark in colour to prevent light damage, airtight and made of glass. You should never store essential oils in plastic bottles as these are permeable – air may reach the oil and damage it.

Composition of essential oils

Essential oils consist of many chemical components, including:

- terpene
- ester
- ketone
- alcohol
- aldehyde
- phenol

It is these chemical components that give the essential oils their specific properties.

Tip

Always buy essential oils from a reputable supplier and never from a supplier who charges the same for each type of oil. The price of each oil should represent the yield of each essential oil when extracted from its source.

Tip

Never store essential oils in plastic bottles. Polythene is essentially a solidified oil, so essential oils can escape from polythene bottles or air can enter the bottle and damage the oil.

Table 11.1 Composition of essential oils

Component	Properties	Where they are found
Terpene	Antiseptic, antiviral	Lemon, peppermint, pine, thyme, tea tree
Alcohol	Anti-inflammatory, antiseptic, diuretic, stimulates the immune system	Thyme, lemon, sandalwood, peppermint, bergamot
Ester	Anti-inflammatory, antispasmodic, sedative, fungicidal	Lemon, rosemary, lavender, bergamot
Aldehyde	Antiseptic, antiviral, anti-inflammatory, sedative	Melissa, lemongrass
Ketone	Helps formation of scar tissue, eases congestion by aiding in flow of mucus	Rosemary, peppermint, fennel, camphor, eucalyptus
Phenol	Antiseptic, antispasmodic, stimulating	Thyme, eucalyptus

Methods of extracting essential oils

Enfleurage

Enfleurage is a method using cold fat. A thin layer of fat is spread on a glass frame and fresh flowers that continue to produce essential oils even after they are picked are put in layers on top of this. The essential oils are absorbed into the fat. The glass frame is then turned and the flowers fall off to be replaced with new ones. This process is continued for about two months. When the fat has been saturated with essential oil, it is washed in pure alcohol and the oil passes into the alcohol, known as an absolute. The alcohol is then evaporated leaving the pure essential oil. This method has now been superseded by other methods.

Distillation

This is an ancient method, but it is still the most widely used technique for extracting essential oils from plants. Distillation involves heating the plants with water in a still. Steam is produced that contains the essential oil and it passes into a condenser where the vapour turns into a liquid consisting of water and the essential oils. The essential oil floats on the water, because it is less dense, which allows it to be siphoned off.

This method is usually used to produce lavender, rose and ylang ylang.

Expression

In expression, a machine is used to crush the rind of the fruit and extract the oil. Years ago, this was extracted by holding a sponge around the rind of the fruit and squeezing until the sponge was filled with oil. Citrus fruits such as lemon and orange are extracted using this method.

Maceration

This method involves dipping plants into hot fat. The process is repeated with fresh supplies of flowers until the fat becomes saturated. The fat is then washed in alcohol, which evaporates and leaves the essential oil. This method is rarely used any more.

Solvent

The solvent used is dependent on the source of the essential oils. For flowers, ether, benzine or petroleum is used, while for gums such as rosewood and pine and resins such as myrrh and benzoin, the solvent used is acetone. The plants are covered with a solvent and heated gradually until the essential oil is extracted. The solvent is then filtered and the dark paste that is left is mixed with alcohol and left to cool. The essential oil dissolves in the alcohol, which then evaporates leaving the oil.

Methods of entry of essential oils into the body

Skin

Essential oils can enter the skin via sebaceous glands, sudoriferous glands and hair follicles. Penetration of essential oils into the skin can take up to 100 minutes. Carrier oils, especially acids, alkalis and alcohols, can pass through only to the epidermis as the modular structure is too large for them to penetrate any further. Because essential oils have small molecular structures however, once the oils have entered the skin, they can penetrate through to the dermis and then pass through to the bloodstream via the capillary walls. The blood then transports essential oils around the body.

Respiratory system

Essential oils can be inhaled. They pass through the lung tissue lining, through the capillary walls into the blood stream and are transported around the body.

Olfactory system

Responsible for the sense of smell, the olfactory system is stimulated when we smell something and the body responds. Volatile essential oils penetrate the olfactory system when inhaled. The olfactory surface is coated with a thin layer of mucus, the oils pass through the mucous membranes and fatty tissues where they stimulate the olfactory nerves and the odour is registered. If the mucous membranes are blocked, for example when you have a cold, substances have difficulty passing through and it is difficult to differentiate smells.

Elimination of essential oils

Essential oils stay in the body for some time, in particular the ones that are in the deeper organs. They are eliminated by a number of methods including perspiration, exhalation and in the urine.

Effects of essential oils

Essential oils can have psychological and physiological effects. Often, the physiological effects can be directly attributed to the mental effects. In many cases, an essential oil can affect both mood and physiology.

Table 11.2 *Psychological effects of essential oils*

Effect	Essential oils
Calming	Camomile, geranium, juniper, lavender, sandalwood, ylang ylang, marjoram
Uplifting	Basil, geranium, lavender, lemongrass, peppermint
Soothing	Cypress, lavender
Energising	Marjoram
Relaxing	Camomile, cypress, sandalwood, ylang ylang
Stimulating	Basil, juniper, lemon, lemongrass, rosemary, peppermint
Sedative	Cedarwood, cypress, lavender, lemon, marjoram, sandalwood, patchouli
Revitalising	Lemongrass, juniper

Table 11.3 *Physiological effects of essential oils*

Effect	Essential oils
Raising body temperature	Camphor
Lowering body temperature	Camomile
Increasing circulation	Rosemary, eucalyptus, black pepper
Lowering blood pressure	Lavender
Respiratory – decrease muscle spasms	Fennel, peppermint, rose, clary sage
Respiratory – expectorant effect	Eucalyptus, benzoin lemon
Sedative effect on nervous system	Melissa, lavender, sandalwood, ylang ylang
Stimulating effect on nervous system	Lemon, fennel, cinnamon
Antispasmodic effect on digestive system	Lavender, rosemary, sandalwood
Laxative effect	Marjoram, rosemary
Diuretic effect	Juniper, fennel, sandalwood
Stimulate oestrogen production	Fennel, aniseed, garlic
Antibacterial effect	Most oils

Safety of essential oils

The majority of essential oils should never be used undiluted. The most common risks of essential oils are:

Toxicity: this is similar to poisoning. If the oil is toxic it could prove to be fatal if taken orally or applied to the skin. Toxicity is a matter of dose, which varies according to the person's size, for example a child should have a much lower percentage of essential oils blended in the carrier oil than an adult, and the treatment should be less frequent. Certain oils are **phototoxic**, which means that the skin will be more sensitive to the sunlight.

Irritation: irritation to the skin and mucous membrane is most likely.

Sensitisation: this is an allergic reaction to the essential oil. It only requires a small amount to cause a reaction.

Some essential oils used in aromatherapy massage are contraindicated to certain conditions. If medical consent is given to massage a client suffering from a specific condition, you should check for any associated contraindicated oils.

Conditions with contraindicated oils include:

High blood pressure: avoid rosemary, sage, thyme and hyssop.

Epilepsy: avoid hyssop, sage and fennel.

Pregnancy: avoid basil, aniseed, cinnamon, carrot seed, clove, clary sage, cypress, cedarwood, fennel, lemongrass, marjoram, origanum, parsley, peppermint, rose, rosemary, sage and thyme.

Bergamot, lemon, orange, lime and angelica should be avoided prior to exposure to sunlight.

Health & safety

The following aromatherapy oils are unsafe and should never be used in massage:

- bitter almond
- boldo leaf
- calamus
- horseradish
- jaborandi leaf
- mugwort

- mustard
- pennyroyal
- rue
- sassafras
- savin
- southernwood

- tansy
- thuja
- wintergreen
- wormseed
- wormwood
- yellow camphor

Tip

Always keep a record of the oils you use on the client. In the event of a problem such as irritation the therapist can identify the oil involved and make the changes accordingly.

Table 11.4 Essential oils for use in aromatherapy massage

Essential oil	Latin name	Extraction	Uses	Properties	Caution
Basil	Ocimum basilicum	Steam distillation from tops of flowers and leaves	Digestive problems, muscular aches and pains, asthma, sinusitis, bronchitis, coughs, irregular periods, anxiety, depression, migraine	Antidepressant, antiseptic, expectorant, emmenagoguic, stimulates and clears the mind	May cause irritation and sensitisation, avoid during pregnancy
Benzoin	Styrax benzoin	Solvent extraction from the resin, which is collected from the bark of the tree	Nervous tension and exhaustion, muscular aches and pains, respiratory ailments, digestive conditions, dry, chapped skin types, helps expel excess body fluid	Nerve sedative, antiseptic, astringent, anti-inflammatory, circulatory, stimulant	Can cause sensitisation
Bergamot	Monarda didyma	Expressed from the rind	Digestive problems, respiratory conditions, urinary infections, stress, anxiety, nervous tension and depression	Antiseptic, astringent, laxative diuretic, uplifting, antidepressant, stimulant	Avoid contact with strong sunlight after using this oil – photosensitive
Black pepper (middle note)	Piper nigrum	Steam distillation of the dried fruit, i.e. peppercorns	Poor circulation, muscular aches and pains, loss of appetite, nausea, colds and flu, lethargy and mental fatigue	Analgesic, antiseptic, antispasmodic, antitoxic, appetite stimulant, bactericidal, diuretic, laxative, stimulant of nervous, circulatory and digestive systems	Use in lowest concentration as it may irritate the skin
Camomile Roman (middle note)	Chamaemelum nobile	Steam distillation of the flowering heads	Acne, allergies, boils, burns, eczema, inflamed skin conditions, earache, wounds, menstrual pains, headaches, premenstrual syndrome, nervous tension and other stress-related disorders	Analgesic, anti-allergenic, anti-inflammatory, antispasmodic, bactericidal, carminative, digestive, emmenagoguic, fungicidal, hepatic and sedative	Avoid during the first few months of pregnancy

Essential oil	Latin name	Extraction	Uses	Properties	Caution
Cedarwood (base note)	*Juniperus virginiana*	Steam distillation from the wood	Anxiety, nervous tension, eczema, dermatitis, insect repellent	Antiseptic, sedative, astringent	Do not use during pregnancy. Use low concentrations as it may cause skin irritation
Clary sage (top note)	*Salvia sclarea*	Steam distillation of the flowering tops and leaves	High blood pressure, muscular aches and pains, respiratory problems, irregular menstruation, premenstrual syndrome, depression, migraine, nervous tension and stress-related disorders	Anticonvulsive, antidepressant, antispasmodic, antiseptic, astringent, bactericidal, deodorant, digestive and sedative	Not to be used in pregnancy or immediately before or after drinking alcohol
Cypress	*Cupressus sempervivens*	Steam distillation from the twigs, cones and needles	Respiratory problems – asthma and bronchitis; menstrual problems and menopause symptoms; oedema; poor circulation, rheumatism	Antiseptic, astringent, anti-rheumatic, diuretic, regulates menstrual cycle	Emmenagoguic
Eucalyptus (top note)	*Eucalyptus globulus*	Steam distillation of the young leaves and twigs	Burns, blisters, chickenpox, measles, cold sores, cuts, insect bites and stings, insect repellant, head lice, skin infections, wounds, arthritis, muscular aches and pains, sprains, poor circulation, cystitis, hay fever, cold and flu, and headaches	Analgesic, anti-rheumatic, antiseptic, antiviral, deodorant, diuretic, expectorant, parasiticidal, stimulant and vulnerary	Allergy sufferers may need a skin test prior to use
Fennel (middle note)	*Foeniculum vulgare*	Steam distillation from the herb's crushed seeds	Digestive problems, constipation, flatulence, cellulite, menstrual/menopausal problems, poor circulation	Diuretic properties, circulatory stimulant, antiseptic, tonic, laxative, detoxicant, anti-inflammatory	Phototoxic, avoid during pregnancy and with epileptics, only use sweet fennel and not bitter fennel in aromatherapy

Table 11.4 (continued)

Essential oil	Latin name	Extraction	Uses	Properties	Caution
Frankincense (base note)	Botswellia carteri	Steam distillation of the tears of the resin produced by making incisions in the bark	Skincare (particularly ageing skin), acne, abscesses, scars, wounds, haemorrhoids, respiratory ailments such as asthma, bronchitis, coughs and catarrah, cystitis, painful menstruation, uterine bleeding outside menstruation, premenstrual syndrome, nervous tension and stress-related disorders	Anti-inflammatory, antiseptic, astringent, carminative, digestive, diuretic, emmenagoguic, expectorant, sedative and tonic	As the oil is an emmenagogue do not use in the first few months of pregnancy
Geranium (middle note)	Pelargonium ordoratissimum, Pelargonium robertianum	Steam distillation of the leaves, stalks and flowers	Burns, eczema, head lice, ringworm, cellulite, haemorrhoids, poor circulation, engorgements of the breasts, menopausal problems, premenstrual syndrome, nervous tension and stress-related disorders	Antidepressant, anti-inflammatory, antiseptic, astringent, deodorant, diuretic, fungicidal, stimulant of the adrenal cortex, tonic and vulnerary	May irritate sensitive skin
Ginger (base note)	Zingiber officinale	Distillation from dried ground root	Digestive, poor circulation, respiratory problems, muscular aches and pains	Warming effect on muscular system, stimulant, antiseptic, bactericidal, tonic	Use in low concentration, may cause irritation and skin sensitivity
Grapefruit	Citrus paradisi	Expressed from fruit peel	Respiratory problems, fluid retention, cellulite, depression and nervous exhaustion, acne and oily skin	Antiseptic, antitoxic, astringent, stimulant (lymphatic system), bactericidal, diuretic, calming, uplifting antidepressant	This oil oxidises quickly and once this occurs it can cause irritation
Jasmine (base note)	Jasminum officinale	Solvent extraction of the flower	Respiratory problems, menstrual pain, labour pain, depression, effective when used on scarring	Relaxing, relieves emotional stress and depression, antiseptic, aids childbirth (parturient),	Never use in pregnancy but can be used to

Essential oil	Latin name	Extraction	Uses	Properties	Caution
Jasmine (continued)				expectorant	help in labour, use in small amounts, very expensive
Juniper (middle note)	Juniperus communis	Steam distillation of the crushed, dried berries	Poor circulation, fluid retention, weeping eczema, wounds, cellulite, haemorrhoids, arthritic and rheumatic complaints, muscular aches and pains, loss of periods outside pregnancy, painful menstruation, cystitis, premenstrual syndrome nervous tension and stress-related disorders	Warming, helps to heal wounds, antiseptic, antispasmodic, astringent, carminative, diuretic, emmenagoguic, nervine, parasiticidal, sedative and tonic	Can be a skin irritant, avoid use during pregnancy, very stimulating so use sparingly, avoid with severe kidney disorders
Lavender (middle note)	Lavandula officinalis	Steam distillation from the flowery heads of the plant	Headaches, depression, digestive problems, menstrual pain, respiratory problems	Antiseptic, balancing, harmonising, promotes healing of burns, wounds and sores, bactericidal, decongestant, sedative, antidepressant, calming, soothing, builds up the immune system, diuretic, antibiotic, warming	Avoid in the first part of pregnancy
Lemon (top note)	Citrus limonia	Cold compression from the rind of the fruit. A distilled oil is also available	Oily skin, acne, boils, warts, chilblains, arthritis, high blood pressure, poor circulation, rheumatism, asthma, sore throats, bronchitis, catarrh, indigestion, colds and flu	Anti-rheumatic, antiseptic, antispasmodic, antitoxic, astringent, carminative, bactericidal, diuretic, hypotensive, insecticidal and tonic	Lemon like other citrus fruits is phototoxic

Table 11.4 (continued)

Essential oil	Latin name	Extraction	Uses	Properties	Caution
Lemongrass (top note)	Cymbopogon citratus	Steam distillation from the grass	General tonic, stimulates circulation in cellulite conditions, digestive problems, tired aching muscles, respiratory conditions, fatigue	Sedative, antiseptic, fungicidal, insect-repelling properties, antidepressant, bactericidal, tonic, headaches, stress, acne, skin infections	Can cause skin irritation and sensitisation therefore use in low dilutions
Marjoram (middle note)	Origanum majorana	Steam distillation from the dried flowering herb	Chilblains, bruises, arthritis, muscular aches and pains, sprains and strains, respiratory ailments, constipation, absence of periods outside pregnancy, painful menstruation, colds and flu, headaches, high blood pressure, insomnia, migraine, nervous tension and other stress-related disorders	Analgesic, antioxidant, antiseptic, bactericidal, carminative, digestive, emmenagoguic, expectorant, fungicidal, hypotensive, laxative, nervine, sedative and vasodilator	Avoid during pregnancy
Melissa (middle note)	Melissa officinalis	Steam distillation from leaves and tops	Insomnia, tension, stress, asthma, menstrual pain	Soothing, calming, good general tonic, uplifting and refreshing	Only buy Melissa officinalis – cheaper version
Neroli (base note)	Citrus aurantium	Steam distillation from the blooms	Stress, shock, muscular tension, nervousness, dry/sensitive skins, scars, stretch marks, acne, insomnia	Soothing, antiseptic, bactericidal, strengthens the nervous system, antidepressant, tonic	An expensive oil so beware of blended versions
Orange	Citrus aurantium sinensis	Expression of the outer rind	Colds, flu, digestive conditions, nervous tension and depression, insomnia, dry skin types	Antispasmodic, antiseptic, tonic, bactericidal, stimulant, antidepressant, mild sedative	Phototoxic

Essential oil	Latin name	Extraction	Uses	Properties	Caution
Patchouli	*Pogostemon cablin*	Steam distillation from the dried flowers	Fluid retention, poor circulation, muscular aches and pains, stress-related conditions. Particularly good for both bacterial and fungal skin infections	Anti-inflammatory, diuretic, sedative, antiseptic, fungicidal, astringent; this oil improves with age	Highly odiferous therefore use sparingly
Peppermint (top note)	*Mentha piperita*	Steam distillation of the flowering tops	Bruises, sprains and strains, swellings, ringworm, scabies, toothache, respiratory disorders, colic, indigestion, irritable bowel syndrome, nausea, colds and flu, fainting, headaches, mental fatigue and migraine	Analgesic, anti-inflammatory, antispasmodic, astringent, antiseptic, carminative, emmenagoguic, antiviral, expectorant, digestive, diuretic, hepatic, nervine, stimulant and sudorific	As the oil promotes menstruation avoid during the first few months of pregnancy. May irritate sensitive skin
Petitgrain (top note)	*Citrus aurantium var. amara*	Steam distillation of the leaves and twigs	Oily skin and hair, indigestion, flatulence, insomnia, premenstrual syndrome, nervous exhaustion and other stress-related disorders	Antiseptic, antispasmodic, deodorant, digestive, nervine and tonic	None
Rose (base note)	*Rosa damascene, Rosa centifolia*	Steam distillation or solvent extraction from the petals	Thread veins, conjunctivitis, eczema, palpitations, respiratory ailments, liver congestion, nausea, irregular menstruation, excessive menstruation, depression, insomnia, headaches, premenstrual syndrome, nervous tension and other stress-related disorders	Antiseptic, anti-inflammatory, antiviral, astringent, bactericidal, emmenagoguic, hepatic, laxative, sedative and tonic	*Rosa absoluta* is more likely to cause skin irritation on hypersensitive skin
Rosemary (middle note)	*Rosmarinus officinalis*	Steam distillation of the flowering tops	Oily skin, dandruff, to promote growth of healthy hair, head lice, insect repellent, scabies, respiratory ailments, muscular aches and pains, rheumatism, poor circulation, painful	Analgesic, antioxidants, anti-rheumatic, carminative, diuretic, emmenagoguic, fungicidal, hypertensive, parasiticidal, stimulant of the adrenal cortex and vulnerary	Avoid during pregnancy and do not use on anyone with high blood pressure.

Table 11.4 (continued)

Essential oil	Latin name	Extraction	Uses	Properties	Caution
Rosemary (continued)			menstruation, colds and flu, headaches, mental fatigue, depression, nervous exhaustion and other stress-related disorders		Rosemary can also trigger epileptic attacks and can irritate sensitive skin
Sandalwood (base note)	Santalum album	Steam distillation from the roots and heartwood	Acne, eczema, cracked and chapped lips, respiratory ailments, laryngitis, cystitis, nausea, insomnia, premenstrual syndrome, depression and other stress-related disorders	Antidepressant, anti-inflammatory, antiseptic, antispasmodic, astringent, bactericidal, carminative, diuretic, expectorant, fungicidal, insecticidal, tonic and sedative	Can cause dermatitis if applied neat on to the skin
Tea tree (top note)	Melaleuca hypericifolia	Steam distillation of the leaves and twigs	Acne, athlete's foot, abscesses, cold sores, dandruff, ringworm, warts, burns, wounds, insect bites and stings, respiratory ailments, colds and flu, thrush and cystitis. Can use directly on the skin	Antiseptic, anti-inflammatory, antibiotic, antiviral, fungicidal and parasiticidal	Some minor skin reactions have been reported on certain skin types
Thyme	Thymus vulgaris	Steam distillation from tops of flowers and leaves	Respiratory problems – asthma, catarrh, colds, flu, sore throats; cystitis; digestive problems – diarrhoea, flatulence; stress; cellulite	Antiseptic, astringent, diuretic, tonic, antitoxic, carminative, immunostimulant	Avoid during pregnancy or in cases of high blood pressure, may cause skin irritation and sensitisation
Ylang ylang (base note)	Cananga odorata	Distillation of the fresh flowers	Insomnia, anxiety, panic attacks, hormonal problems	Sedative, calming, aphrodisiac, antiseptic, tonic helps to build up immune system, hormone regulator, antidepressant	Can give headaches to client and/or therapist because of its sickly sweet smell. Can cause sensitisation

Carrier or fixed oils

Fixed oils are very different from essential oils. They are less volatile, hence their use as carrier oils.

Table 11.5 *Carrier oils*

Properties	Carrier oils	Essential oils
Smell	Very little smell	Pleasant
Volatility	Low	High
Soluble in alcohol	No	Yes
Viscosity	Medium	Low

Essential oils must be mixed with an oily medium before they are massaged into the skin. The skin will absorb fat-soluble substances more readily than water-based substances, therefore essential oils will be absorbed more efficiently if applied to the skin after being blended with a carrier oil. The most effective carrier oils for massage are vegetable based. Mineral oils such as baby oil are not suitable as the molecular structures are too large for them to penetrate through the epidermis.

Any vegetable oil can be used as a carrier oil but one that has been cold pressed and not processed is the most suitable, as it contains all the valuable nutrients for the body and will not adversely affect the properties of the essential oil it is blended with. Creams can also be used to blend essential oils prior to a massage and although a vegetable oil is more effective for this purpose, creams can be ideal on smaller areas such as the face, feet and hands.When a cream is used, it should ideally be non-perfumed and unmedicated. Less essential oil is needed when blending with base creams due to their denser consistency: use about one drop of essential oil per five grams of cream and blend with a glass rod.

Methods of extracting carrier oils

Solvent

Solvents such as petroleum are heated and washed through plant material dissolving any oil that is present. The solvents are evaporated, leaving the refined oil that will be suitable for aromatherapy massage.

Table 11.6 *Carrier oils for use in aromatherapy massage*

Carrier oil Extraction Colour	Latin name	Properties/uses	Caution
Almond oil Warm pressed	*Prunus dulcis*	Light textured. Particularly good for facial massage on dry, sensitive skins. [Almond trees that bear white blossoms produce bitter almonds and the pink blossoms produce sweet almonds]	
Aloe vera	*Aloe barbadenesis*	Soothing, anti-inflammatory properties. Good for sensitive skin types	Tends to be a low viscosity and therefore is blended with thicker oils to improve the texture for massage
Apricot kernel Pale yellow	*Persea americana*	Very nourishing, ideal for facial massage	
Avocado Green	*Prunus armeniaca*	Rich, heavy. Penetrates deep into the epidermis. Ideal for dry skin types. High in vitamin E	Thick oil, usually blended with other lighter carrier oils. Expensive
Evening primrose Pale yellow	*Oenothera biennis*	Ideal for irritated skin conditions like eczema. Particularly good for dry skin.	Very expensive
Grapeseed Pale yellow/green	*Vitis vinifera*	Inexpensive. Light can be used on all skin types	
Jojoba Cold pressed	*Simmondsia chinesis*	Semi-solid at room temperature, needs to be warmed in the hands	Very expensive, can be blended with cheaper oils
Macadamia nut oil Pale yellow	*Macadamia ternifolia*	Good for mature, dry skin as it easily absorbed. Slight odour	
Olive oils Cold pressed Green	*Olea europea*	Soothing	Quite thick, therefore needs to be blended with an oil with lighter properties prior to massaging
Rose hip oil Solvent Warm gold	*Rosa canina*		
Safflower oil Pale yellow	*Carthamus tictorius*	Light textured	Not a very stable oil, needs addition of an antioxidant, e.g. wheat germ to stop it from spoiling
Sunflower Pale yellow	*Helianthus annus*	Contains vitamin A, B, C, D and E	
Wheat germ Cold pressed Orange	*Triticum vulgare*	Heavy, rich in vitamins E and C. Particularly good for dry and mature skin types. Add to other blends, as it will prolong their shelf life	Avoid if client is allergic to wheat

Cold pressing

This is the method most desirable for extracting a carrier oil for use in aromatherapy. The plant is crushed using great pressure, literally squeezing the oil from the plant, leaving the pure, unrefined oil.

Health & safety

Always wear disposable gloves when blending oils so that your skin does not come into contact with neat essential oils.

Aromatherapy massage

Health & safety

It is essential that, during the consultation, you establish if the client has any contraindications that will prevent or restrict massage. (See Chapter 3.)

Consultation

Prior to carrying out any aromatherapy treatment, you should carry out a full consultation in much the same way as you would for a traditional body massage (see Chapter 3). It is beneficial to find out as much as you can about the client's lifestyle, for example whether they are under stress, how demanding their job is and how they cope with this, what their energy levels are like and whether they have any specific problems they would like you to address. You should also find out which, if any, essential oils they have used before.

Health & safety

Patch test
A patch test should ALWAYS be carried out 24 hours prior to the treatment being carried out. This will determine if the client is suitable for the treatment.

Procedure
Ensure that the client's skin is clean and apply an essential oil blend (two drops of essential oil in 2ml of carrier oil) to the crook of the client's elbow. If the client experiences redness, swelling or itching to the area they must inform the clinic immediately. If contra-actions occur the treatment must not be carried out.

As with body massage, it is essential that you have their personal and medical details prior to any treatment and that the consultation card is signed by the client. Use the consultation as an opportunity to build a good rapport with your client and to put them at ease.

Do not forget to use open-ended questions and encourage the client to ask questions. You should find out their reasons for seeking treatment, their expectations from the treatment and discuss and agree a treatment plan during the consultation.

At the end of the consultation, you should identify the oils to be used in the treatment. Since essential oils work synergistically, it is most effective to choose one base, one middle and one top note oil. This is not essential, however, and on occasions you may wish to use only one oil.

Blending oils

After the consultation has taken place and the oils have been identified, you should select the appropriate oils to suit the client's requirements.

For this unit you are required to use pre-blended aromatherapy oils to meet the client's needs:

- For body massage the oils should be mixed using one drop of essential oil to each 2ml of carrier oil, i.e for 10ml of carrier oil five drops of essential oils should be used.
- For facial massage one drop of essential oil should be used for every 4ml of carrier oil.

Oils can be used in various ways to help the client feel as follows:

Uplifted	Relaxed	A sense of well-being
Eucalyptus	Camomile Roman	Camomile Roman
Grapefruit	Clary sage	Clary sage
Lemon	Geranium	Geranium
Lemongrass	Lavender	Lavender
Rosemary	Marjoram	Neroli
Tea tree	Neroli	Rose
	Rose	Ylang ylang
	Ylang ylang	

General contraindications to aromatherapy body massage:

- radiotherapy patients
- chemotherapy patients
- pregnancy
- immediately after a heat treatment such as steam bath or sauna treatment
- before or after alcohol consumption
- in the presence of cuts and abrasions
- contagious diseases and disorders
- fever
- varicose veins.

Treatment procedure

Having greeted the client, carried out a full consultation and agreed a treatment plan with which you and the client are both happy, you should instruct your client to undress and assist them on to the massage couch, if necessary. You should then blend the oils and wash your hands prior to commencing treatment. Once you have applied the aromatherapy massage techniques in accordance with the client's requirements (see later), you should give the client homecare advice, not forgetting to ask the client if they have any questions. You should use this opportunity to evaluate the treatment as discussed in Chapter 3. You should then assist the client from the massage couch and leave them to shower and dress. While they are doing this, you should add any comments to the client's record card, including oils used and homecare advice given, and make their next appointment if appropriate.

Techniques

The massage techniques used in aromatherapy massage are designed to get the oils into the body, warm the body so the oils are more easily absorbed into the skin and relax the client.

There are three types of massage that can be used.

Shiatsu

Shiatsu massage employs a range of oriental massage techniques. The strokes relate to the energy pathways within the body. An adapted form of shiatsu is often incorporated into the aromatherapy massage. The techniques used are long flowing strokes applied to the meridian lines or *tsubo* (pressure points). These are applied very firmly.

Neuromuscular

This massage technique is designed to stimulate the nerves. The strokes are firmer and applied in the direction of the sensory nerve roots rather than in the direction of the blood and lymph flow.

Swedish

This type of massage includes the following techniques:

- effleurage
- petrissage
- tapotement
- vibrations.

These are used to increase the blood and lymph circulation and can either relax or stimulate the client. This massage is the focus of the rest of this chapter.

Order of work

It is always better to start on the back, as this is the largest area and the oils will begin to penetrate through the skin into the bloodstream very quickly.

You should then progress in the following order:

- back
- backs of legs
- neck and chest
- face (optional)
- arms
- abdomen
- fronts of legs.

Checklist

Equipment check

✓ Treatment couch
✓ Towels
✓ Pillows
✓ Trolley
✓ Client's footstool – to assist the
   client to step onto the treatment couch
✓ Stool
✓ Bowls
✓ Tissues
✓ Record card/pen
✓ Gown
✓ Cleansing lotion – to remove
   client's makeup prior to the treatment
✓ Damp cotton wool – to gently wipe
   away the client's makeup
✓ Toner – to freshen the client's
   skin after cleansing
✓ A range of essential oils and carrier oils
✓ Glass measuring jug – to ensure that the
   quantity of carrier oil is accurate
✓ Blending bottles – ensure that the
   essential oil and carrier oils are
   thoroughly blended. These can
   also store the remaining oil after
   treatment and can be given to the
   client to take home
✓ Bin

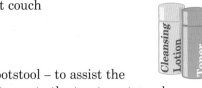

Client Record Card

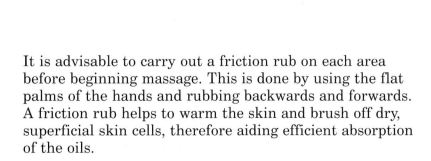

Eau De Cologne

It is advisable to carry out a friction rub on each area before beginning massage. This is done by using the flat palms of the hands and rubbing backwards and forwards. A friction rub helps to warm the skin and brush off dry, superficial skin cells, therefore aiding efficient absorption of the oils.

Procedure

Back

1   Apply oil.

2   In the stride standing position, perform friction rub.

3   Effleurage/reverse effleurage – standing at the client's head, effleurage from the back of the neck down either side of the spine, across the base of the back and back up to the starting position. (6 times)

4   Effleurage downwards – standing at the side of the client in the walk standing position, start from the base of the back and effleurage up either side of the spine, across the shoulders and back down to the starting position. (6 times)

5   Deep reinforced kneading – standing behind the client in the stride standing position, place one hand on top of the other and massage first around one scapula and then the other in one flowing movement forming a figure of eight. (10 times, very slowly)

6   Flat-handed kneading – starting at one shoulder, in walk standing, place hands side by side and knead together, compressing the tissue between the hands. Work hands down to base of the back and slide back up to the starting position. Move slightly towards the trapezius area and work down again to the base of the back. Continue until all the back has been covered. It usually it takes about 3/4 goes to do this. (3 times)

7   Reinforced kneading to the trapezius (ironing movement) – walk standing, starting at one shoulder, place one hand on top of the other and knead the tissues. Work down to the base of the back, then slide the hands back up and move slightly towards the trapezius area and work down again to the base of the back. Continue until all the back has been covered. (3 times)

8   Kneading the intercostal nerves – walk standing, starting at the base of the spine with one hand on either side of the spine, start to work outwards with both hands simultaneously. Using the first and middle fingers of each hand, knead in tiny circles, working gradually to the sides of the body. Slide fingers back to original position then move up slightly and repeat. When fingers reach the ribs, the kneading should continue in between the ribs on the intercostal nerves and fingers slide back on the rib. Continue until you reach the occiput. (2 times)

9   Single-handed stroking to intercostal nerves – stride standing, start at the bottom of spine using the

whole hand alternately stroke away from the spine in the direction of intercostal nerves. Stroke down one side of spine and then repeat on the other side. (2 times)

10   Thumb kneading to erector spinae – walk standing, starting at base of spine, place thumbs one in front of the other on the erector spinae. Slowly circle thumbs, moving up the muscle. Repeat on the other side. (3 times)

11   Double-handed stroking to intercostal nerves – walk standing, place both hands on either side of spine gently stroke both hands out simultaneously in the direction of the intercostal nerves. Repeat movement while working down towards the base of spine. (3 times)

12   Repeat Steps 3 and 4.

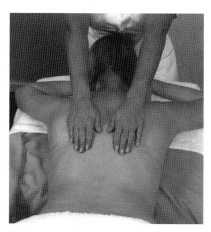

Reverse effleurage, step 3

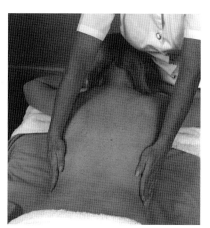

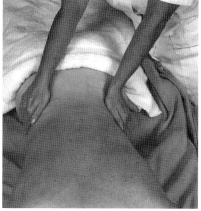

Effleurage downwards, step 4

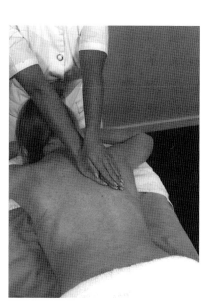

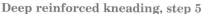

Deep reinforced kneading, step 5

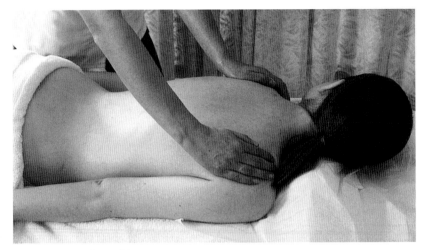

Flat-handed kneading, step 6

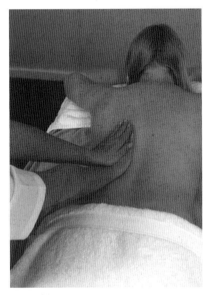

Reinforced kneading to the trapezius, step 7

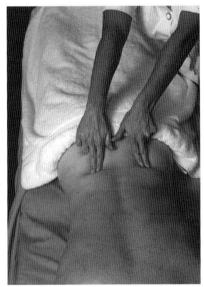

Kneading to the intercostal nerves, step 8

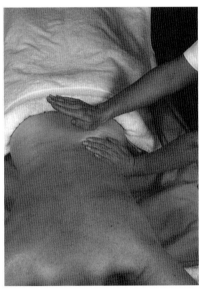

Single-handed stroking to the intercostal nerves, step 9

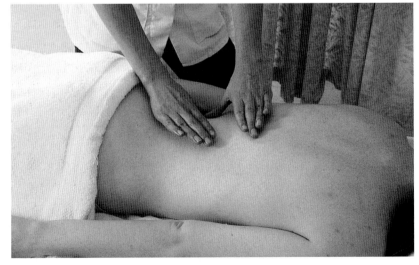

Thumb kneading to erector spinae, step 10

Backs of legs

1 Apply oil.

2 Stride standing, perform friction rub.

3 **a** Effleurage – in the walk standing position and using the whole of the hands, effleurage the whole leg starting from the toes working up to the gluteals. (3 times)

3 **b** In the stride standing position and starting with one hand on the Achilles' tendon and the other on popliteal glands, slide both hands up the leg together towards the gluteal fold. When the hands reach the gluteal fold, lift off and start again from the Achilles' tendon, with both hands sliding up at the same time. One hand should always remain in contact with the client. (6 times)

4 Alternate handed kneading – walk standing, starting at the top of thigh, hands on either side, knead the tissues in an alternate movement. Work down to and including the foot. Pressure should be applied on the upward movement. (3 times)

5 Covering the whole area, stride standing, pick up and wring the hamstrings. (3 times)

6 Effleurage to lower leg – stride standing, elevate the leg with one hand supporting the ankle. Stroke firmly with the other hand down towards the popliteal glands. Lift off and repeat. (6 times)

7 Thumb kneading – walk standing, work upwards to the popliteal glands and back to Achilles' tendon. (3 times)

8 Thumb stroking sciatic nerve – walk standing, place both thumbs one in front of the other on the Achilles' tendon and slide gently up the centre of the calf towards the popliteal glands. Slide back to starting position. (6 times)

9 Repeat Steps 3 a and/or b.

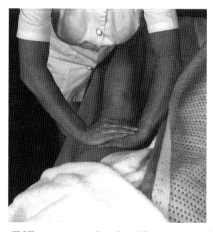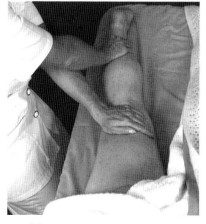

Effleurage to back of legs, steps 3a and b

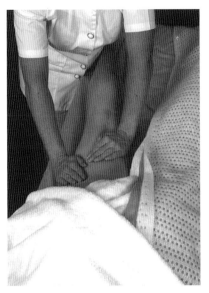

Alternate handed kneading, step 4

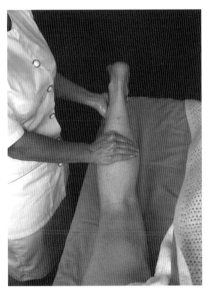

Effleurage to lower leg, step 6

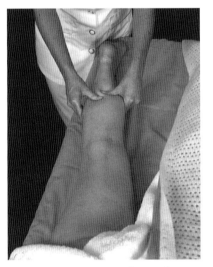

Thumb kneading to lower leg, step 7

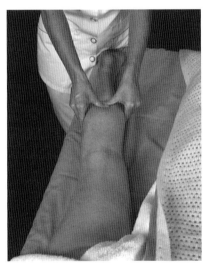

Thumb stroking sciatic nerve, step 8

Neck and chest

1 Apply oil.

2 Stand at head, effleurage to chest, shoulders, back of neck and scalp. In the walk standing position, place both hands on the sternum and effleurage out across the chest, behind the shoulders, up the back of the neck and behind the scalp if desired. Slide back gently muscles to starting position over sternocleidomastoid. (2 times)

3 Knuckling to chest, shoulders and back of neck – standing behind client, place both hands in relaxed fists

with the fingers underneath the hand onto the sternum. Using circular movements, knead out across the chest, behind the shoulders, over the upper trapezius area and back of the neck. Slide gently back to the starting position. (2 times)

4 Alternate stroking – in the stride standing position, apply alternate stroking across the chest from axilla to axilla. Ensure one hand starts as the other hand is lifting off. (6 times)

5 Double-handed kneading – remaining in the same area, stride standing, perform double-handed kneading, adapting the pressure to suit the client.

6 Repeat Step 2.

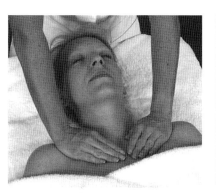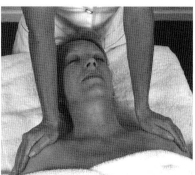

Effleurage to chest, back of neck and shoulders, step 2

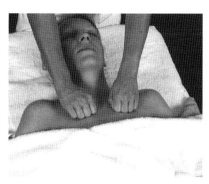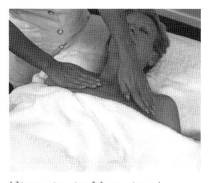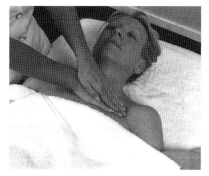

Knuckling to chest, shoulders and back of neck, step 3

Alternate stroking, step 4

Double-handed kneading, step 5

Tip

If the client is wearing makeup and would like a face massage, makeup must be removed first.

Holistic face (optional)

If you are going to massage the face and scalp, a different essential oil and carrier oil may be used to suit the client's skin type. Remember to use only one drop of essential oil for every 4ml of carrier oil when blending.

Stand behind the client in the stride standing position throughout the treatment:

1   Effleurage scalp – place both hands on hairline above the forehead and start to firmly effleurage over the scalp, moving a little further out each time to ensure that all the scalp is covered.

2   Finger kneading to scalp – starting at the temple, use the fingertips to slowly but firmly knead the scalp all over. This movement is similar to that made when shampooing the hair, but with a slower action.

3   Repeat Step 1 a further three times.

4   Effleurage to neck – place both hands on the sternum and effleurage up the neck to the chin, out across the jawline and gently back to starting position.

5   Effleurage across chin:

   a   Supporting the side of the head with one hand, apply a smooth effleurage stroke with the other hand from one angle of the jaw to the other. Swap hands and repeat on the other side. (4 times)

   b   Place hands on the jaw move up over cheeks to the temples. Circle temples and slide back down to starting position. (3 times)

6   One-finger effleurage around lips – with the ring fingers of both hands placed beneath the centre of the lower lip, apply a light effleurage stroke around the mouth to the nose. Take the fingers off the skin and repeat the movement three times.

7   Effleurage from nose to ears:

   a   Place the first and middle finger of each hand on either side of the nostrils. With a light, even pressure work across the cheeks and beneath the cheekbones to the ear. (3 times)

   b   Place both middle fingers on the bridge of the nose one in front of the other and stroke alternately down the nose. (6 times)

8   Circle around eyes – place both thumbs on the forehead with one hand placed on the side of the head for support. With the fingers of the other hand, circle around the eyes towards the nose. (3 times)

   Keeping the thumbs in contact with the skin, support the other side of the head with the fingers of the free hand. (3 times)

   Repeat the whole of this step twice more.

9   Alternate stroking to forehead – place one hand on the forehead and stroke from the eyebrows to the hairline

using slow, controlled effleurage movement. Repeat with alternative hands, covering the whole forehead.

10 Place both hands, fingers facing each other, on the forehead and at the same time stroke out to the temples. (3 times)

11 Finish by applying gentle pressure to the temples.

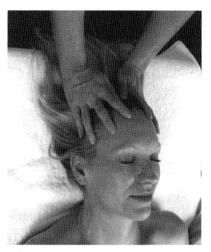

Effleurage to scalp, step 1

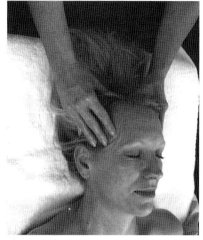

Finger kneading to scalp, step 2

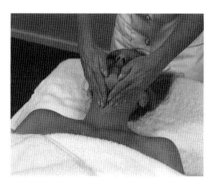

Effleurage to neck, step 4

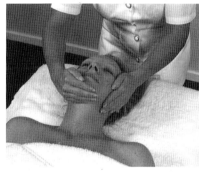

Effleurage across chin, step 5a

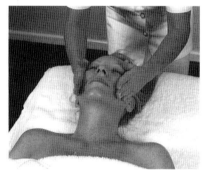

Effleurage across chin, step 5b

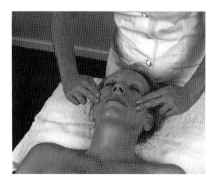

Effleurage from nose to ears, step 7a

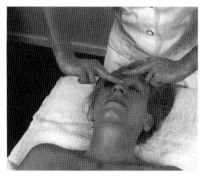

Effleurage down nose, step 7b

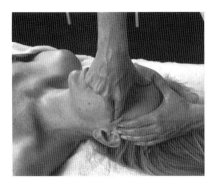

Circle around eyes, step 8

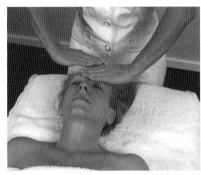

Alternate stroking to forehead, step 9

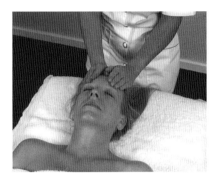

Alternate stroking to forehead, step 10

Arms

1 Apply oil.

2 Perform friction rub in the stride standing position.

3 Effleurage to the whole arm – walk standing, starting from tips of fingers, effleurage to the shoulders and back to starting position using each hand alternately. (6 times)

4 Effleurage elbow to shoulder – walk standing. (6 times)

5 Kneading – walk standing, using both hands, cup the deltoid and knead the area alternately. (10 times)

6 Picking up biceps and triceps – stride standing, using both hands alternately, pick up the tissues of the biceps and triceps. (3 times)

7 Picking up forearm – using both hands alternately, pick up tissues of forearm. (3 times)

8 Finger kneading – walk standing, apply circular movements to the elbow with one hand while using the other hand to support the elbow.

9 Thumb kneading to the forearm – walk standing, covering the whole area. (3 times)

10 Effleurage to hand – walk standing, alternate from finger tips to wrist. (6 times)

11 Thumb kneading:

   a Apply thumb kneading to the palms. (3 times)

   b Apply thumb kneading to the back of the hand. (3 times)

   c Apply thumb kneading to the wrist bone. (6 times)

   d Apply thumb kneading to the tendons on top of the hand. (3 times)

12 Repeat Step 3.

Effleurage to whole arm, step 3

Effleurage elbow to shoulder, step 4

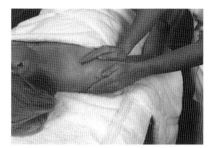

Kneading, step 5

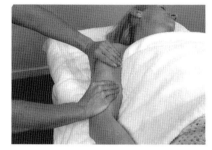

Picking up over forearm, biceps and triceps, step 6

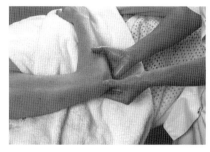

Picking up forearm, step 8

Thumb kneading to forearm, step 9

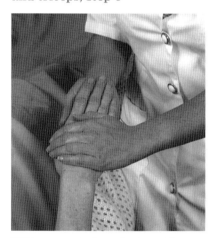

Effleurage to hand, step 10

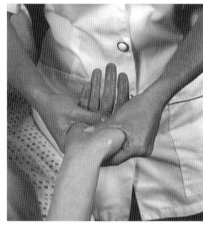

Thumb kneading to palm, step 11a

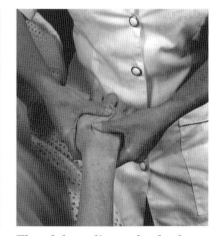

Thumb kneading to back of hand, step 11b

Thumb kneading to wrist bone, step 11c

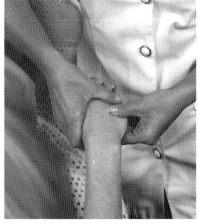

Thumb kneading to tendons on top of hand, step 11d

Abdomen

1 Apply oil.

2 Diamond effleurage – in the walk standing position, place both hands on the abdomen just below sternum. Stroke out to the waist then inwards towards pubic bone. Repeat this stroke in reverse. (3 times)

3 Single-handed stroking to rectus abdominus – in the walk standing position, place one hand below the sternum and apply a smooth stroke down the rectus abdominus. Repeat using alternate hands. (6 times)

4 Alternate kneading to abdominal walls – in the walk standing position, place hands either side of waist just below ribcage. Using circular movements, knead down towards the hip. (6 times)

5 Finger circles to abdomen – in the stride standing position and with one hand on top of the other, gently apply finger circles to the navel. (3 times)

6 Finger kneading to colon (optional) – apply gentle pressure up the ascending colon (walk standing), across the transverse (stride standing) and down the descending colon (walk standing). (2 times **only**)

7 Repeat Step 2.

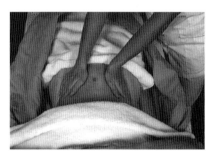 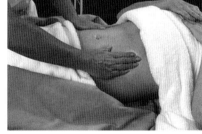

Diamond effleurage to abdomen, step 2

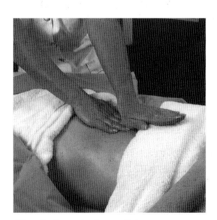 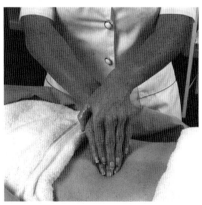 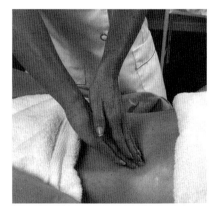

Single-handed stroking to rectus abdominus, step 3

Finger circles to abdomen, step 5

Finger kneading to colon, step 6

Fronts of legs

1   Apply oil.

2   In the stride standing position, perform friction rub.

3   Effleurage whole leg – starting at the toes, walk standing, use whole hands and effleurage up the whole anterior aspect of leg, finishing off at the inguinal glands. (3 times)

4   Alternate kneading to whole leg – starting at the top of thigh, walk standing, with hands on either side of leg, knead the tissues in an alternate movement, working down to the foot, include the plantar aspect of the foot. (3 times)

5   Reverse diagonal effleurage – with your back to the client, walk standing, stroke from the medial aspect of the knee across the thigh using alternate hands. Perform with light pressure. (6 times)

6   Double-handed kneading to thigh – walk standing, keeping your back to the client and with your hands on either side of the thigh just above knees, knead the tissues applying firm pressure. Work towards the top of the leg. (3 times)

7   Finger or thumb kneading around knee – walk standing, using first two fingers or both thumbs, apply small circular movements around the patella. (3 times)

8   Thumb kneading to tibialis anterior – walk standing, starting just below the knee and using the thumb, apply small circular kneading movements to the tibialis anterior. Work towards the ankle. (3 times)

9   Apply effleurage from toes to the ankle, walk standing. (6 times)

10 Cross-thumb kneading:

    a   Stand at the bottom of the massage couch in the stride standing position. With the fingers of both hands supporting the plantar surface of the foot and the thumbs on the dorsal surface, firmly zigzag thumbs back and forth covering the whole surface, up to the ankles.

    b   With fingers of both hands supporting the dorsal surface and thumbs on the plantar surface, firmly zigzag thumbs back and forth.

11 Palm kneading to sole of foot – walk standing, support the foot on the dorsal aspect with one hand, use the other hand to apply deep circular kneading to the plantar surface of the foot. Movements should be deep and slow. (3 times)

12 Kneading around the ankle bones – walk standing, using the first two fingers of both hands, circle around the ankle bones using small circular movements. (10 times)

13 Walk standing, apply thumb frictions in between tendons on top of the foot.

14 Repeat Step 3 six times.

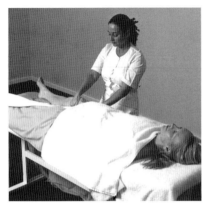

Perform friction rub in walk standing, step 2

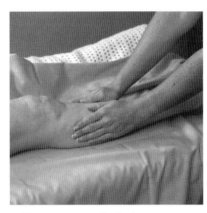

Effleurage to whole leg, step 3

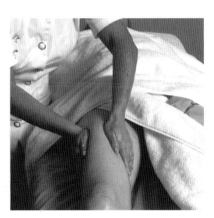

Alternate kneading to whole leg, step 4

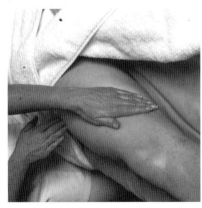

Reverse diagonal stroking across thigh, step 5

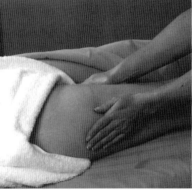

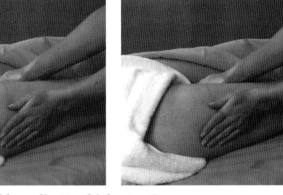

Double-handed kneading to thigh, step 6

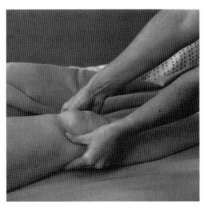

Thumb kneading behind knee, step 7

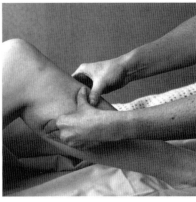

Thumb kneading to tibialis anterior, step 8

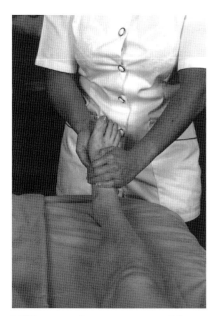

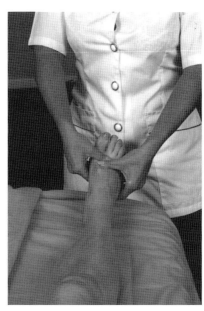

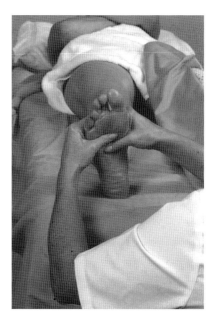

Effleurage from toes to ankles, step 9

Cross-thumb kneading, steps 10a and b

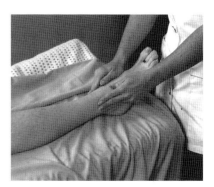

Palm kneading to sole of foot, step 11

Kneading around the ankle bones, step 12

Contra-actions to aromatherapy

● Some essential oils bring about extreme relaxation and can make the client drowsy. Clients who react in this way should be advised not to drive home or operate any machinery until they feel sufficiently alert to do so.

● Certain essential oils may cause some clients to experience headaches or feelings of light-headedness.

It is essential that you ask the client to report any adverse effects immediately so that notes not to use these oils in any future treatment can be added to the client's record card.

Tip

Remember that if the product has a short shelf life, it should not be ordered in large quantities unless it is a popular product that sells quickly.

Retailing

Whether an aromatherapist is self-employed using a room in a clinic or at home or working in a large clinic with many other practitioners, she can only carry out so many treatments in a working week. This means that there will always be a maximum amount of money that it will be possible to earn. Taking away the costs incurred on the premises (heat, lighting, oils etc.) and deducting tax and national insurance, this will always remain the same unless the number of clients decreases.

Retailing can be introduced to increase earnings, while still working the same number of hours and treating the same number of clients. Although aromatherapy is a caring profession, the aromatherapist still needs to earn a living!

It is essential to choose the right manufacturers or to sell your own-blended products. Own blended products can be made personal to the client and you know exactly what has gone into the products, but it can prove to be very time consuming to decide on the ingredients and messy to blend, with no national advertising campaigns and no quality control systems in place.

Ready-made products will usually have a recognised brand name, good advertising systems in place and a wide range of products. They do, however, tend to be costly when the minimum orders are imposed. Also, the aromatherapist cannot know exactly what the products contain.

Once the aromatherapist has decided what products are going to be sold in the place of work, a retail display needs to be organised, displaying all the products available for the clients to see. Each product needs to be labelled, clearly stating the price.

Knowledge review

1 Explain the properties of an essential oil.

2 Describe the differences between top, middle and base note essential oils.

3 Why should you not use a product that has reached its expiry date?

4 How do essential oils enter the body?

5 How is the olfactory system affected by the inhalation of aromatherapy oils?

6 Describe three physiological effects of essential oils on the body.

7 What are the risks of using an undiluted oil on the skin?

8 Why is it important to ensure that records are kept accurate and up to date?

9 What carrier oil would be most suitable for a client with eczema?

10 State four contraindications to essential oils.

11 State three conditions that would affect the choice of carrier oil.

12 Name four oils that could achieve the following effects:

- relaxing
- uplifting
- sense of well-being.

13 Why is it important to determine the client's lifestyle pattern prior to the treatment being carried out?

14 Give two conditions that would require adaptation of the treatment.

15 Why is it important to agree the content of the client's consultation record before asking the client to sign the record?

16 Explain how you could help your client relax during the treatment preparation.

17 How is the quantity of oil selected for the client?

18 Why is it important to use the correct quantity of oil?

19 Why is a patch test carried out?

20 Explain briefly why it is important to agree the treatment objectives prior to treatment planning.

21 Explain briefly how you could identify whether or not a client is satisfied with the treatment.

22 What is the commercially acceptable time for a full body aromatherapy massage?

23 How does massage help with the penetration of the oils?

24 Give two risks associated with using essential oils that have not been diluted.

25 How could the client use aromatherapy oils at home?

26 Explain three different massage techniques that can be used in aromatherapy body massage.

27 List the equipment and material required for an aromatherapy full body massage.

28 Briefly explain how you would prepare the treatment area.

29 Why is it important to have everything to hand during the treatment?

30 Give three products that may be recommended to the client for retail following the aromatherapy massage treatment.

31 Explain why it is important for the client's record card to be kept up to date on the essential oil blends used for treatment.

Body massage case studies

12

This chapter offers a selection of case studies representative of those that you might come across while practising body massage, Indian head massage and aromatherapy body massage. They demonstrate the effectiveness of massage and give an insight into the kind of feedback you can expect from clients. Each of the following case studies covers a period of four treatments.

Body massage

Case study 1

Gender: Female

Age: 47 years

Occupation: Nurse

Reasons for treatment: High blood pressure and pain in left shoulder

Frequency of visits: Once a week, due to time constraints arising from working a shift pattern

General information:

- Marion works as a nurse in a community home for psychiatric patients. Her job is very demanding, both mentally and physically and she has to work shifts that include night duty. On some occasions, her feet swell due to long periods of standing.
- Marion is quite fit and tends to do a lot of walking when she has the time.
- During the consultation, I discovered Marion had high blood pressure and therefore requested permission from her doctor for massage treatment. When she returned the following week, she had a letter from her doctor giving his consent for massage, as he thought this would be beneficial to her.

First treatment:

- A full body massage was carried out, omitting tapotement movements, as Marion had stated she wanted a relaxing and not a stimulating massage.
- Her left shoulder was very tender. This turned out to be tension nodules, which I only worked on for a short time (to try and disperse the tension), as Marion found the area very tender. Conversation revealed that this condition was probably at least partially due to lifting at work so at the end of the session, we discussed lifting techniques.
- Despite being extremely apprehensive at the start, Marion said that she thoroughly enjoyed the massage.

Outcome of first treatment: At the second session, Marion reported that after the first session, she became very conscious every time she lifted anything heavy at work and made a special effort to do it correctly, which seemed to have helped the shoulder. She reported that after the massage her shoulder was extremely sore for a few days, but after this had passed, she noticed an improvement.

Second treatment: I carried out the full massage, concentrating on the left shoulder for a little longer than the previous treatment, as this seemed to have increased her mobility slightly.

Outcome of second treatment: Marion reported that the shoulder was not as painful at the beginning of the week, but as the week went on it started to niggle slightly.

Third treatment: Marion's shoulder seemed to be a lot better. The mobility had increased, and it was not as painful. I still spent more time massaging the shoulder area, which was beginning to feel a lot more supple.

Outcome of third treatment: Marion felt her shoulder had greatly improved.

Fourth treatment: Another full massage treatment was carried out, still omitting any stimulating movements. There was no need to spend any extra time on the shoulder as it had improved considerably. During this massage I spent more time on Marion's legs, as her feet were very swollen from being on them for long periods of time since work had been very hectic. Lymph drainage was applied to reduce the oedema.

Conclusion:

- Marion felt she was no longer feeling stressed at work particularly in the first few days following a massage. If she felt herself getting worked up, she would practise breathing exercises.
- Marion continued to be aware of correct lifting techniques at work and this has prevented any further problems with her shoulder.
- Marion continues to have a weekly massage.

Case study 2

Gender: Female

Age: 62 years

Occupation: Retired teacher

Reasons for treatment: Car accident a few years ago and arthritis

Frequency of visits: Once a week

General information:

- Shirley was involved in a bad car accident in 1997 when a car ran into the back of hers. She received injuries to her neck and clavicle for which she had physiotherapy. This treatment ended in 1998.

- Her neck still becomes quite painful and she still has problems turning her head. As a result of the accident and her arthritis, her mobility has been greatly reduced.

First treatment: The first massage was a very gentle one, eliminating all tapotement movements. She particularly enjoyed the hand massage as her joints did not feel as stiff.

Outcome of first treatment: Shirley reported that she slept very well that evening and her arthritis felt a little easier.

Second treatment: I performed a full massage, slightly firmer than for the first treatment but still not applying any tapotement movements. I spent more time on the neck area.

Outcome of second treatment: Shirley felt she had a little more mobility in her neck and said that it did not seem as 'creaky'.

Third treatment: I applied paraffin wax to the hands, feet and the neck area prior to carrying out a full massage, paying particular attention to these areas during the massage.

Outcome of third treatment: Shirley reported that she felt a definite improvement, particularly in her neck and hands which were not as painful. Her neck seemed to have regained most of its mobility.

Fourth treatment: Again, I applied the paraffin wax prior to the massage. I carried out a firm massage concentrating on the hands, feet and neck areas.

Conclusion:

- Shirley reports feeling far more relaxed and her pain has eased.

- She now uses paraffin wax on herself in between each massage, as it brings a lot of pain relief to her arthritic joints. She still continues to have the wax applied to her neck and cervical vertebrae prior to the massage.

- Her neck now has more mobility and she can now turn her head from side to side, although it is still a little stiff from time to time.

- Shirley continues to have a full massage every week.

Case study 3

Gender: Male

Age: 45 years

Occupation: Lecturer

Reasons for treatment: Very stressed and tired

Frequency of visits: Twice a week

General information:

- Stuart has a very stressful job with a lot of responsibility. At present he is feeling very tense and down.
- He is also suffering from stomach ache, through stress-related constipation.

First treatment: Stuart was extremely apprehensive about the treatment and not really looking forward to having a massage. On this first treatment I massaged:

- His stomach, as he was not in any pain, concentrating on the colon to try to alleviate the constipation.
- His back and, once he was facing down, he seemed to relax more. The shoulder and neck region were very tight to the touch with a lot of tension nodules present. I used lots of stroking and kneading movements to stretch and relax these muscles.

All the movements were carried out slowly and firmly avoiding all stimulating manipulations. At the end of the treatment Stuart was very relaxed and reported feeling quite 'high'.

Outcome of first treatment: Stuart said that after the treatment he had gone to bed early that evening and slept really well.

Second treatment: As Stuart did not feel as self-conscious, I performed a full body massage, still concentrating on the stomach, the neck and shoulders. Once the back massage started, he fell asleep. After the treatment had finished, he was very relaxed.

Outcome of second treatment: Stuart reported his constipation had started to alleviate itself and he was not getting as worked up. As he was now sleeping better, he was better able to cope at work.

Third treatment: I performed a full massage, again concentrating on the stomach and upper back areas.

Outcome of third treatment: Stuart reported that he felt extremely well. He was sleeping very well, having broken the routine of only sleeping for a few hours each night and was not having any bowel problems.

Fourth treatment: I carried out a full massage treatment. The tension seemed to have dispersed from the upper back region and was now feeling quite soft and pliable. Once again, Stuart fell asleep when I was massaging his back.

Conclusion:

- Stuart's treatment now continues on a regular weekly basis. If he feels that he is getting worked up, he has a massage in between regular treatments, but this is occurring less and less frequently.
- He feels he can cope better with work and has not been constipated for quite a long time and so is not experiencing any abdominal pain.

Case study 4

Gender: Male

Age: 25 years

Occupation: Office worker

Reasons for treatment: Lack of energy and feeling of debilitation

Frequency of visits: Once a week

General information:

- After carrying out a full consultation, there was clearly no medical indication as to why Alan was so lacking in energy. He felt he needed a boost.
- Once he got home from work he just lay in front of the television and then went to bed, feeling too tired to do anything else.

First treatment: Alan was looking forward to his massage. I carried out a full massage, using very light and quick movements particularly percussion and tapotement movements. After the massage Alan said he felt very refreshed.

Outcome of first treatment: Even though Alan still continued to sit in front of the television each night, he reported that he did feel better.

Second treatment: I carried out the same massage as the previous week and again Alan said he felt quite invigorated.

Outcome of second treatment: Alan had been out for a walk on two nights the previous week, as he had felt restless.

Third treatment: Once again, I carried out a full body massage using light and quick movements, particularly percussion and tapotement.

Outcome of third treatment: Alan informed me that after his previous massage he had not gone straight home but had gone swimming, something he had not done for years. He is also considering joining some colleagues from work to play five-a-side football twice a week. He does not think that he is up to this yet, but is going to build himself up to it.

Conclusion:

- Alan still continues to walk and swim each week.
- He has a full body massage once a month.

Aromatherapy body massage

Case study 1

Gender: Female

Age: 20 years

Occupation: Customer services adviser

Reasons for treatment: Headaches and stiffness in upper and lower back region

Frequency of visits: Once a week

General information:

- Tracy works as a customer services adviser and sits at a desk for most of the day.
- Her job is quite stressful as she is answering the telephone most of the day, dealing with difficult customers.
- Tracy is otherwise fit and healthy.

First treatment: consultaltion:

- During consultation, Tracy was rather tense and unsure as she had never had an aromatherapy treatment before and did not know what it entailed.

- I selected oils for anxiety, stress and headaches: pre-blended oils of camomile and jasmine, blended with almond oil
  - camomile for its tension-releasing and calming properties
  - jasmine for its relaxing properties
  - almond oils as Tracy had slightly dry and sensitive skin.
- A full body aromatherapy massage was carried out.

First treatment:

- Tracy's shoulders were very tight with lots of tension nodules. As the area was very tender I worked for a short time to try and disperse the tension.
- The lower back was also very tight and conversation revealed that this was probably due to the way she was sitting at her desk when working.
- At the end of the massage, we discussed her posture and correct sitting techniques.
- Despite being extremely tense and apprehensive at the start of treatment, Tracy said she had thoroughly enjoyed the treatment.

Outcome of first treatment: At the second session Tracy reported that after the first session she became very conscious of her posture when sitting at her desk at work and now made a special effort to sit correctly. Tracy reported that the day after the treatment she felt quite tender particularly in the shoulder area.

Second treatment:

- Tracy reported that her headaches had much improved but she was still feeling very lethargic and quite stressed.
- Oils selected: basil, lavender and jasmine, pre-blended in almond oil.
  - basil for muscular aches and pains and anxiety
  - lavender for headaches
  - jasmine for relaxation.
- I carried out a full aromatherapy massage, concentrating on the shoulders and lower back for a little longer than the previous treatment.

Outcome of second treatment: Tracy reported her shoulders and lower back were not as painful at the beginning of the week, but as the week went on they started to ache slightly.

Third treatment: Tracy's shoulders and back seemed to be a lot better. Mobility had increased and the area was not as painful. I decided to use the same the oils as the previous week. The area was now beginning to feel a lot more supple.

Outcome of third treatment: Tracy felt her shoulders, in particular, had greatly improved and did not ache as much.

Fourth treatment: Another full aromatherapy massage was carried out using the same oils. Tracy's headaches had ceased altogether and there was far less tension in her shoulders and lower back area. Tracy has decided to continue having her weekly massage session and continues to check her posture at work when sitting at her desk.

Conclusion:

- I advised Tracy to use pre-blended peppermint oil in the bath before going to bed, to try and help with her mental fatigue and headaches.

Case study 2

Gender: Female

Age: 30 years

Occupation: Full-time hairdresser working in a busy hairdressing salon

Reasons for treatment: Aching legs and back due to being on her feet all day long

General information: Gill has recently been made manager of the salon, and is working extremely hard to ensure that everything runs smoothly

Frequency of visits: Once a week

Objective: Relaxation, and to ease general aches and pains resulting from work

First treatment:

- Choice of oils: eucalyptus, lavender and ginger, blended in grapeseed:
    - eucalyptus to aid poor circulation, muscular aches and pains
    - lavender for its calming, soothing, balancing, harmonising properties
    - ginger for its warming effect, and to aid poor circulation
    - grapeseed, which is light, so can be used for all skin types.

- Gill was really looking forward to the treatment, particularly as she had not had much time to relax recently.

- I found that Gill's trapezius muscle was very high and her ankles were slightly swollen. I therefore concentrated on the back region and drainage of the lower legs and ankles.

Outcome of first treatment: Gill said that she felt extremely tired that evening and went to bed early, but felt very refreshed the next day.

Second treatment: Gill was really looking forward to her treatment.

- Choice of oils: I concentrated on choosing oils suitable for general aches, lymphatic drainage as ankles still swollen and relaxation: eucalyptus, rosemary and sandalwood mixed in grapeseed oil:
  - rosemary for muscular aches and pains, poor circulation
  - sandalwood, an anti-inflammatory
  - grapeseed, a light oil.

- I performed a full aromatherapy massage treatment but concentrated on draining the lymphatic in the legs. Gill particularly liked the smell of the oils.

Outcome of second treatment: Gill felt her legs did not ache quite as much and her ankles had not been quite as swollen.

Third treatment: I decided to use the same oils as the last treatment.

I wanted to concentrate on the lymphatic drainage in the legs and the back (trapezius area). Gill totally relaxed but felt very tired throughout the massage.

Outcome of third treatment: Gill reported that her back had not felt as stiff and did not ache as much – it was beginning to feel more flexible. She felt that her ankles had much improved and were not nearly as swollen as previously.

Fourth treatment: I used the same oils as previous treatment. I felt that her back was not as tense as previously, and was far more relaxed and supple. Her ankles had definitely improved.

Conclusion:

Gill appeared very relaxed and reported that she felt much better, but would continue to have her weekly treatment.

Case study 3

Gender: Female

Age: 40 years

Occupation: Unemployed due to family problems

Reasons for treatment: Insomnia, stress, general aches and pains

Frequency of visits: Once a week

General information:

● Mary has three children, one of whom is very demanding with behavioural problems.

● Mary had decided to try aromatherapy instead of taking sleeping tablets and was hoping the treatment would help her by relaxing her mentally and physically and also help her to get an undisturbed night's sleep.

First treatment: consultation:

● Choice of oils: bergamot, camomile, sandalwood, pre-blended with almond oil:
  - bergamot, which relieves stress, anxiety, nervous tension
  - camomile, a sedative, that relieves nervous tension
  - sandalwood, a sedative, that relieves stress, tension, insomnia
  - almond oil, a light textured oil.
● A full aromatherapy massage was carried out.

First treatment: I carried out a very relaxing and deep aromatherapy massage treatment. Mary slept through most of the treatment.

Outcome of first treatment: Mary slept well that evening for the first time in months, but felt very agitated the next day.

Second treatment: I used the same oils, as they seemed effective in reducing her tension, aches and pains. Carried out a general, deep, relaxing aromatherapy massage. Mary fell into a deep sleep halfway through the massage, but felt her legs ached slightly after treatment.

Outcome of second treatment: Mary reported that even though she had slept well her legs ached the next day.

Third treatment: I used the same oils as previously. Tension seemed to have reduced and her overall mood had lifted. Mary fell asleep straightaway and awoke feeling very relaxed and content.

Outcome of third treatment: Mary had had a good week, felt less stressed and continued to sleep well.

Fourth treatment: I decided to change the oils to bergamot, lavender and jasmine for stress and relaxation:

– bergamot, uplifting, stimulant helps stress, anxiety, nervous tension

– lavender, balancing, harmonising, calming, soothing

– jasmine, relaxing, relieves emotional stress.

- Mary fell asleep straightaway but felt very groggy after treatment.
- She reported that she had felt extremely tired the next day, but was now feeling much better within herself, far less stressed.
- Mary has decided to continue with her treatment once every two weeks.

Conclusion:

- Mary was given the oils that were left over from her treatment to use in the bath or apply to her body before going to bed.
- Mary often used lavender in a burner just before bedtime as she felt that this helped her to relax.

Case study 4

Gender: Male

Age: 55 years

Occupation: Unemployed due to redundancy four months earlier

Reasons for treatment: Feeling very low

Frequency of visits: Once a week

General information: George worked for 20 years in a factory and was recently made redundant.

First treatment: consultation:

- During consultation George said he was feeling 'under the weather', could not pull himself together and felt as though he had no energy.
- Choice of oils: basil for depression and stimulation and marjoram to energise blended with wheatgerm oil which is particularly good for dry skin.

- A full aromatherapy massage was carried out.

First treatment

- Carried out a very relaxing and deep aromatherapy massage treatment.
- George was very tense throughout the massage.

Outcome of first treatment: At the second session George reported that after the massage he did not feel any better – if anything he felt worse.

Second treatment: I used the same oils as previously and carried out a very relaxing and deep massage treatment. George continued to be very tense throughout the treatment.

Outcome of second treatment: George reported that he was still feeling low and uninterested in anything, but had gone out for a couple of walks.

Third treatment:

- I decided to changed the oils:
  - geranium to uplift
  - marjoram to energise
  - wheatgerm
- George was still very tense throughout the massage but seemed to relax a little near the end.
- I gave George lemongrass (for its uplifting properties), blended in wheatgerm to use in his bath every morning

Outcome of third treatment: George had started to feel a little better, he had started to walk every other day and had started to look for a part-time job.

Fourth treatment:

- Continued to use geranium, marjoram and wheatgerm.
- George relaxed more readily and reported that he had been looking forward to his massage.

Outcome of fourth treatment: George reported he felt more cheerful, enjoyed his now daily walk and had an interview lined up for the following week. George has decided to continue with his treatment every other week.

Conclusion; George was given more lemongrass blended in wheatgerm to continue to use in his morning bath.

Indian head massage

Case study 1

Gender: Male

Age: 36 years

Occupation: Hairdressing salon owner

Reasons for treatment: Tension across the shoulders and sinus problems

Frequency of visits: Once a week

General information:

- Mark owns a busy hairdressing salon. His job is very demanding both mentally and physically. He works six days a week and therefore finds he has very little time for either relaxation or exercise.
- During the consultation, I discovered that Mark had had meningitis when he was a boy and has since suffered from headaches as well as sinus problems.
- Mark's GP regularly prescribes him penicillin to treat his sinuses.
- Mark also has constant pain in his shoulders due to tension and the nature of his job. Correct posture techniques were discussed as Mark did admit that he tended to stoop at work when carrying out hair treatments.

First treatment:

- A full Indian head massage was carried out using lots of effleurage and champissage, and only very few tapotement and friction movements.
- Mark was very tense around the shoulder region accompanied with lots of tension nodules, which I concentrated on for a period of time, to try and disperse them.
- Later on in the massage, Mark did tend to relax a little.

Outcome of first treatment: At the second treatment Mark reported that he had felt more relaxed, his sinuses had felt a 'little stuffy', but he had slept well that evening. He had also tried to correct his posture at work when he had thought about it.

Second treatment: This time I used a few more tapotement and friction movements, but still used lots of effleurage movements concentrating on his shoulders and face for the sinus problems.

Mark was a lot more relaxed this time and seemed to enjoy the massage.

Outcome of second treatment: Tension in his shoulders seemed to be a lot less tender. He was consciously concentrating on correct posture techniques at work. His nose had felt like it was 'cleaning itself' and he had not had a headache for a full week.

Third treatment: Again, I tended to concentrate more on the shoulders, which now felt quite supple with no tension nodules evident and also on his face and head region. Mark was totally relaxed and at one point fell asleep for a few minutes.

Outcome of third treatment: Mark had not had a headache all week, his sinuses had much improved and his shoulders were not as tender.

Fourth treatment: Mark fell asleep almost straightaway and slept for the majority of the treatment. His shoulders were much more supple, with no signs at all of any tension nodules. Again, I tended to use lots of effleurage and champissage movements, with very few tapotement and friction movements.

Conclusion:

- Mark no longer felt as stressed.
- His sinuses were much improved, he had had just one mild headache and his shoulder tension was almost non-existent.
- Mark also concentrated on correct posture when carrying out hair treatments in his salon.
- Mark continues to have regular weekly Indian head massage treatments.

Case study 2

Gender: Female

Age: 29 years

Occupation: Full-time student

Reasons for treatment: Tension around neck, shoulder and upper back

Frequency of visits: Once a week

General information: Sarah was a full-time recruitment consultant who gave this up to train as a teacher. Sarah is finding it quite stressful going back to college after all these years, coping with all the course work.

First treatment:

- A full Indian head massage was carried out, using lots of effleurage and champissage movements, as her neck and upper back region was extremely painful.
- Sarah did tend to relax a little towards the end of the treatment.

Outcome of first treatment: Sarah reported that after the first treatment, she felt quite tender around her neck and had felt as though she had been drinking alcohol: she 'felt drunk'. That evening she had slept very heavily.

Second treatment: Again concentrated on the neck and upper back avoiding petrissage and friction movements on these areas, as Sarah still felt quite sore and tender. Sarah seemed to relax about halfway through the treatment

Outcome of second treatment: Sarah reported that the tension in her neck and back had started to ease.

Third treatment: Again, I concentrated on the neck and upper back but incorporating some petrissage and friction movements on these areas. I worked quite deeply into the upper back region. Sarah fell asleep straightaway, her upper back felt a lot more relaxed and more supple.

Outcome of third treatment: Sarah reported that she had felt bruised for the first couple of days following her treatment, but after that had felt the area much improved.

Fourth treatment: The area felt less tight, so I carried out a full treatment concentrating on the neck and upper back for less time than previously. Sarah tended to drift in and out of sleep throughout the treatment and seemed extremely relaxed at the end.

Conclusion:

- Sarah felt far more relaxed and reported she could cope better with her workload from college.
- Her neck and upper back had much improved.
- Sarah continues with her weekly treatment to de-stress and stay relaxed.

Case study 3

Gender: Female

Age: 55 years

Occupation: Unemployed, due to a car accident

Reasons for treatment: Julie had a car accident last year. Someone ran into the back of her car, leaving her with a very stiff neck and sometimes limited movement when turning her head to the right.

First treatment: Julie seemed very relaxed and did not feel any discomfort as I massaged, concentrating on her neck region.

Outcome of first treatment: Julie reported that she had suffered a very severe headache after her previous treatment, but realised that this was part of the healing crisis and had followed the aftercare advice.

Second treatment: Julie again seemed completely relaxed. I spent some time on the neck region, but did not use as much pressure as previously. Julie fell asleep towards the end of the treatment.

Outcome of second treatment: Julie informed me that she had had a good week. She had suffered from a couple of headaches that week, but her neck was not as stiff and she had felt that there was more mobility than previously.

Third treatment: I carried out the same massage as previously, but concentrated on her head and scalp as she had informed me she had a bit of a headache. Julie fell asleep towards the end of the massage.

Outcome of third treatment: Julie had had a good week. She had more mobility in her neck and could almost put her right ear down to touch her right shoulder as well as turn to look over her shoulder, although it still remained a little tender.

Fourth treatment: I carried out the same massage as previously, still tending to concentrate a little more on the neck area.

Conclusion:

- Julie felt that the pain in her neck and upper back had much improved, as well as gaining more mobility in her neck region, without causing any pain.
- Julie's headaches had also become increasingly less frequent.
- Julie continues to have her massage on a regular basis.

Case study 4

Gender: Female

Age: 46 years

Occupation: Teacher

Reason for treatment: Joan wants Indian head massage treatment for relaxation – she is quite stressed at work and this is affecting her psoriasis, which is becoming worse.

First treatment: I carried out a full Indian head massage using all movements, but limited the friction movements. Joan chatted throughout the treatment and seemed very tense.

Outcome of first treatment: Joan reported that she had felt very restless after the treatment and had slept very badly that evening.

Second treatment: I carried out the same massage as previously, but did not use too many friction movements on the scalp area. Joan started to chatter – halfway through the treatment she stopped talking but kept her eyes open.

Outcome of second treatment: Joan reported that she had felt much more relaxed and had slept quite well that evening. The psoriasis on her knees and thighs seemed much the same.

Third treatment: I carried out the same massage as previously. Joan chatted for the first few minutes but then went quiet. She kept her eyes open until a few minutes before the end of the treatment, then closed them and seemed to relax more.

Outcome of third treatment: Joan felt far more relaxed. She had slept very deeply that evening and had continued to sleep well throughout the week. Joan reported that her psoriasis did not seem to be as red and angry looking.

Fourth treatment: I carried out the same massage routine as previously. This time Joan chatted for the first couple of minutes then went quiet and shut her eyes for the remainder of the treatment.

Conclusion:

- Joan felt far more relaxed and her psoriasis had started to clear up, which made her feel better.
- Work was still stressful, but her weekly treatment was helping her to cope a little better with it.
- She was now sleeping more soundly.

Find out more

Associations

British Massage Therapy Council
7 Rymers Lane
Oxon OX4 3JU
Tel 01865 774 123
www.bmtc.co.uk

Federation of Holistic Therapies
18 Shakespeare Business Centre
Hathaway Close
Eastleigh
Hants SO50 4SR
Tel 023 8062 4399
www.fht.org.uk

Hair and Beauty Industry Authority (HABIA)
Fraser House
Nether Hall Road
Doncaster
South Yorks DN1 2PH
Tel 01302 380 000
www.habia.org.uk

Institute Federation of Aromatherapists
182 Chiswick High Road
London W4 1PP
Tel 020 8742 2605
www.ifparoma.org

Institute of Indian Head Massage
PO Box 1
Windsor
Berks SL4 4UZ
Tel 01753 831 841
www.indianheadmassage.org

Websites

Have a look at these websites for more details on different massage types, careers, courses and information.

http://www.aromatherapy-regulation.org.uk/
Aromatherapy Consortium – Formed by previous members of the Aromatherapy Organisations Council (AOC) to extend and promote the voluntary regulatory process. Represents many aromatherapy associations and aromatherapists. Includes information on training.

http://www.bcma.co.uk/
British Complementary Medicine Association – organisation representing 60 organisations, schools and colleges. Aims to represent therapists and protect the interests of the public.

http://www.gcmt.org.uk/
General Council for Massage Therapy – organisation for the self-regulation of massage therapy in the UK.

http://www.i-c-m.org.uk/careers.htm
Institute for Complementary Medicine (ICM) – registered charity formed to provide the public with information on complementary medicine. This page takes you straight to a guide on choosing complementary medicine as a career.

http://www.massagetherapy.co.uk/
Massage Therapy UK – information and descriptions of the main massage and holistic therapies. Promotes awareness and increases understanding of alternative treatments.

http://www.fihealth.org.uk/
Prince of Wales' Foundation for Integrated Health – supports the complementary healthcare profession in developing nationally recognised standards of education and training. Includes a guide to choosing courses.

http://www.scotmass.co.uk/SMTO/frames.htm
Scottish Massage Therapists' Organisation (SMTO) – works

with the General Council for Massage Therapy in developing and maintaining standards.

http://www.shiatsu.org/
Shiatsu Society – network linking individuals, students, practitioners and teachers of shiatsu, fulfilling the role of the professional association for shiatsu practitioners. Includes a good introduction to the subject, information on training and related links.

Suppliers

Dale Sauna
www.dalesauna.co.uk

Depilex
www.depilex.co.uk

Ellisons
www.ellisons.co.uk

Sorisa
www.sorisa.co.uk

Index